WCFL Chicago Top 40 Charts 1965–1976

To JIM--

Ron Smith

2007

WCFL Chicago Top 40 Charts 1965–1976

Compiled by Ron Smith

iUniverse, Inc.
New York Lincoln Shanghai

WCFL Chicago Top 40 Charts 1965–1976

iUniverse books may be ordered through booksellers or by contacting:

iUniverse
2021 Pine Lake Road, Suite 100
Lincoln, NE 68512
www.iuniverse.com
1-800-Authors (1-800-288-4677)

ISBN-13: 978-0-595-43180-9 (pbk)
ISBN-13: 978-0-595-87523-8 (ebk)
ISBN-10: 0-595-43180-1 (pbk)
ISBN-10: 0-595-87523-8 (ebk)

Printed in the United States of America

To the staff of the late, lamented and now legendary Real Oldies 1690 in Chicago: Tommy, Larry, Kathy, Len, Scotty, "World", Jerry, Herb, Scott, Erv, Tony and John. Never have so few done so much with so little.

CONTENTS

ACKNOWLEDGEMENTS

Thank you to those who inspired, encouraged and helped as I compiled and promoted my books: Chuck Bern, Clark Besch, Dick Biondi, John Charleson, Scott Childers, Steve Dahl, Bob Dearborn, Dave Douglas, Dennis Dvorshak, J.R. Dykema, Tommy Edwards, Mike Elder, Robert Feder, Scott Fischer, Jim Furholmen, Bill Ganson, John Gehron, John Govi, Wayne Jancik, Barbara Jastrab, Kent Kotal, Randy Lane, Jack Levin, Larry Lujack, Donald Liebenson, Dan Lusk, Jack Miller, Mark Morris, Dale Noble, Len O'Kelly, Lorna Ozmon, Mike Palesh, Scott Paulson, Rich Potts, Robert Pruter, Jeff Roteman, Randy Rowley, Kurt Scholle, Mary Shumanis, Hank Shurba, Bob Sirott, Jim Smith, Bill Stedman, Constantine Vigderman and Clark Weber. As always, a special thanks goes to the person who inspires every book of this type, Joel Whitburn.

INTRODUCTION

Just as Coke has Pepsi, McDonald's has Burger King and Hertz has Avis, it was inevitable that the success of top 40 WLS in Chicago would invite competition and spark a battle for radio supremacy in the Windy City.

For awhile that competition was assumed to be WJJD, who published their own list of the city's top songs (including artists like Bill Haley and Little Richard) going back to 1956. But the daytime-only station was never able to shed its "middle-of-the-road" image, and by 1965, it had switched to country music. Likewise, WIND had become as conservative musically as its morning man, the great Howard Miller, was politically. WYNR offered some competition to WLS between 1962 and 1964 under top 40 pioneer Gordon McLendon, but its poor signal led the "Old Scotchman" to try another experimental format with the station—all-news as WNUS.

WCFL was an odd choice for Chicago's second top 40 station. It had been owned by the Chicago Federation of Labor (hence the call letters) and Industrial Union Council since 1926—though not always at 1000 kilohertz. By 1965, the station's eclectic mix of easy listening music, jazz and sports had left it behind the other 50,000 watt signals in Chicago, as well as less powerful stations like WAIT.

While WLS' switch to the top 40 format on May 2, 1960 was sudden and complete, WCFL's was an evolution that can't be traced to a single date. General Manager Tom Haviland hired Ken Draper away from KYW, Cleveland's top station, in April of 1965. Draper, in turn, initially brought two of his jocks, Jim Runyon and Jimmy P. Stagg, along with him for morning and afternoon drives at WCFL. But the new jocks were still playing the old music as Draper slowly changed the direction of "Big 10 WCFL." It was two months before the press took note of the evolution. Draper was quoted as saying, "We're going to do whatever is necessary to be number one." He also pointed out that the station was getting ready to distribute its music surveys to area record stores. That wouldn't happen, however, until December of 1965.

It is those surveys that are documented in *WCFL Chicago Top 40 Charts 1965–1976*. But no mere black-and-white listing of the songs the station played can evoke the excitement WCFL brought to Chicago. WLS was personable, professional and yes, fun. WCFL, though, had attitude. Twin spins, mini-spins and capsule countdowns kept the station's energy up while song-length jingles from the legendary Chuck Blore, with their references to Wendella Boats and the Cheetah Nightclub, left no doubt that this was *Chicago's* top 40 station. WLS had Officer Vic for traffic—WCFL had Trooper 36-24-36 (Jane Roberts, who later became Runyon's wife). With production ace Dick Orkin providing the adventures of *Chickenman*—the White Winged Warrior and ex-Milwaukeean Barney Pip blowing his trumpet and turning teenagers "into peanut butter", WCFL was perfectly positioned to take on WLS in the city's great "radio war."

Even its music had attitude. While WLS was reluctant to play controversial tunes like Lou Christie's "Rhapsody In The Rain" (with its reference to "making out in the rain") and "Society's Child", Janis Ian's ode to inter-racial dating, WCFL had no such qualms. And it forced WLS into fierce competition to be the first to play local groups like the Buckinghams, the Cryan' Shames and the New Colony Six.

Despite their initial success, though, WCFL was unable to topple WLS in the sixties. "Superjock" Larry Lujack spent one month on the overnight shift at WCFL before crossing the river to anchor afternoons at WLS. And though nearly doubling WCFL's billing over the previous year, Draper left them in 1967 over budget cuts and joined Blore as a programming consultant. Meanwhile, John Rook at WLS brought in younger jocks like Chuck Buell and Kris Erik Stevens to re-connect the "Big 89" with its teen-aged core.

Rook left WLS in the early seventies however, and ironically, was responsible for WCFL's greatest success. Hired as the station's consultant in 1972, he lured Lujack back to WCFL and even renamed it "Super CFL" in his honor. Within a year, CFL was finally number one. But without Rook the station just as quickly fell back to its runner-up position, as WLS countered by hiring the top FM jocks of the day—Bob Sirott, Steve King and Yvonne Daniels (who, strangely enough, had played jazz all-nights at WCFL before Lujack arrived there).

The handwriting was on the wall. With its high overhead offsetting its billing, the Chicago Federation of Labor pulled the plug on top 40 in favor of automated beautiful music on March 15, 1976—"the day the music died"—as Lujack appropriately played Super CFL's last song, Don McLean's "American Pie."

WCFL was sold to the Mutual Broadcasting System in 1978 and the new owners even attempted a personality adult contemporary format in the early eighties. But the station was sold again in 1983 to a religious radio chain. After several mergers, AM 1000 eventually became WMVP and is now the flagship station for the ESPN radio sports network.

The WCFL call letters were revived in the early nineties by a station in Morris, Illinois, who even brought back the old "Super CFL" jingles. But the station went into receivership in 1993 and now plays contemporary Christian music under its new owners.

WCFL's status as Chicago's second great top 40 radio station should in no way diminish the memory of what it accomplished and the enjoyment it brought to the city in a little over a decade. As you look through this listing of the incredible music we heard during Chicago top 40 radio's "golden age", let your own memories of "the Voice of Labor" flow.

METHODOLOGY

This book is a continuation of my three *Chicago Top 40 Charts* books covering the WLS and WYTZ surveys of the '60s, '70s and '80s. It lists every tune that charted on the WCFL-AM weekly music surveys from December 23, 1965 through the final survey on February 21, 1976, less than a month before the station itself stopped playing top 40 music altogether.

Since the very first printed WCFL "Sound 10 Survey", however, listed positions for the previous week, I've given those 16 songs credit for that week, as well.

As in the previous books, **Debut** is the date the song first appears on the charts. **Peak** is the date it first reaches its highest position. **Pos** is the highest position reached on the charts and **Wks** is the number of weeks it appears on the charts.

In the very early years, the charts consisted of the top twenty songs, followed by 3-to-5 unnumbered "Very Important Premieres". I have chosen to use the week a song appeared as a "premiere" as its debut date, even when it doesn't appear again on the chart for several weeks. In fact, many of those songs never appeared again at all, and so are listed in the book with **pr** as their Peak. However, when entire albums were listed as premieres they are not listed in this book.

By February of 1966, WCFL added a "Sound 10 Stairway" of ten songs in addition to the top twenty. Bear in mind that these songs were never those going down the charts, only moving up. Since they were only listed alphabetically, no numeric value can be assigned to them. So a song that peaked on the "Stairway" is listed with an **xx** in this book. It can reasonably be assumed, though, that these songs actually peaked between 21 and 30 on the charts.

In most years, special year-end charts took the place of the normal survey. As in my previous books, songs that appeared on the charts before and after the special survey are given credit for the missing week with their positions "frozen." Songs debuting after the special survey are not credited for the previous week, even when their debut position is rather high. Songs that drop off the chart after a special survey are not credited for the missing week. This is also true of surveys missing for no real reason. There was no WCFL survey on May 30, 1968; August 20, 1969 and January 10, 1976.

In June of 1968, WCFL abandoned their printed surveys in favor of a poster-sized top thirty sent only to record stores. That practice ended with the October

8, 1969 survey and the printed surveys resumed on January 12, 1970. Therefore, no surveys were issued at all from October 15, 1969 through January 5, 1970. No song is given credit for this period, however, since none appeared both before and after the gap. This accounts for the poor showing of songs in late 1969, such as Elvis Presley's "Suspicious Minds" and the complete absence of the Beatles' "Come Together" or "Something".

When the printed surveys resumed, the "Big 10 Countdown" sheets listed 40 songs, with up to five "Hit Bound" extras. Since the extras were not alphabetical, I have credited them as if numbering continued. So those songs debut at #41 or lower. The last "Hit Bound" songs showed up on January 25, 1971, at which time the station issued a standard top forty list until the final survey in 1976.

There was one exception. Larry Lujack's novelty song, "The Ballad Of The Mad Streaker" appeared on four surveys in April and May of 1974. While the song is listed as #99, 98, 97 and 96 during those weeks, it's obvious that it was simply an unnumbered "extra" and I've chosen to give it's peak as **xx** in this book.

The WCFL surveys are generally for the "week ending" the date listed with the exception of charts from January 12, 1970 through March 1, 1971, which are the "week of".

At times, "two-sided hits" appeared on the charts. Both the "A" and "B" sides of a record would be listed. Any time both sides were listed, the "B" side also received credit for the position reached and for that week on the chart. However, often the "B" side was only listed during part of the record's run on the chart. Only the weeks a "B" side was actually listed is credited. Therefore, while the Guess Who's "No Sugar Tonight" receives the same chart credit as its "A" side, "American Woman", because both songs were listed every week; "Hey Tonight" by Creedence Clearwater Revival receives credit for eight less weeks and fifteen lower positions than its "A" side, "Have You Ever Seen The Rain", because it was only listed one-quarter of the time. In the artist listing, "B" sides are preceded by a slash and listed under their "A" sides.

Artists often recorded under different variations of their names. Name variations are indented under the original artist name. Totally different groups or names are listed separately, with a notation to "also see" the other artist.

The yearly top 40 lists are not the printed WCFL year-end lists, but rather my own objective ranking of the year's (and decade's) top songs, based on highest position reached, weeks at that highest position, weeks on the chart, followed by weeks in the top ten, twenty and top five, in that order.

Finally, the top artists of the decade is based on a point system for the highest position reached for every charted song by an artist with bonus points for each week on the chart.

ALPHABETICAL LISTING BY ARTIST

Artist	Title	Debut	Peak	Pos	Wks
ABBA					
	Waterloo	5/25/74	7/20/74	2	15
	SOS	9/27/75	11/22/75	4	17
	I Do, I Do, I Do, I Do, I Do	2/21/76	2/21/76	38	1
Ace					
	How Long	3/22/75	5/24/75	5	17
Acklin, Barbara					
	Love Makes A Woman	8/15/68	9/5/68	17	5
Adams, Johnny					
	Reconsider Me	7/2/69	7/30/69	23	5
Adderley, "Cannonball"					
	Mercy, Mercy, Mercy	2/9/67	3/2/67	20	4
Addrisi Brothers					
	I Can Feel You	5/18/72	6/22/72	20	7
Aerosmith					
	Dream On	2/7/76	2/21/76	20	3
Akens, Jewel					
	Little Bitty Pretty One	10/26/67	10/26/67	pr	1
Albert, Morris					
	Feelings	11/22/75	12/20/75	1	13
Alive And Kicking					
	Tighter, Tighter	6/15/70	7/13/70	4	14

Artist	Title	Debut	Peak	Pos	Wks
Allan, Davie & the Arrows					
	Blue's Theme	7/13/67	8/3/67	3	8
Allman, Gregg					
	Midnight Rider	12/15/73	1/26/74	15	10
Allman Brothers Band					
	Ramblin Man	8/18/73	10/20/73	3	14
Alpert, Herb & the Tijuana Brass					
	Taste Of Honey	12/16/65	12/16/65	3	4
	Zorba The Greek	1/20/66	2/3/66	13	5
	What Now My Love	3/24/66	3/24/66	xx	2
	The Work Song	6/23/66	7/7/66	xx	5
	Flamingo	8/25/66	9/22/66	xx	4
	Mame	11/10/66	12/8/66	19	4
	Casino Royale	4/6/67	6/8/67	17	7
	The Happening	7/6/67	8/3/67	30	2
	A Banda	8/31/67	8/31/67	pr	1
	Carmen	1/4/68	1/4/68	pr	1
Alpert, Herb					
	This Guy's In Love With You	5/9/68	6/13/68	1	10
	To Wait For Love	9/19/68	9/19/68	28	1
Amazing Rhythm Aces					
	Third Rate Romance	8/9/75	9/20/75	10	14
Amboy Dukes					
	Journey To The Center Of The Mind	7/25/68	8/22/68	6	7
America					
	A Horse With No Name	2/17/72	4/6/72	1	13
	I Need You	5/25/72	7/15/72	5	11
	Ventura Highway	10/21/72	12/16/72	5	13
	Don't Cross The River	1/27/73	2/17/73	26	6
	Tin Man	11/2/74	11/30/74	2	12
	Lonely People	2/15/75	3/29/75	4	12
	Sister Golden Hair	5/10/75	6/21/75	1	17

Artist	Title	Debut	Peak	Pos	Wks
American Breed					
	Step Out Of Your Mind	6/8/67	7/13/67	10	7
	Bend Me, Shape Me	11/30/67	1/18/68	1	12
	Green Light	1/25/68	3/21/68	18	5
	Ready, Willing And Able	4/25/68	5/16/68	27	4
	also see Rufus				
Ames, Ed					
	My Cup Runneth Over	2/23/67	3/23/67	14	5
	Who Will Answer	12/7/67	1/18/68	15	5
Amesbury, Bill					
	Virginia (Touch Me Like You Do)	3/2/74	4/20/74	11	12
Anders, Peter					
	Sunrise Highway	6/22/67	6/22/67	pr	1
Anderson, Lynn					
	Rose Garden	12/14/70	1/25/71	21	7
Animals					
	It's My Life	12/16/65	1/20/66	8	8
	Inside-Looking Out	3/17/66	3/17/66	xx	2
	Don't Bring Me Down	5/19/66	6/2/66	11	6
Eric Burdon & the Animals					
	See See Rider	10/20/66	11/3/66	16	6
	Help Me Girl	12/15/66	12/15/66	xx	2
	When I Was Young	3/30/67	5/11/67	21	5
	Sky Pilot (Part One)	7/18/68	8/8/68	11	5
	also see Burdon, Eric & War				
Anka, Paul					
	Goodnight My Love	1/8/69	1/22/69	17	3
	Do I Love You	10/28/71	12/30/71	8	10
	Times Of Your Life	1/24/76	2/7/76	19	5
Anka, Paul with Odia Coates					
	(You're) Having My Baby	8/3/74	9/7/74	1	14
	One Man Woman/One Woman Man	11/9/74	1/18/75	5	16
	I Don't Like To Sleep Alone	3/29/75	5/17/75	9	14
	(I Believe) There's Nothing Stronger Than Our Love	8/9/75	8/30/75	22	9

Artist	Title	Debut	Peak	Pos	Wks

Apollo 100
| | Joy | 1/13/72 | 3/2/72 | 1 | 12 |

April Wine
| | You Could Have Been A Lady | 3/30/72 | 5/18/72 | 7 | 11 |

Arbors
| | The Letter | 3/12/69 | 4/9/69 | 20 | 6 |

Archies
	Bang-Shang-A-Lang	11/7/68	11/21/68	10	4
	Sugar, Sugar	8/6/69	9/3/69	1	10
	Jingle Jangle	1/12/70	1/12/70	4	4
	Who's Your Baby	2/23/70	3/30/70	13	8

also see the Cuff Links and Kim, Andy

Argent
| | Hold Your Head Up | 7/22/72 | 9/16/72 | 2 | 13 |

also see the Zombies

Arnold, Eddy
| | I Want To Go With You | 3/3/66 | 3/3/66 | xx | 1 |

Ashton, Gardner & Dyke
| | Resurrection Shuffle | 7/22/71 | 9/2/71 | 8 | 10 |

Assembled Multitude
| | Overture From Tommy (A Rock Opera) | 7/20/70 | 8/24/70 | 8 | 10 |

Association
	Along Comes Mary	6/23/66	7/14/66	10	6
	Cherish	8/4/66	9/15/66	1	12
	Pandora's Golden Heebie Jeebies	11/17/66	11/17/66	pr	1
	No Fair At All	2/9/67	3/2/67	18	6
	Windy	5/18/67	6/8/67	1	12
	Never My Love	8/31/67	10/5/67	2	10
	Everything That Touches You	1/25/68	2/29/68	11	8
	Time For Livin'	5/9/68	6/13/68	14	5
	Six Man Band	8/29/68	9/5/68	25	2
	Names, Tags, Numbers & Labels	3/3/73	4/7/73	12	8

Artist	Title	Debut	Peak	Pos	Wks

AWB
| | Pick Up The Pieces | 1/11/75 | 3/8/75 | 3 | 13 |

Bachelors
| | Can I Trust You | 6/30/66 | 6/30/66 | pr | 1 |

Bachman-Turner Overdrive
	Blue Collar	11/24/73	12/22/73	27	6
	Let It Ride	3/9/74	4/13/74	21	8
	Takin' Care Of Business	6/15/74	8/10/74	5	14
	You Ain't Seen Nothing Yet	10/12/74	11/16/74	1	12
	Roll On Down The Highway	2/1/75	3/22/75	4	12
	Hey You	5/17/75	6/28/75	7	15

also see the Guess Who

Bad Company
	Can't Get Enough	9/14/74	11/2/74	1	14
	Movin' On	2/8/75	3/15/75	13	9
	Feel Like Makin' Love	8/9/75	9/27/75	4	16

also see Free

Badfinger
	Come And Get It	2/23/70	3/30/70	4	11
	/Rock Of All Ages	1/26/70	2/23/70	32	5
	No Matter What	11/9/70	12/14/70	10	10
	Day After Day	11/25/71	1/27/72	2	13
	Baby Blue	3/16/72	5/4/72	4	12

Baez, Joan
| | The Night They Drove Old Dixie Down | 8/12/71 | 9/23/71 | 2 | 11 |

Baker, George, Selection
| | Little Green Bag | 3/23/70 | 4/27/70 | 3 | 13 |
| | Paloma Blanca | 1/17/76 | 2/7/76 | 29 | 5 |

Balloon Farm
| | A Question Of Temperature | 2/15/68 | 3/21/68 | 11 | 6 |

Artist	Title	Debut	Peak	Pos	Wks
Band					
	Up On Cripple Creek	1/12/70	1/12/70	24	2
	Life Is A Carnival	9/30/71	11/11/71	17	8
	also see Dylan, Bob				
Banks, Darrell					
	Open The Door To Your Heart	7/28/66	7/28/66	xx	1
Barry, Len					
	1-2-3	12/16/65	12/16/65	6	3
	It's That Time Of The Year	6/2/66	6/2/66	pr	1
Bass, Fontella					
	Recovery	12/23/65	12/23/65	pr	1
Baxter, Duke					
	Everybody Knows Matilda	7/30/69	8/6/69	27	3
Bay City Rollers					
	Saturday Night	11/22/75	1/17/76	2	14
	Money Honey	2/14/76	2/21/76	28	2
Bazuka					
	Dynamite—Part I	7/5/75	8/23/75	4	12
Beach Boys					
	The Little Girl I Once Knew	12/23/65	12/23/65	18	2
	Barbara Ann	1/6/66	2/17/66	2	9
	Sloop John B	3/24/66	5/12/66	10	8
	God Only Knows	7/21/66	8/25/66	4	8
	/Wouldn't It Be Nice	8/11/66	8/25/66	4	7
	Good Vibrations	10/27/66	11/17/66	1	10
	Heroes And Villians	7/27/67	8/31/67	14	6
	Darlin'	12/7/67	2/8/68	30	2
	Friends	4/11/68	4/11/68	pr	1
	Do It Again	8/8/68	9/12/68	1	9
	I Can Hear Music	3/26/69	4/16/69	7	7
	also see Wilson, Brian				

Artist	Title	Debut	Peak	Pos	Wks

Beatles

We Can Work It Out		12/16/65	1/13/66	1	11
/Day Tripper		12/30/65	1/13/66	1	9
Nowhere Man		3/3/66	3/31/66	4	7
/What Goes On		3/10/66	3/17/66	5	2
Paperback Writer		6/2/66	6/30/66	2	8
/Rain		6/2/66	6/30/66	2	8
Yellow Submarine		8/11/66	9/8/66	3	10
/Eleanor Rigby		8/11/66	9/8/66	3	10
Penny Lane		2/16/67	3/23/67	4	9
/Strawberry Fields Forever		2/16/67	3/23/67	4	9
All You Need Is Love		7/13/67	8/31/67	4	9
/Baby You're A Rich Man		7/13/67	8/31/67	4	8
Hello Goodbye		11/23/67	12/21/67	1	9
/I Am The Walrus		11/23/67	12/21/67	1	8
Lady Madonna		3/14/68	4/11/68	1	8
/The Inner Light		3/14/68	4/11/68	1	8
Hey Jude		9/5/68	9/26/68	2	11
/Revolution		9/5/68	9/26/68	2	11
Get Back		4/30/69	5/21/69	1	9
/Don't Let Me Down		4/30/69	5/21/69	1	6
The Ballad Of John And Yoko		6/4/69	7/16/69	8	8
/Old Brown Shoe		6/4/69	7/16/69	8	7
Let It Be		3/2/70	3/23/70	1	13
The Long And Winding Road		5/18/70	6/22/70	9	10
/For You Blue		5/18/70	6/22/70	9	10

also see Lennon, John; McCartney, Paul; Harrison, George and Starr, Ringo

Bee Gees

New York Mining Disaster 1941		6/1/67	6/29/67	21	5
(The Lights Went Out In) Massachusetts		12/7/67	12/14/67	26	2
Words		1/18/68	1/18/68	pr	1
I've Gotta Get A Message To You		9/19/68	10/31/68	2	9
I Started A Joke		1/8/69	2/5/69	5	7
Lonely Days		11/30/70	1/4/71	6	9
How Can You Mend A Broken Heart		6/17/71	7/29/71	1	12
Don't Wanna Live Inside Myself		10/14/71	11/25/71	17	8
My World		1/20/72	3/9/72	7	11
Run To Me		8/5/72	9/16/72	16	8
Jive Talkin'		6/14/75	8/23/75	1	20

Artist	Title	Debut	Peak	Pos	Wks
	Nights On Broadway	10/4/75	11/29/75	4	17
	Fanny (Be Tender With My Love)	12/27/75	2/21/76	7	9

Beginning Of The End
	Funky Nassau-Part 1	6/17/71	7/22/71	4	11

Bell, Archie & the Drells
	Tighten Up	4/4/68	5/16/68	3	10
	I Can't Stop Dancing	8/1/68	9/5/68	10	6
	There's Gonna Be A Showdown	1/22/69	2/12/69	12	5

Bell, Madeline
	I'm Gonna Make You Love Me	3/7/68	3/7/68	24	2

also see Blue Mink

Bell, Vincent
	Airport Love Theme (Gwen And Vern)	3/30/70	4/20/70	26	7

also see Ferrante & Teicher

Bells
	Stay Awhile	3/11/71	4/15/71	1	11
	I Love You Lady Dawn	6/17/71	7/15/71	27	6

Bent Bolt & the Nuts
	The Mechanical Man	2/9/67	2/23/67	24	3

Benton, Brook
	Rainy Night In Georgia	1/19/70	2/23/70	5	10

Berkeley Kites
	Hang Up City	2/8/68	2/8/68	pr	1

Berry, Chuck
	My Ding-A-Ling	9/16/72	10/7/72	1	8

Big Brother & the Holding Company
	Down On Me	9/5/68	9/26/68	20	4
	Piece Of My Heart	10/17/68	10/31/68	23	3

also see Joplin, Janis

Black, Cilla
	A Fool Am I	11/10/66	11/10/66	pr	1

Artist	Title	Debut	Peak	Pos	Wks
Black, Terry & Laurel Ward					
	Goin' Down (On The Road To L.A.)	2/3/72	3/16/72	20	9
Black Oak Arkansas					
	Jim Dandy	12/29/73	3/2/74	5	14
Blanchard, Jack & Misty Morgan					
	Tennessee Bird Walk	3/23/70	4/13/70	20	6
Blood, Sweat & Tears					
	You've Made Me So Very Happy	3/19/69	4/16/69	1	8
	Spinning Wheel	6/25/69	7/16/69	13	6
	/More And More	6/25/69	7/16/69	13	4
	Hi-De-Ho	7/20/70	8/17/70	22	11
	Lucretia Mac Evil	10/12/70	11/2/70	25	5
Bloodstone					
	Natural High	6/9/73	7/14/73	18	10
Bloom, Bobby					
	Montego Bay	10/19/70	11/30/70	2	14
Blue Cheer					
	Summertime Blues	3/14/68	4/25/68	5	9
Blue Haze					
	Smoke Gets In Your Eyes	1/13/73	2/24/73	11	10
Blue Magic					
	Sideshow	7/6/74	8/3/74	15	9
Blue Mink					
	Our World	8/31/70	9/28/70	19	7
	also see Bell, Madeline					
Blue Ridge Rangers					
	Jambalaya (On The Bayou)	12/16/72	2/10/73	5	13
	also see Creedence Clearwater Revival					

Artist	Title	Debut	Peak	Pos	Wks
Blue Swede					
	Hooked On A Feeling	2/16/74	4/13/74	1	16
	Never My Love	9/7/74	10/12/74	11	10
Blues Image					
	Ride Captain Ride	5/4/70	6/15/70	3	14
also see Iron Butterfly					
Blues Magoos					
	(We Ain't Got) Nothin' Yet	12/29/66	1/26/67	5	9
Bones					
	Roberta	10/21/72	11/25/72	19	7
Booker T. & the MG's					
	Groovin'	9/21/67	9/21/67	26	2
	Soul-Limbo	8/1/68	8/29/68	17	5
	Hang 'Em High	11/28/68	1/15/69	6	10
	Time Is Tight	3/26/69	4/16/69	13	5
	Mrs. Robinson	6/18/69	7/2/69	22	4
Boone, Daniel					
	Beautiful Sunday	8/26/72	10/21/72	1	13
Boone, Pat					
	Wish You Were Here, Buddy	11/3/66	11/3/66	xx	1
	Break My Mind	8/27/69	8/27/69	29	1
Bowie, David					
	Fame	9/6/75	10/18/75	1	15
Box Tops					
	The Letter	8/31/67	9/21/67	1	12
	Neon Rainbow	11/23/67	12/28/67	8	7
	Cry Like A Baby	3/21/68	4/25/68	2	9
	Choo Choo Train	6/13/68	6/20/68	26	3
	I Met Her In Church	9/19/68	9/26/68	26	3
	Soul Deep	7/16/69	9/3/69	4	10

Artist	Title	Debut	Peak	Pos	Wks

Boyce, Tommy & Bobby Hart
	Out & About	8/10/67	8/17/67	29	3
	I Wonder What She's Doing Tonite	1/4/68	2/8/68	2	10
	Alice Long (You're Still My Favorite Girlfriend)	7/25/68	8/29/68	7	8
	L.U.V. (Let Us Vote)	3/5/69	4/2/69	23	5

Boys In The Band
	(How Bout A Little Hand For) The Boys In The Band	6/22/70	7/20/70	20	7

Brass Ring
	The Phoenix Love Theme (Senza Fine)	3/3/66	3/17/66	19	3

Bread
	Make It With You	6/29/70	7/27/70	1	12
	It Don't Matter To Me	9/21/70	10/19/70	7	10
	If	3/25/71	5/13/71	4	12
	Mother Freedom	7/15/71	8/26/71	12	10
	Baby I'm-A Want You	10/21/71	12/9/71	2	11
	Everything I Own	1/20/72	3/16/72	2	12
	Diary	5/11/72	6/29/72	5	9
	The Guitar Man	7/29/72	9/16/72	10	11
	Sweet Surrender	11/25/72	1/20/73	10	12

Bremers, Beverly
	Don't Say You Don't Remember	12/23/71	2/10/72	4	11

Brenda & the Tabulations
	Right On The Tip Of My Tongue	4/29/71	6/10/71	12	9

Brewer & Shipley
	One Toke Over The Line	3/11/71	3/11/71	36	1

Brighter Side Of Darkness
	Love Jones	1/20/73	3/17/73	8	12

Bristol, Johnny
	Hang On In There Baby	6/29/74	8/10/74	13	11

Brooklyn Bridge
	Worst That Could Happen	12/19/68	2/12/69	2	9

Artist	Title	Debut	Peak	Pos	Wks

Brotherhood Of Man
United We Stand · 5/11/70 · 6/8/70 · 9 · 9

also see Edison Lighthouse, First Class, the Pipkins and White Plains

Brown, Crazy World Of Arthur
Fire · 9/12/68 · 9/26/68 · 1 · 8

Brown, James
It's A Man's Man's Man's World · 5/26/66 · 5/26/66 · xx · 2
There Was A Time · 1/18/68 · 2/1/68 · 14 · 5
I Got The Feelin' · 3/14/68 · 4/25/68 · 10 · 9
Licking Stick—Licking Stick (Part 1) · 6/6/68 · 6/13/68 · 20 · 4
Say It Loud—I'm Black And I'm Proud (Part 1) · 10/10/68 · 10/24/68 · 21 · 3
Give It Up Or Turnit A Loose · 2/19/69 · 2/26/69 · 21 · 2
Mother Popcorn (You Got To Have A Mother For Me) Part 1 · 6/25/69 · 7/16/69 · 9 · 7

Brown, Polly
Up In A Puff Of Smoke · 1/25/75 · 3/8/75 · 12 · 10

Browne, Jackson
Doctor My Eyes · 3/2/72 · 5/11/72 · 1 · 15
Rock Me On The Water · 8/19/72 · 9/2/72 · 26 · 4

Brownsville Station
Smokin' In The Boy's Room · 11/10/73 · 1/12/74 · 2 · 14
I'm The Leader Of The Gang · 5/18/74 · 6/29/74 · 10 · 13
Kings Of The Party · 9/7/74 · 10/5/74 · 18 · 8

B.T. Express
Do It ('Til You're Satisfied) · 11/16/74 · 12/28/74 · 5 · 12
Express · 3/8/75 · 4/19/75 · 9 · 11

Bubble Puppy
Hot Smoke & Sasafrass · 2/26/69 · 3/26/69 · 8 · 6

Buchanan Brothers
Medicine Man (Part I) · 4/30/69 · 5/28/69 · 5 · 10

Buckinghams
I'll Go Crazy · 4/7/66 · 5/5/66 · 19 · 6
I Call Your Name · 6/16/66 · 7/7/66 · 17 · 4

Artist	Title	Debut	Peak	Pos	Wks
	I've Been Wrong	9/1/66	9/22/66	15	4
	Kind Of A Drag	11/24/66	12/22/66	2	11
	Laudy Miss Clawdy	3/9/67	3/16/67	24	2
	Don't You Care	3/16/67	5/18/67	2	11
	Mercy, Mercy, Mercy	6/15/67	7/27/67	7	9
	Hey Baby (They're Playing Our Song)	9/7/67	10/19/67	6	8
	Susan	11/23/67	1/18/68	6	9
	Back In Love Again	5/23/68	6/20/68	21	4

Buckwheat
	Simple Song Of Freedom	3/23/72	4/27/72	11	9

Buffalo Springfield
	For What It's Worth (Stop, Hey What's That Sound)	2/16/67	3/23/67	3	10
	Bluebird	6/29/67	6/29/67	pr	1

also see Crosby, Stills & Nash; Loggins & Messina; Poco; Stills, Stephen and Young, Neil

Bulldog
	No	12/2/72	1/13/73	17	9

also see the Young Rascals

Bullet
	White Lies, Blue Eyes	11/25/71	1/27/72	4	13
	Little Bit O' Soul	6/8/72	6/29/72	27	5

Buoys
	Timothy	1/11/71	5/20/71	8	16

Burdon, Eric & War
	Spill The Wine	6/29/70	8/10/70	2	15

also see the Animals and War

Butler, Jerry
	Never Give You Up	6/20/68	7/11/68	17	5
	Hey, Western Union Man	10/10/68	11/7/68	14	5
	Only The Strong Survive	3/12/69	4/16/69	8	7
	Moody Woman	6/4/69	6/18/69	18	3
	What's The Use Of Breaking Up	9/17/69	9/17/69	21	4

also see the Impressions

Artist	Title	Debut	Peak	Pos	Wks
Byrds					
	Turn! Turn! Turn! (To Everything There Is A Season)	12/16/65	12/16/65	8	3
	It Won't Be Wrong	2/24/66	2/24/66	xx	1
	/Set You Free This Time	1/13/66	1/13/66	pr	1
	Eight Miles High	4/14/66	5/19/66	8	7
	So You Want To Be A Rock 'N' Roll Star	1/19/67	2/23/67	22	3
	My Back Pages	3/23/67	3/23/67	pr	1
	Lady Friend	8/3/67	8/3/67	pr	1
also see Crosby, Stills & Nash					
Cale, J.J.					
	Crazy Mama	2/17/72	3/9/72	29	5
	After Midnight	5/25/72	6/8/72	26	4
Campbell, Glen					
	By The Time I Get To Phoenix	12/21/67	12/28/67	18	2
	Dreams Of The Everyday Housewife	7/11/68	7/25/68	23	3
	Gentle On My Mind	10/17/68	10/24/68	28	2
	Wichita Lineman	11/21/68	12/12/68	10	6
	Galveston	3/19/69	4/16/69	4	6
	True Grit	8/13/69	8/13/69	30	1
	Honey Come Back	2/2/70	2/9/70	25	2
	Dream Baby (How Long Must I Dream)	4/8/71	4/29/71	31	4
	Rhinestone Cowboy	7/5/75	9/6/75	1	21
	Country Boy (You Got Your Feet In L.A.)	12/6/75	1/17/76	13	10
also see the Hondells and Sagittarius					
Canned Heat					
	On The Road Again	9/5/68	10/3/68	6	6
	Going Up The Country	12/19/68	1/29/69	7	6
	Let's Work Together	10/19/70	11/23/70	6	8
Cannon, Freddy					
	The Dedication Song	2/3/66	2/24/66	xx	3
Capaldi, Jim					
	Eve	3/23/72	4/27/72	17	8
	It's All Right	1/11/75	2/15/75	22	8
	It's All Up To You	5/31/75	6/21/75	31	5

Artist	Title	Debut	Peak	Pos	Wks
Capes Of Good Hope					
	Winters Children	12/22/66	12/22/66	pr	1
Capitols					
	Cool Jerk	5/26/66	6/23/66	7	6
Captain & Tennille					
	Love Will Keep Us Together	6/14/75	7/12/75	1	15
	The Way I Want To Touch You	10/25/75	11/29/75	2	15
	Lonely Night (Angel Face)	2/7/76	2/21/76	19	3
Captain Beefheart & his Magic Band					
	Diddy Wah Diddy	6/30/66	6/30/66	pr	1
Cargill, Henson					
	Skip A Rope	12/28/67	1/25/68	14	6
Carlin, George					
	Al Sleet, Your Hippy-Dippy Weatherman	3/30/67	4/6/67	20	2
Carlton, Carl					
	Everlasting Love	10/5/74	11/30/74	10	13
Carmen, Eric					
	All By Myself	12/20/75	2/21/76	6	10
also see the Raspberries					
Carpenters					
	Ticket To Ride	1/12/70	2/9/70	14	8
	(They Long To Be) Close To You	6/22/70	7/13/70	1	15
	We've Only Just Begun	9/7/70	10/26/70	1	16
	Merry Christmas Darling	12/14/70	12/14/70	xx	2
	For All We Know	2/1/71	4/8/71	3	13
	Rainy Days And Mondays	5/13/71	6/17/71	2	13
	Superstar	9/9/71	10/21/71	1	10
	Hurting Each Other	1/13/72	2/17/72	1	11
	It's Going To Take Some Time	5/4/72	6/8/72	7	10
	Goodbye To Love	7/15/72	9/9/72	2	13
	Sing	3/17/73	5/12/73	1	13
	Yesterday Once More	6/23/73	7/28/73	1	13
	Top Of The World	10/13/73	12/15/73	1	18

Artist	Title	Debut	Peak	Pos	Wks
	I Won't Last A Day Without You	4/20/74	6/1/74	8	13
	Please Mr. Postman	12/21/74	2/1/75	1	13
	Only Yesterday	5/3/75	6/14/75	2	16
Carr, Vikki					
	It Must Be Him	9/21/67	11/9/67	8	9
	With Pen In Hand	6/11/69	6/25/69	26	3
Carter, Clarence					
	Looking For A Fox	3/7/68	3/7/68	29	1
	Slip Away	8/1/68	8/29/68	12	5
	Too Weak To Fight	12/19/68	1/8/69	19	6
	Patches	7/27/70	9/7/70	4	14
Cash, Johnny					
	A Boy Named Sue	7/23/69	8/13/69	6	8
	What Is Truth	3/30/70	4/20/70	21	8
Casinos					
	Then You Can Tell Me Goodbye	2/2/67	2/23/67	13	8
Cassidy, David					
	Cherish	11/11/71	12/23/71	3	11
	Could It Be Forever	2/10/72	3/30/72	5	10
	How Can I Be Sure	5/11/72	6/15/72	15	7
also see the Partridge Family					
Castor, Jimmy					
	Hey Leroy, Your Mama's Callin' You	1/26/67	1/26/67	xx	1
	Troglodyte (Cave Man)	6/1/72	7/6/72	1	10
	The Bertha Butt Boogie-Part 1	3/15/75	4/19/75	19	9
Cat Mother & the All Night News Boys					
	Good Old Rock 'N Roll	7/2/69	7/23/69	20	4
Chad & Jeremy					
	Distant Shores	8/4/66	8/4/66	xx	3
Chairmen Of The Board					
	Give Me Just A Little More Time	1/26/70	2/23/70	3	11

Artist	Title	Debut	Peak	Pos	Wks
Chakachas					
	Jungle Fever	3/9/72	4/13/72	5	8
Chambers Brothers					
	Time Has Come Today	9/26/68	10/17/68	9	5
	I Can't Turn You Loose	11/28/68	12/19/68	15	5
Chandler, Gene					
	Groovy Situation	8/10/70	9/14/70	2	10
Chantay's					
	Pipeline	11/3/66	11/17/66	19	3
Chapin, Harry					
	Cat's In The Cradle	11/2/74	12/14/74	1	13
Charles, Ray					
	Crying Time	12/30/65	2/17/66	xx	2
	Here We Go Again	6/22/67	7/6/67	21	4
	Yesterday	12/7/67	12/7/67	30	2
Charles, Sonny & the Checkmates, Ltd.					
	Black Pearl	5/28/69	7/2/69	8	8
Cheech & Chong					
	Basketball Jones Featuring Tyrone Shoelaces	9/29/73	11/3/73	3	11
	Sister Mary Elephant (Shudd-Up!)	12/15/73	1/19/74	2	11
	Earache My Eye Featuring Alice Bowie	8/31/74	9/28/74	6	12
	also see Taylor, Bobby				
Cher					
	Bang Bang (My Baby Shot Me Down)	3/17/66	4/7/66	8	9
	Behind The Door	10/27/66	10/27/66	pr	1
	You Better Sit Down Kids	11/2/67	12/14/67	3	7
	Gypsys, Tramps & Thieves	9/23/71	10/28/71	1	11
	The Way Of Love	2/3/72	3/9/72	5	10
	Living In A House Divided	5/18/72	7/6/72	4	11
	Half-Breed	8/18/73	10/13/73	1	15
	Dark Lady	1/19/74	3/2/74	2	13
	Train Of Thought	6/1/74	6/29/74	13	9
	also see Sonny & Cher				

Artist	Title	Debut	Peak	Pos	Wks

Chicago

	Make Me Smile	4/20/70	6/1/70	5	13
	25 Or 6 To 4	7/20/70	8/24/70	3	12
	Does Anybody Really Know What Time It Is	11/2/70	12/21/70	5	12
	Free	2/15/71	3/18/71	15	8
	Beginnings	7/1/71	7/29/71	6	9
	Saturday In The Park	8/5/72	9/23/72	3	12
	Dialogue (Parts I & II)	11/4/72	12/23/72	8	11
	Feelin' Stronger Every Day	7/7/73	9/1/73	2	12
	Just You 'N' Me	9/29/73	11/24/73	4	14
	(I've Been) Searchin' So Long	3/23/74	5/18/74	7	15
	Wishing You Were Here	10/26/74	12/7/74	15	10
	Harry Truman	3/1/75	4/12/75	14	10
	Old Days	5/17/75	6/14/75	9	12

Chicago Loop

	(When She Needs Good Lovin') She Comes To Me	12/1/66	12/1/66	xx	1

Chicory

	Son Of My Father	2/24/72	4/20/72	9	11

Chiffons

	Sweet Talkin' Guy	5/26/66	6/16/66	18	5
	Stop, Look And Listen	9/15/66	9/15/66	pr	1

Chi-Lites

	Have You Seen Her	11/4/71	12/16/71	2	11
	Oh Girl	4/27/72	6/8/72	5	12

Christie

	Yellow River	10/19/70	11/9/70	4	9

Christie, Lou

	Lightnin' Strikes	1/20/66	2/10/66	1	8
	Outside The Gates Of Heaven	3/17/66	3/17/66	xx	3
	Rhapsody In The Rain	3/17/66	5/12/66	14	10
	Shake Hands And Walk Away Cryin'	4/27/67	5/11/67	22	4
	I'm Gonna Make You Mine	9/3/69	9/24/69	2	6

Artist	Title	Debut	Peak	Pos	Wks

Christie, Susan
	I Love Onions	7/28/66	7/28/66	xx	1

Clapton, Eric
	After Midnight	11/9/70	12/21/70	6	10
	I Shot The Sheriff	8/3/74	9/21/74	1	15

also see Cream, Delaney & Bonnie & Friends, Derek & the Dominos and the Yardbirds

Clark, Dave, Five
	Over And Over	12/16/65	12/16/65	4	5
	At The Scene	1/27/66	3/10/66	13	6
	Try Too Hard	3/24/66	4/14/66	14	7
	Please Tell Me Why	6/16/66	6/16/66	xx	4
	Satisfied With You	8/4/66	8/25/66	xx	3
	Nineteen Days	11/17/66	11/17/66	xx	3
	I've Got To Have A Reason	12/29/66	1/19/67	xx	4
	You Got What It Takes	3/23/67	5/4/67	6	8
	You Must Have Been A Beautiful Baby	6/1/67	6/29/67	23	5
	A Little Bit Now	8/3/67	8/24/67	28	2
	Everybody Knows	1/4/68	1/4/68	28	3

Clark, Petula
	My Love	1/20/66	2/10/66	11	7
	A Sign Of The Times	3/17/66	3/31/66	xx	6
	I Couldn't Live Without Your Love	7/7/66	8/18/66	5	9
	Who Am I	10/13/66	11/24/66	20	4
	Color My World	12/15/66	1/19/67	xx	3
	This Is My Song	3/16/67	3/30/67	9	7
	Don't Sleep In The Subway	5/25/67	7/13/67	14	7
	The Cat In The Window (The Bird In The Sky)	8/24/67	9/14/67	29	4
	The Other Man's Grass Is Always Greener	12/28/67	1/4/68	25	2
	Kiss Me Goodbye	2/8/68	3/14/68	10	7

Clark, Roy
	Yesterday, When I Was Young	7/16/69	7/16/69	30	1

Classics IV
	Spooky	1/11/68	2/22/68	2	9

Artist	Title	Debut	Peak	Pos	Wks
Classics IV featuring Dennis Yost					
	Stormy	11/14/68	1/8/69	4	10
	Traces	2/26/69	3/26/69	3	7
	Everyday With You Girl	5/28/69	6/25/69	13	5
Cliff, Jimmy					
	Wonderful World, Beautiful People	1/12/70	1/12/70	16	3
Climax					
	Precious And Few	12/30/71	2/3/72	4	9
also see the Outsiders					
Clique					
	Sugar On Sunday	9/17/69	10/8/69	21	4
Cocker, Joe					
	She Came In Through The Bathroom Window	1/12/70	1/26/70	32	4
	The Letter	4/13/70	6/1/70	7	11
	Cry Me A River	10/26/70	11/23/70	10	9
	High Time We Went	6/17/71	7/22/71	10	9
	You Are So Beautiful	2/15/75	4/19/75	2	15
Coffey, Dennis & the Detroit Guitar Band					
	Scorpio	12/2/71	1/13/72	4	11
	Taurus	4/6/72	5/18/72	12	8
also see Kent, Al					
Cold Blood					
	You Got Me Hummin	1/12/70	2/16/70	29	7
Cole, Natalie					
	This Will Be	9/27/75	11/8/75	8	12
Collins, Judy					
	Both Sides Now	11/14/68	12/19/68	11	7
	Amazing Grace	12/14/70	2/8/71	20	7
Colter, Jessi					
	I'm Not Lisa	5/31/75	7/12/75	6	13
Coltrane, Chi					
	Thunder And Lightning	9/30/72	11/18/72	4	12

Artist	Title	Debut	Peak	Pos	Wks

Commander Cody & his Lost Planet Airmen
	Hot Rod Lincoln	3/16/72	4/27/72	2	10

Commodores
	Machine Gun	7/20/74	8/10/74	12	8

Como, Perry
	Seattle	4/30/69	5/21/69	21	5
	It's Impossible	12/14/70	1/4/71	27	5

Conley, Arthur
	Sweet Soul Music	4/13/67	5/11/67	4	9
	Funky Street	4/4/68	5/9/68	10	8
	People Sure Act Funny	7/11/68	7/11/68	28	1
	Ob-La-Di, Ob-La-Da	1/22/69	1/29/69	25	2

Conniff, Ray
	Somewhere, My Love	7/28/66	7/28/66	xx	1

Cooper, Alice
	Eighteen	2/15/71	4/15/71	4	13
	School's Out	6/15/72	8/5/72	2	11
	Elected	10/14/72	11/11/72	22	8
	No More Mr. Nice Guy	4/28/73	6/30/73	6	12
	Teenage Lament '74	12/22/73	2/9/74	9	12
	Only Women	4/26/75	6/14/75	6	14
	Welcome To My Nightmare	10/25/75	11/29/75	16	9

Cornelius Brothers & Sister Rose
	Treat Her Like A Lady	5/27/71	7/1/71	10	9
	Too Late To Turn Back Now	6/8/72	7/29/72	2	11
	Don't Ever Be Lonely (A Poor Little Fool Like Me)	9/30/72	11/4/72	25	8

Cosby, Bill
	Little Ole Man (Uptight-Everything's Alright)	9/7/67	10/12/67	2	8
	Funky North Philly	2/29/68	2/29/68	pr	1
	Grover Henson Feels Forgotten	4/13/70	4/13/70	43	1

Count Five
	Psychotic Reaction	9/29/66	10/27/66	9	7

Artist	Title	Debut	Peak	Pos	Wks
Country Coalition					
	Time To Get It Together	2/16/70	3/9/70	31	5
Coven					
	One Tin Soldier, The Legend Of Billy Jack	12/15/73	1/26/74	1	12
Cowsills					
	The Rain, The Park & Other Things	10/12/67	11/16/67	1	10
	We Can Fly	1/4/68	2/8/68	21	5
	In Need Of A Friend	3/7/68	3/7/68	pr	1
	Indian Lake	5/23/68	7/25/68	5	6
	Poor Baby	9/19/68	10/3/68	20	4
	Hair	3/19/69	4/2/69	1	10
Crabby Appleton					
	Go Back	8/17/70	9/14/70	12	9
Crazy Elephant					
	Gimme Gimme Good Lovin'	3/26/69	5/7/69	3	9

also see Kasenetz-Katz, Ohio Express, Reunion and the Third Rail

Artist	Title	Debut	Peak	Pos	Wks
Crazy Paving					
	Anytime Sunshine	2/22/71	3/18/71	30	4
Cream					
	Sunshine Of Your Love	1/11/68	2/15/68	10	6
	Sunshine Of Your Love	8/8/68	8/22/68	11	3
	White Room	10/3/68	11/14/68	5	8
	Crossroads	2/12/69	3/5/69	18	5

also see Clapton, Eric

Artist	Title	Debut	Peak	Pos	Wks
Creedence Clearwater Revival					
	Suzie Q. (Part One)	9/19/68	10/17/68	10	6
	Proud Mary	2/5/69	3/19/69	4	9
	Bad Moon Rising	5/21/69	6/11/69	2	8
	/Lodi	5/21/69	6/11/69	2	5
	Green River	7/30/69	8/27/69	6	10
	/Commotion	7/30/69	8/27/69	6	5
	Down On The Corner	1/12/70	1/12/70	22	2
	Travelin' Band	1/19/70	2/23/70	7	8
	/Who'll Stop The Rain	1/19/70	2/23/70	7	8

Artist	Title	Debut	Peak	Pos	Wks
	Up Around The Bend	4/13/70	5/11/70	3	10
	Lookin' Out My Back Door	8/3/70	9/21/70	2	14
	Have You Ever Seen The Rain	1/18/71	3/1/71	4	11
	/Hey Tonight	1/18/71	2/1/71	19	3
	Sweet Hitch-Hiker	7/8/71	8/12/71	9	10

also see the Blue Ridge Rangers

Crewe, Bob, Generation
	Music To Watch Girls By	1/19/67	2/16/67	13	5

Critters
	Mr. Dieingly Sad	9/15/66	9/29/66	12	6
	Don't Let The Rain Fall Down On Me	8/24/67	8/24/67	26	2

Croce, Jim
	You Don't Mess Around With Jim	7/29/72	9/9/72	1	13
	Operator (That's Not The Way It Feels)	11/4/72	12/16/72	7	11
	Bad, Bad Leroy Brown	5/12/73	7/14/73	5	15
	I Got A Name	10/13/73	12/1/73	2	14
	Time In A Bottle	12/1/73	1/12/74	6	13
	I'll Have To Say I Love You In A Song	3/9/74	4/27/74	4	14
	Workin' At The Car Wash Blues	6/29/74	8/3/74	11	10

Crosby, Stills & Nash
	Marrakesh Express	7/9/69	8/13/69	17	6
	Suite: Judy Blue Eyes	10/8/69	10/8/69	25	1

Crosby, Stills, Nash & Young
	Teach Your Children	6/15/70	6/22/70	34	2

also see Buffalo Springfield; the Byrds; the Hollies; Stills, Stephen and Young, Neil

Cross Country
	In The Midnight Hour	9/1/73	10/13/73	20	9

also see the Tokens

Crow
	Evil Woman Don't Play Your Games With Me	1/12/70	1/12/70	17	3
	Cottage Cheese	7/13/70	8/24/70	4	12
	Don't Try To Lay No Boogie Woogie On The "King Of Rock & Roll"	10/12/70	11/16/70	13	8

Artist	Title	Debut	Peak	Pos	Wks
Crusaders					
	Put It Where You Want It	8/12/72	9/9/72	21	6
Cryan' Shames					
	Sugar And Spice	7/7/66	7/28/66	7	8
	I Wanna Meet You	10/27/66	11/17/66	9	9
	Mr. Unreliable	3/16/67	4/6/67	12	8
	It Could Be We're In Love	6/29/67	8/17/67	1	13
	Up On The Roof	2/22/68	3/14/68	7	8
	Young Birds Fly	5/23/68	6/27/68	12	6
	Greenburg, Glickstein, Charles, David Smith & Jones	9/26/68	10/10/68	9	6
	First Train To California	2/26/69	3/5/69	26	2
Cuff Links					
	Tracy	9/17/69	10/8/69	5	4
also see the Archies					
Curb, Mike, Congregation					
	Burning Bridges	1/4/71	2/1/71	9	8
Cymarron					
	Rings	7/22/71	8/26/71	3	10
Cyrkle					
	Red Rubber Ball	6/9/66	7/21/66	6	8
	Turn-Down Day	9/8/66	9/22/66	13	4
	Please Don't Ever Leave Me	12/1/66	12/1/66	xx	4
Daddy Dewdrop					
	Chick-A-Boom (Don't Ya Jes' Love It)	2/22/71	4/29/71	7	15
Damon's, Liz, Orient Express					
	1900 Yesterday	12/14/70	1/18/71	9	8
Dana, Vic					
	If I Never Knew Your Name	1/12/70	1/19/70	18	5
Daniels, Charlie					
	Uneasy Rider	6/16/73	8/11/73	10	13
	The South's Gonna Do It	2/8/75	3/15/75	18	9

Artist	Title	Debut	Peak	Pos	Wks
Darin, Bobby					
	If I Were A Carpenter	10/27/66	11/17/66	15	4
	The Girl That Stood Beside Me	11/24/66	11/24/66	pr	1
	Lovin' You	1/12/67	2/9/67	24	4
Darren, James					
	All	1/5/67	2/2/67	15	6
Davis, Mac					
	Baby Don't Get Hooked On Me	8/12/72	9/23/72	4	12
	Stop And Smell The Roses	9/7/74	10/26/74	3	14
Davis, Jr., Sammy					
	I've Gotta Be Me	1/29/69	3/5/69	3	8
	The Candy Man	6/15/72	7/15/72	2	9
Davis, Spencer, Group					
	Gimme Some Lovin'	1/19/67	2/16/67	6	6
	I'm A Man	4/6/67	4/20/67	22	5
	Somebody Help Me	7/20/67	8/10/67	20	4
Davis, Tyrone					
	Can I Change My Mind	1/15/69	2/5/69	16	4
	Turn Back The Hands Of Time	3/16/70	4/20/70	8	10
Dawn					
	Candida	8/10/70	9/21/70	1	15
	Knock Three Times	11/9/70	1/4/71	1	14
	I Play And Sing	3/11/71	4/8/71	14	9
	Summer Sand	6/10/71	7/22/71	13	11
Dawn featuring Tony Orlando					
	What Are You Doing Sunday	9/23/71	11/25/71	3	14
	Tie A Yellow Ribbon Round The Ole Oak Tree	3/10/73	5/5/73	3	13
	Say, Has Anybody Seen My Sweet Gypsy Rose	7/14/73	9/22/73	8	13
Tony Orlando & Dawn					
	Who's In The Strawberry Patch With Sally	11/17/73	12/22/73	20	9
	Steppin' Out (Gonna Boogie Tonight)	10/5/74	11/2/74	14	8
	He Don't Love You (Like I Love You)	3/15/75	5/17/75	2	15
	Mornin' Beautiful	7/5/75	8/2/75	15	9

also see Wind

Artist	Title	Debut	Peak	Pos	Wks

Daybreak
| | Good Morning Freedom | 5/18/70 | 6/15/70 | 25 | 5 |

Deal, Bill & the Rhondels
	May I	2/19/69	3/26/69	11	6
	I've Been Hurt	4/16/69	5/21/69	11	6
	What Kind Of Fool Do You Think I Am	8/27/69	9/10/69	16	3
	Nothing Succeeds Like Success	4/6/70	4/27/70	16	5

Dee, Dave; Dozy, Beaky, Mick & Tich
| | Save Me | 2/9/67 | 2/9/67 | pr | 1 |

Dee, Kiki, Band
| | I've Got The Music In Me | 10/19/74 | 11/30/74 | 13 | 10 |

Deep Purple
	Hush	9/5/68	9/26/68	6	6
	Kentucky Woman	11/28/68	12/19/68	22	5
	Smoke On The Water	6/2/73	8/4/73	3	15

DeFranco Family featuring Tony DeFranco
	Heartbeat—It's A Lovebeat	9/8/73	11/10/73	1	16
	Abra-Ca-Dabra	12/29/73	2/23/74	3	13
	Save The Last Dance For Me	4/27/74	5/25/74	19	9

Dekker, Desmond & the Aces
| | Israelites | 5/28/69 | 6/25/69 | 5 | 8 |

Delaney & Bonnie & Friends
	Soul Shake	8/10/70	8/24/70	27	4
	Never Ending Song Of Love	6/3/71	8/12/71	1	15
	Only You Know And I Know	9/16/71	11/11/71	6	11
	also see Clapton, Eric				

Delegates
| | Convention '72 | 10/28/72 | 11/11/72 | 5 | 7 |

Delfonics
	La-La-Means I Love You	2/29/68	4/4/68	7	7
	Didn't I (Blow Your Mind This Time)	2/9/70	3/2/70	4	10
	Over And Over	7/15/71	7/29/71	30	4
	also see Harris, Major				

Artist	Title	Debut	Peak	Pos	Wks

Dells

	There Is	1/18/68	2/1/68	16	5
	Wear It On Our Face	4/4/68	4/4/68	pr	1
	Stay In My Corner	7/11/68	8/22/68	15	7
	Always Together	11/14/68	11/14/68	20	2
	Oh, What A Night	9/3/69	9/3/69	28	3
	The Glory Of Love	2/8/71	2/15/71	32	2
	Give Your Baby A Standing Ovation	6/16/73	7/28/73	14	10
	I Miss You	1/19/74	2/23/74	20	8

Del-Vetts

	Last Time Around	7/14/66	7/14/66	xx	1

also see the Pride & Joy

Denver, John

	Take Me Home, Country Roads	7/1/71	8/19/71	2	12
	Rocky Mountain High	1/20/73	3/10/73	4	13
	Sunshine On My Shoulders	1/26/74	3/9/74	2	15
	Annie's Song	6/15/74	8/3/74	1	16
	Back Home Again	10/12/74	11/16/74	9	10
	Sweet Surrender	1/18/75	2/15/75	20	8
	Thank God I'm A Country Boy	5/3/75	6/14/75	4	13
	I'm Sorry	9/20/75	11/1/75	1	14
	Fly Away	1/17/76	1/24/76	20	5

Deodato

	Also Sprach Zarathustra (2001)	2/24/73	3/24/73	1	9

Derek

	Cinnamon	10/3/68	11/28/68	7	13
	Back Door Man	3/12/69	3/19/69	28	2

Derek & the Dominos

	Layla	3/11/71	4/8/71	18	6

also see Clapton, Eric

Derringer, Rick

	Rock And Roll, Hoochie Koo	2/23/74	3/16/74	24	5

also see the McCoys

Artist	Title	Debut	Peak	Pos	Wks

DeShannon, Jackie

	I Can Make It With You	9/1/66	9/1/66	pr	1
	Put A Little Love In Your Heart	7/2/69	8/13/69	7	9

Detroit Emeralds

	Do Me Right	4/1/71	4/15/71	32	3
	Baby Let Me Take You (In My Arms)	8/12/72	9/16/72	6	10

Diamond, Neil

	Solitary Man	4/21/66	4/21/66	pr	1
	Cherry, Cherry	9/15/66	10/27/66	4	8
	I Got The Feelin' (Oh No No)	10/27/66	11/24/66	xx	7
	You Got To Me	2/9/67	3/9/67	16	5
	Girl, You'll Be A Woman Soon	3/30/67	5/11/67	8	7
	I Thank The Lord For The Night Time	7/27/67	8/24/67	9	9
	Kentucky Woman	10/5/67	11/9/67	15	6
	New Orleans	12/28/67	12/28/67	pr	1
	Brooklyn Roads	5/23/68	6/6/68	18	3
	Two-Bit Manchild	7/18/68	7/25/68	22	3
	Brother Love's Travelling Salvation Show	3/26/69	4/16/69	12	6
	Sweet Caroline (Good Times Never Seemed So Good)	7/9/69	8/13/69	2	9
	Holly Holy	1/12/70	1/12/70	39	1
	Shilo	1/26/70	4/6/70	12	8
	Until It's Time For You To Go	2/2/70	3/2/70	30	5
	Soolaimón (African Trilogy II)	4/20/70	5/11/70	11	8
	Solitary Man	8/3/70	9/7/70	2	12
	Cracklin' Rosie	8/10/70	9/28/70	2	15
	He Ain't Heavy … He's My Brother	12/7/70	12/21/70	26	3
	Do It	1/4/71	1/18/71	25	4
	I Am … I Said	3/18/71	4/29/71	16	9
	/Done Too Soon	5/20/71	6/24/71	21	7
	Stones	11/4/71	12/9/71	7	9
	Song Sung Blue	4/27/72	6/22/72	2	14
	Play Me	8/26/72	10/7/72	4	11
	"Cherry Cherry" from Hot August Night	3/31/73	5/19/73	8	12
	Be	10/20/73	11/24/73	16	10
	Longfellow Serenade	10/12/74	12/7/74	5	15

Artist	Title	Debut	Peak	Pos	Wks
Diddley, Bo					
	Ooh Baby	2/2/67	2/2/67	xx	1
Dino, Desi & Billy					
	Two In The Afternoon	5/11/67	6/29/67	26	3
Dion					
	Abraham, Martin And John	11/7/68	11/28/68	1	8
Dirksen, Senator Everett McKinley					
	Gallant Men	12/29/66	12/29/66	xx	3
Disco Tex & the Sex-O-Lettes featuring Sir Monti Rock III					
	Get Dancin'	12/21/74	2/8/75	15	12
	I Wanna Dance Wit' Choo (Doo Dat Dance), Part 1	5/3/75	5/24/75	26	5
Dolenz, Micky					
	Don't Do It	2/2/67	2/2/67	pr	1
also see the Monkees					
Donaldson, Bo & the Heywoods					
	Billy, Don't Be A Hero	4/20/74	6/15/74	2	16
	Who Do You Think You Are	8/17/74	9/28/74	10	12
Donovan					
	Sunshine Superman	8/11/66	9/8/66	1	10
	Mellow Yellow	11/3/66	12/8/66	3	10
	Epistle To Dippy	2/23/67	3/9/67	24	3
	There Is A Mountain	9/7/67	9/21/67	22	3
	Wear Your Love Like Heaven	12/21/67	1/18/68	22	3
	Jennifer Juniper	3/28/68	5/2/68	12	6
	Hurdy Gurdy Man	7/4/68	8/1/68	7	7
	Atlantis	4/23/69	5/21/69	6	6
Doobie Brothers					
	Listen To The Music	9/16/72	11/4/72	3	11
	Long Train Runnin'	5/19/73	7/14/73	3	15
	China Grove	8/25/73	10/13/73	2	13
	Another Park, Another Sunday	5/11/74	6/22/74	10	11
	Black Water	2/1/75	3/1/75	1	12
	Take Me In Your Arms (Rock Me)	5/17/75	7/5/75	4	15

Artist	Title	Debut	Peak	Pos	Wks
Doors					
	Light My Fire	7/6/67	8/10/67	2	12
	People Are Strange	9/21/67	10/26/67	20	5
	The Unknown Soldier	4/11/68	4/11/68	pr	1
	Hello, I Love You	7/11/68	8/8/68	1	8
	Touch Me	1/8/69	2/12/69	1	9
	Love Her Madly	4/1/71	5/27/71	3	13
	Riders On The Storm	7/1/71	8/12/71	2	11
Dorsey, Lee					
	Working In The Coal Mine	9/1/66	9/1/66	xx	3
Douglas, Carl					
	Kung Fu Fighting	10/19/74	12/21/74	1	17
Douglas, Carol					
	Doctor's Orders	12/28/74	2/15/75	8	12
Douglas, Mike					
	The Men In My Little Girl's Life	1/6/66	1/20/66	13	5
Dove, Ronnie					
	When Liking Turns To Loving	1/13/66	2/17/66	xx	2
	Let's Start All Over Again	5/5/66	5/5/66	xx	3
	Happy Summer Days	7/7/66	7/7/66	xx	1
	I Really Don't Want To Know	10/6/66	10/6/66	xx	1
	Cry	12/8/66	12/15/66	18	4
	My Babe	5/11/67	5/11/67	27	1
Dozier, Lamont					
	Trying To Hold On To My Woman	2/23/74	3/23/74	24	7
Dr. Hook & the Medicine Show					
	Sylvia's Mother	4/13/72	6/8/72	1	12
	The Cover Of "Rolling Stone"	1/13/73	3/3/73	5	13
Dr. Hook					
	Only Sixteen	1/31/76	2/21/76	21	4
Dr. John					
	Iko Iko	4/6/72	5/11/72	25	7
	Right Place Wrong Time	5/12/73	7/7/73	3	14

Artist	Title	Debut	Peak	Pos	Wks

Drafi
	Marble Breaks And Iron Bends	4/21/66	4/21/66	pr	1

Dramatics
	Whatcha See Is Whatcha Get	7/29/71	9/16/71	8	10
	In The Rain	4/6/72	5/25/72	5	11

Drew, Patti
	Workin' On A Groovy Thing	8/1/68	8/22/68	25	4

Drifters
	Baby What I Mean	12/1/66	12/1/66	pr	1

also see King, Ben E.

Dusk
	Angel Baby	1/18/71	2/8/71	27	5
	I Hear Those Church Bells Ringing	5/27/71	7/8/71	9	10

Dylan, Bob
	Rainy Day Women #12 & 35	4/14/66	5/12/66	3	8
	I Want You	7/7/66	7/7/66	xx	4
	Just Like A Woman	9/29/66	9/29/66	xx	1
	Lay Lady Lay	7/30/69	8/27/69	1	9
	Knockin' On Heaven's Door	10/6/73	11/17/73	16	10

also see the Band

Dyson, Ronnie
	(If You Let Me Make Love To You Then) Why Can't I Touch You	6/22/70	8/3/70	4	13
	One Man Band (Plays All Alone)	2/17/73	4/7/73	11	10

Eagles
	Take It Easy	5/18/72	7/22/72	2	13
	Witchy Woman	10/7/72	12/2/72	6	11
	Peaceful Easy Feeling	1/20/73	2/17/73	22	7
	Already Gone	6/22/74	7/13/74	14	9
	Best Of My Love	12/14/74	2/15/75	1	15
	One Of These Nights	5/24/75	7/26/75	3	17
	Lyin' Eyes	9/27/75	11/8/75	4	14
	Take It To The Limit	1/17/76	2/21/76	17	6

also see Poco, the Stone Poneys and Walsh, Joe

Artist	Title	Debut	Peak	Pos	Wks
Earth, Wind & Fire					
	Shining Star	5/10/75	6/21/75	6	14
	That's The Way Of The World	9/6/75	9/20/75	18	9
	Sing A Song	12/27/75	1/31/76	14	9
Edison Lighthouse					
	Love Grows (Where My Rosemary Goes)	2/9/70	3/9/70	3	11
	It's Up To You Petula	12/21/70	1/18/71	15	6
also see the Brotherhood Of Man, First Class, the Pipkins and White Plains					
Edmunds, Dave					
	I Hear You Knocking	12/14/70	1/18/71	1	11
Edward Bear					
	Last Song	1/13/73	2/24/73	2	14
Edwards, Jonathan					
	Sunshine	11/18/71	12/30/71	1	12
El Chicano					
	Tell Her She's Lovely	11/17/73	12/29/73	20	9
Elbert, Donnie					
	Where Did Our Love Go	12/2/71	1/27/72	3	12
Electric Indian					
	Keem-O-Sabe	8/27/69	9/3/69	16	3
Electric Light Orchestra					
	Roll Over Beethoven	7/7/73	9/1/73	6	13
	Can't Get It Out Of My Head	2/15/75	3/29/75	7	12
	Evil Woman	12/20/75	2/14/76	4	10
Electric Prunes					
	I Had Too Much To Dream (Last Night)	1/5/67	2/16/67	4	9
	Get Me To The World On Time	3/2/67	3/2/67	pr	1
Elephant's Memory					
	Mongoose	10/12/70	11/23/70	5	11
Elliman, Yvonne					
	I Don't Know How To Love Him	4/15/71	6/10/71	4	12

Artist	Title	Debut	Peak	Pos	Wks
Elliot, Mama Cass					
	Dream A Little Dream Of Me	7/25/68	8/29/68	11	6
also see the Mamas & the Papas and the Mugwumps					
Ely, Jack & the Courtmen					
	David's Mood	5/5/66	5/5/66	pr	1
also see the Kingsmen					
Emerson, Lake & Palmer					
	From The Beginning	10/21/72	11/25/72	14	8
Emotions					
	So I Can Love You	5/21/69	5/21/69	27	1
English Congregation					
	Softly Whispering I Love You	12/30/71	2/24/72	3	12
	Jesahel	6/29/72	8/5/72	17	9
Equals					
	Baby, Come Back	9/26/68	10/17/68	12	4
Ernie (Jim Henson)					
	Rubber Duckie	8/24/70	9/14/70	7	7
Esquires					
	Get On Up	9/14/67	10/19/67	21	6
Essex, David					
	Rock On	1/19/74	3/9/74	3	14
Everett, Keith					
	Don't You Know	3/24/66	5/5/66	10	8
Everly Brothers					
	Bowling Green	4/27/67	4/27/67	pr	1
Every Mothers' Son					
	Come On Down To My Boat	6/8/67	7/20/67	1	11
Faces					
	Stay With Me	12/23/71	2/3/72	1	12
also see the Small Faces and Stewart, Rod					

Artist	Title	Debut	Peak	Pos	Wks
Fairchild, Barbara					
	Teddy Bear Song	4/28/73	5/19/73	28	5
Faith Hope & Charity					
	So Much Love	5/4/70	5/18/70	32	3
Fame, Georgie					
	Get Away	9/29/66	9/29/66	xx	2
	The Ballad Of Bonnie And Clyde	2/22/68	3/21/68	12	9
Family					
	Face The Autumn	11/2/67	11/23/67	13	5
Fancy					
	Wild Thing	6/29/74	8/17/74	5	14
Fanny					
	Charity Ball	9/9/71	10/28/71	3	11
Fantastic Johnny C					
	Boogaloo Down Broadway	11/30/67	12/21/67	9	7
Fantastics					
	(Love Me) Love The Life I Lead	1/20/72	2/24/72	23	7
Fardon, Don					
	(The Lament Of The Cherokee) Indian Reservation	9/5/68	9/26/68	5	5
Fargo, Donna					
	The Happiest Girl In The Whole U.S.A.	6/22/72	8/5/72	16	9
	Funny Face	12/2/72	1/27/73	14	12
Feather					
	Friends	5/4/70	6/8/70	29	6
Feliciano, José					
	Light My Fire	8/1/68	8/22/68	1	7
	Hi-Heel Sneakers	10/17/68	10/31/68	17	4
	Feliz Navidad	12/14/70	12/14/70	xx	2

Artist	Title	Debut	Peak	Pos	Wks
Fender, Freddy					
	Before The Next Teardrop Falls	4/12/75	5/31/75	3	12
	Wasted Days And Wasted Nights	8/30/75	9/13/75	20	9
	Secret Love	11/22/75	12/6/75	26	6
Ferrante & Teicher					
	Midnight Cowboy	1/12/70	1/12/70	12	3
also see Bell, Vincent					
Fever Tree					
	San Francisco Girls (Return Of The Native)	9/19/68	10/10/68	26	4
Field, Sally					
	Felicidad	11/23/67	11/30/67	22	2
5th Dimension					
	Go Where You Wanna Go	12/29/66	3/16/67	17	5
	Another Day, Another Heartache	4/13/67	4/13/67	pr	1
	Up-Up And Away	6/1/67	6/22/67	5	7
	Paper Cup	11/16/67	11/30/67	27	4
	Stoned Soul Picnic	5/16/68	7/18/68	2	10
	Sweet Blindness	10/31/68	11/14/68	18	4
	California Soul	1/15/69	2/5/69	19	4
	Aquarius/Let The Sunshine In (The Flesh Failures)	3/19/69	4/23/69	1	10
	Workin' On A Groovy Thing	7/30/69	8/13/69	14	6
	Wedding Bell Blues	10/1/69	10/8/69	15	2
	Blowing Away	1/12/70	1/26/70	16	6
	Puppet Man	4/13/70	5/11/70	15	7
	Save The Country	6/8/70	6/29/70	19	6
	One Less Bell To Answer	11/23/70	12/14/70	2	10
	Love's Lines, Angles And Rhymes	2/15/71	4/1/71	9	10
	Never My Love	10/14/71	11/11/71	23	5
	(Last Night) I Didn't Get To Sleep At All	5/11/72	6/29/72	2	12
	If I Could Reach You	9/30/72	12/2/72	5	13
	Living Together, Growing Together	1/20/73	2/24/73	19	9
Fifth Estate					
	Ding Dong! The Witch Is Dead	6/1/67	6/15/67	16	5

Artist	Title	Debut	Peak	Pos	Wks
Fireballs					
	Bottle Of Wine	12/28/67	1/4/68	17	4
	Long Green	2/19/69	3/19/69	18	5
First Class					
	Beach Baby	8/17/74	9/28/74	2	15
also see the Brotherhood Of Man, Edison Lighthouse, the Pipkins and White Plains					
First Edition					
	Just Dropped In (To See What Condition My Condition Was In)	2/22/68	3/14/68	4	6
	But You Know I Love You	2/5/69	2/26/69	18	4
Kenny Rogers & the First Edition					
	Ruby, Don't Take Your Love To Town	6/18/69	7/23/69	2	7
	Ruben James	10/1/69	10/8/69	19	2
	Something's Burning	3/23/70	4/20/70	2	11
Five Americans					
	I See The Light	12/23/65	2/24/66	14	5
	Evol-Not Love	3/31/66	6/2/66	7	8
	Western Union	3/2/67	3/30/67	7	8
	Sound Of Love	5/4/67	6/15/67	17	7
	Zip Code	8/17/67	8/31/67	17	4
also see Gladstone					
Five By Five					
	Fire	10/10/68	11/7/68	5	7
Five Flights Up					
	Do What You Wanna Do	8/3/70	9/28/70	9	14
Five Man Electrical Band					
	Absolutely Right	10/7/71	11/25/71	2	12
Five Stairsteps					
	O-o-h Child	6/8/70	7/13/70	2	14
5000 Volts					
	I'm On Fire	10/18/75	11/29/75	12	11

Artist	Title	Debut	Peak	Pos	Wks
Flack, Roberta					
	The First Time Ever I Saw Your Face	3/2/72	4/13/72	1	12
	Killing Me Softly With His Song	2/3/73	3/3/73	1	11
	Jesse	9/29/73	10/27/73	28	6
	Feel Like Makin' Love	7/27/74	8/31/74	1	12
Flack, Roberta & Donny Hathaway					
	Where Is The Love	6/22/72	8/12/72	2	11
Flaming Ember					
	I'm Not My Brothers Keeper	11/30/70	12/14/70	30	4
Flash					
	Small Beginnings	7/6/72	8/12/72	23	7
Flatt, Lester & Earl Scruggs					
	Foggy Mountain Breakdown	3/28/68	3/28/68	pr	1
Flavor					
	Sally Had A Party	8/29/68	9/5/68	27	2
Fleetwood Mac					
	Over My Head	1/17/76	2/21/76	8	6
Fletcher, Lois					
	I Am What I Am	3/23/74	5/4/74	14	12
Flirtations					
	Nothing But A Heartache	1/29/69	6/4/69	21	9
Flock					
	Can't You See (That I Really Love Her)	1/19/67	1/19/67	xx	3
	Take Me Back	8/3/67	8/24/67	17	3
Floyd, Eddie					
	Bring It On Home To Me	11/21/68	11/28/68	23	2
Floyd, King					
	Groove Me	1/11/71	2/8/71	26	6
Floyd & Jerry					
	Dusty	11/17/66	11/17/66	pr	1

Artist	Title	Debut	Peak	Pos	Wks
Focus					
	Hocus Pocus	4/7/73	5/26/73	1	13
Fogelberg, Dan					
	Part Of The Plan	1/25/75	3/15/75	10	11
Foghat					
	Slow Ride	2/21/76	2/21/76	35	1
Fontana, Wayne					
	Come On Home	7/7/66	7/7/66	pr	1
also see the Mindbenders					
Fortunes					
	Here Comes That Rainy Day Feeling Again	5/6/71	7/8/71	4	13
Foundations					
	Baby, Now That I've Found You	2/1/68	2/29/68	4	5
	Back On My Feet Again	2/22/68	4/4/68	26	3
	Build Me Up Buttercup	1/22/69	2/26/69	2	8
Four Jacks & A Jill					
	Master Jack	5/9/68	6/6/68	6	7
Four Seasons					
	Let's Hang On	12/16/65	12/16/65	1	6
	Little Boy (In Grown Up Clothes)	12/23/65	12/23/65	pr	1
	Working My Way Back To You	1/13/66	3/17/66	12	7
	Opus 17 (Don't You Worry 'Bout Me)	6/2/66	6/2/66	xx	1
	I've Got You Under My Skin	8/25/66	10/27/66	20	5
	Tell It To The Rain	12/8/66	2/2/67	20	5
	Beggin'	2/23/67	4/27/67	20	7
	C'mon Marianne	6/1/67	7/20/67	10	11
	Watch The Flowers Grow	11/2/67	11/30/67	12	5
	Will You Love Me Tomorrow	2/15/68	3/14/68	22	6
	Who Loves You	10/18/75	11/29/75	1	15
	December, 1963 (Oh, What A Night)	12/27/75	2/21/76	3	9
Wonder Who					
	Don't Think Twice	12/16/65	12/23/65	11	5
also see Valli, Frankie					

Artist	Title	Debut	Peak	Pos	Wks

Four Tops

	Shake Me, Wake Me (When It's Over)	2/17/66	2/17/66	pr	1
	Reach Out I'll Be There	9/15/66	11/10/66	1	12
	Standing In The Shadows Of Love	12/8/66	1/26/67	10	10
	Bernadette	3/2/67	4/6/67	15	6
	7 Rooms Of Gloom	5/18/67	6/8/67	24	4
	You Keep Running Away	9/7/67	10/12/67	24	3
	Walk Away Renee	1/18/68	2/22/68	11	6
	If I Were A Carpenter	4/11/68	6/13/68	11	8
	Yesterday's Dreams	8/8/68	8/8/68	30	1
	I'm In A Different World	10/24/68	10/31/68	24	3
	It's All In The Game	5/25/70	6/15/70	23	7
	Still Water (Love)	10/19/70	11/23/70	13	8
	MacArthur Park (Part II)	9/2/71	10/7/71	24	7
	Keeper Of The Castle	11/18/72	1/13/73	2	14
	Ain't No Woman (Like The One I've Got)	2/24/73	4/7/73	4	11
	Are You Man Enough	7/28/73	9/15/73	9	11

also see the Supremes & the Four Tops

Franklin, Aretha

	I Never Loved A Man (The Way I Love You)	3/30/67	3/30/67	30	1
	Respect	5/4/67	6/15/67	7	9
	Baby I Love You	7/20/67	9/7/67	15	8
	A Natural Woman (You Make Me Feel Like)	9/28/67	11/2/67	18	5
	Chain Of Fools	11/30/67	1/11/68	4	9
	(Sweet Sweet Baby) Since You've Been Gone	2/15/68	3/28/68	8	8
	/Ain't No Way	4/4/68	5/9/68	19	4
	Think	5/16/68	6/13/68	12	7
	I Say A Little Prayer	8/15/68	9/12/68	6	7
	/The House That Jack Built	8/15/68	9/12/68	6	7
	See Saw	11/28/68	12/12/68	24	4
	Call Me	3/2/70	3/16/70	18	5
	You're All I Need To Get By	2/22/71	3/25/71	27	5
	Bridge Over Troubled Water	5/6/71	6/3/71	15	7
	Spanish Harlem	7/29/71	9/9/71	3	10
	Rock Steady	10/21/71	12/9/71	13	11
	Day Dreaming	3/16/72	5/4/72	2	11
	Angel	8/4/73	9/8/73	24	8
	Until You Come Back To Me (That's What I'm Gonna Do)	1/12/74	2/23/74	14	10

Artist	Title	Debut	Peak	Pos	Wks
Fred, John & his Playboy Band					
	Judy In Disguise (With Glasses)	12/7/67	1/4/68	1	10
Free					
	All Right Now	8/24/70	10/5/70	3	14
	also see Bad Company				
Free Movement					
	I've Found Someone Of My Own	8/19/71	10/21/71	2	13
Friend & Lover					
	Reach Out Of The Darkness	5/2/68	6/6/68	4	8
Friends Of Distinction					
	Grazing In The Grass	5/7/69	6/4/69	1	7
	Going In Circles	1/12/70	1/12/70	14	3
	Love Or Let Me Be Lonely	3/2/70	4/27/70	8	16
Frijid Pink					
	House Of The Rising Sun	2/16/70	3/9/70	2	9
Frost, Max & the Troopers					
	Shape Of Things To Come	8/29/68	10/3/68	3	9
Fuller, Bobby, Four					
	I Fought The Law	1/27/66	2/17/66	6	7
	Love's Made A Fool Of You	3/24/66	4/21/66	xx	3
Fulsom, Lowell					
	Tramp	1/19/67	1/19/67	xx	3
Fuzz					
	I Love You For All Seasons	4/8/71	5/20/71	20	8
Gallery					
	Nice To Be With You	4/20/72	6/15/72	1	15
	I Believe In Music	10/14/72	12/2/72	7	12
	Big City Miss Ruth Ann	2/17/73	4/7/73	7	11
Garfunkel, Art					
	All I Know	9/22/73	11/3/73	4	12
	also see Simon & Garfunkel				

Artist	Title	Debut	Peak	Pos	Wks
Gary & the Hornets					
	Hi Hi Hazel	11/3/66	11/3/66	pr	1
Gaye, Marvin					
	One More Heartache	2/17/66	2/17/66	pr	1
	You	2/1/68	2/15/68	28	3
	Chained	10/10/68	10/17/68	26	2
	I Heard It Through The Grapevine	11/14/68	12/12/68	1	12
	Too Busy Thinking About My Baby	5/7/69	6/4/69	2	10
	That's The Way Love Is	9/10/69	10/8/69	9	5
	What's Going On	2/8/71	3/25/71	3	12
	Mercy Mercy Me (The Ecology)	7/1/71	8/12/71	6	12
	Inner City Blues (Make Me Wanna Holler)	9/30/71	11/11/71	8	11
	Trouble Man	1/13/73	2/10/73	18	8
	Let's Get It On	7/21/73	9/29/73	1	15
Gaye, Marvin & Tammi Terrell					
	Ain't No Mountain High Enough	8/10/67	8/10/67	25	1
	Your Precious Love	9/28/67	11/2/67	14	6
	If I Could Build My Whole World Around You	12/14/67	1/4/68	18	6
	Ain't Nothing Like The Real Thing	5/9/68	6/13/68	15	6
	You're All I Need To Get By	8/8/68	9/12/68	8	6
	Keep On Lovin' Me Honey	11/14/68	11/14/68	25	1
	Good Lovin' Ain't Easy To Come By	2/26/69	2/26/69	29	1
also see Ross, Diana & Marvin Gaye and Terrell, Tammi					
Gaynor, Gloria					
	Never Can Say Goodbye	1/11/75	2/22/75	2	12
Geddes, David					
	Run Joey Run	8/2/75	9/13/75	7	12
	The Last Game Of The Season (A Blind Man In The Bleachers)	11/15/75	12/13/75	20	7
Geils, J., Band					
	Looking For A Love	12/16/71	1/20/72	16	9
	Give It To Me	4/14/73	6/16/73	7	13
	Must Of Got Lost	11/2/74	12/21/74	16	12
Gentry, Bobbie					
	Ode To Billie Joe	8/17/67	9/7/67	1	9
	Okolona River Bottom Band	11/23/67	11/23/67	pr	1

Artist	Title	Debut	Peak	Pos	Wks
Gentrys					
	Keep On Dancing	12/16/65	12/16/65	5	2
	Why Should I Cry	2/16/70	2/23/70	30	3
Gerry & the Pacemakers					
	Girl On A Swing	9/1/66	10/20/66	11	7
Gladstone					
	A Piece Of Paper	9/2/72	10/14/72	22	8
also see the Five Americans					
Glass Bottle					
	I Ain't Got Time Anymore	8/12/71	9/16/71	17	9
Glitter, Gary					
	Rock And Roll Part 2	7/6/72	9/2/72	1	13
	I Didn't Know I Loved You (Till I Saw You Rock And Roll)	10/28/72	12/9/72	19	10
Godspell					
	Day By Day	6/1/72	7/22/72	12	10
Golden Earring					
	Radar Love	6/29/74	8/10/74	4	12
Goldsboro, Bobby					
	It's Too Late	2/10/66	3/10/66	xx	4
	Honey	3/14/68	4/18/68	1	10
	Autumn Of My Life	7/4/68	8/8/68	16	6
	The Straight Life	11/28/68	12/12/68	23	3
	Watching Scotty Grow	1/11/71	2/22/71	11	8
Goodees					
	Condition Red	1/8/69	1/22/69	14	3
Goodman, Dickie					
	Batman & His Grandmother	5/19/66	5/26/66	10	4
	Energy Crisis '74	2/16/74	3/9/74	12	7
	Mr. Jaws	9/6/75	10/4/75	5	10

Artist	Title	Debut	Peak	Pos	Wks

Goose Creek Symphony
	(Oh Lord Won't You Buy Me A) Mercedes Benz	2/10/72	3/9/72	28	6

Gore, Lesley
	California Nights	3/30/67	4/27/67	8	6

Grand Funk Railroad
	Closer To Home	9/21/70	10/19/70	16	9
	Rock 'N Roll Soul	11/11/72	12/16/72	18	8

Grand Funk
	We're An American Band	7/28/73	9/15/73	3	13
	Walk Like A Man	12/15/73	2/2/74	16	10
	The Loco-Motion	3/9/74	5/11/74	2	16
	Some Kind Of Wonderful	12/21/74	2/22/75	5	14
	Bad Time	4/19/75	6/14/75	3	14

Grass Roots
	Where Were You When I Needed You	8/11/66	8/11/66	xx	2
	Let's Live For Today	5/25/67	6/29/67	4	9
	Things I Should Have Said	8/24/67	8/24/67	30	1
	Wake Up, Wake Up	10/12/67	10/12/67	pr	1
	Midnight Confessions	9/12/68	10/17/68	2	9
	Bella Linda	12/5/68	1/15/69	15	7
	Lovin' Things	2/19/69	3/5/69	22	3
	I'd Wait A Million Years	8/6/69	9/17/69	3	10
	Heaven Knows	1/12/70	1/12/70	27	1
	Temptation Eyes	3/11/71	3/25/71	31	3
	Two Divided By Love	11/18/71	12/23/71	5	10
	Glory Bound	2/10/72	3/30/72	7	11
	The Runway	7/15/72	8/19/72	10	8

Gray, Dobie
	Drift Away	3/24/73	6/9/73	6	15

Grean, Charles Randolph, Sounde
	Quentin's Theme	7/2/69	7/23/69	8	7

Greaves, R.B.
	Always Something There To Remind Me	1/19/70	2/16/70	17	7
	Fire & Rain	3/30/70	4/20/70	29	4

Artist	Title	Debut	Peak	Pos	Wks
Green, Al					
	Tired Of Being Alone	9/23/71	11/4/71	5	10
	Let's Stay Together	12/16/71	2/3/72	7	11
	Look What You Done For Me	4/20/72	6/8/72	9	10
	I'm Still In Love With You	7/29/72	9/9/72	9	9
	You Ought To Be With Me	11/11/72	12/16/72	14	10
	Call Me (Come Back Home)	3/10/73	4/21/73	16	10
	Here I Am (Come And Take Me)	8/4/73	8/25/73	25	6
	Sha-La-La (Make Me Happy)	11/16/74	12/21/74	12	10
	L-O-V-E (Love)	4/12/75	5/3/75	27	6
Green, Garland					
	Jealous Kind Of Fella	9/17/69	9/24/69	26	2
Greenbaum, Norman					
	Spirit In The Sky	2/16/70	3/16/70	1	12
Groce, Larry					
	Junk Food Junkie	2/21/76	2/21/76	32	1
Gross, Henry					
	Simone	3/16/74	4/13/74	25	7
Guess Who					
	These Eyes	4/9/69	5/14/69	2	10
	Laughing	7/23/69	8/13/69	10	7
	No Time	1/12/70	2/2/70	1	9
	American Woman	3/23/70	4/20/70	1	12
	/No Sugar Tonight	3/23/70	4/20/70	1	12
	Hand Me Down World	7/6/70	8/17/70	30	6
	Share The Land	11/23/70	12/14/70	12	8
	Hang On To Your Life	1/11/71	2/15/71	4	8
	Star Baby	4/6/74	6/1/74	3	16
	Clap For The Wolfman	9/21/74	11/2/74	11	12
	also see Bachman-Turner Overdrive					
Gunhill Road					
	Back When My Hair Was Short	4/28/73	6/9/73	13	10
Hall, Tom T.					
	I Love	12/29/73	2/9/74	26	10

Artist	Title	Debut	Peak	Pos	Wks
Hamilton, Joe Frank & Reynolds					
	Don't Pull Your Love	6/10/71	7/22/71	1	13
	Fallin' In Love	7/19/75	9/13/75	1	18
	Winners And Losers	11/1/75	12/27/75	2	16
	also see the T-Bones				
Hamlisch, Marvin					
	The Entertainer	3/30/74	6/1/74	2	16
Hammond, Albert					
	It Never Rains In Southern California	11/18/72	12/30/72	3	13
	I'm A Train	4/13/74	5/11/74	24	8
Happenings					
	See You In September	8/4/66	9/8/66	4	9
	Go Away Little Girl	9/22/66	10/27/66	16	4
	I Got Rhythm	5/4/67	5/25/67	2	8
	My Mammy	7/6/67	7/27/67	17	6
	Crazy Love	7/6/70	8/3/70	19	6
Happy Day					
	Easy To Be Free	5/4/70	5/25/70	24	5
	/Heighty-Hi	6/15/70	7/13/70	24	5
	Everybody I Love You	11/2/70	11/30/70	30	5
Harpers Bizarre					
	The 59th Street Bridge Song (Feelin' Groovy)	3/16/67	4/13/67	16	7
	Anything Goes	9/7/67	9/28/67	19	5
Harpo, Slim					
	Baby Scratch My Back	3/10/66	3/24/66	18	3
Harris, Major					
	Love Won't Let Me Wait	5/24/75	6/28/75	13	12
	also see the Delfonics				
Harris, Richard					
	MacArthur Park	4/18/68	6/20/68	7	8

Artist	Title	Debut	Peak	Pos	Wks
Harrison, George					
	My Sweet Lord	11/23/70	12/7/70	1	10
	/Isn't It A Pity	11/23/70	11/30/70	16	2
	What Is Life	2/22/71	3/25/71	9	9
	/Apple Scruffs	2/22/71	3/11/71	18	3
	Bangla-Desh	8/5/71	9/16/71	15	8
	Give Me Love—(Give Me Peace On Earth)	5/19/73	6/30/73	1	13
also see the Beatles					
Harrison, Noel					
	Suzanne	11/2/67	11/2/67	30	1
Hart, Freddie					
	Easy Loving	10/14/71	11/18/71	13	8
Hart, Trella					
	Two Little Rooms	8/3/70	8/31/70	34	7
Havens, Richie					
	Here Comes The Sun	5/6/71	7/1/71	7	12
Hawkins', Edwin, Singers featuring Dorothy Combs Morrison					
	Oh Happy Day	4/23/69	5/21/69	4	7
Hayes, Isaac					
	Theme From Shaft	10/21/71	11/25/71	1	11
Haywood, Leon					
	I Want'a Do Something Freaky To You	10/18/75	11/22/75	15	10
Head, Murray with the Trinidad Singers					
	Superstar	4/8/71	5/20/71	5	10
Heaven Bound with Tony Scotti					
	He'd Rather Have The Rain	8/26/71	9/30/71	16	8
	Five Hundred Miles	12/9/71	1/27/72	5	10
also see the Sunrays					
Hebb, Bobby					
	Sunny	7/28/66	8/18/66	4	9

Artist	Title	Debut	Peak	Pos	Wks
Hedgehoppers Anonymous					
	It's Good News Week	12/23/65	12/30/65	5	6
	Don't Push Me	2/24/66	3/17/66	xx	3
Hendrix, Jimi, Experience					
	Purple Haze	10/5/67	11/16/67	5	8
	Foxey Lady	11/30/67	11/30/67	pr	1
	All Along The Watchtower	10/17/68	11/7/68	19	4
Herman's Hermits					
	A Must To Avoid	12/30/65	1/13/66	5	6
	Listen People	2/10/66	2/24/66	4	6
	Leaning On The Lamp Post	4/14/66	5/12/66	11	5
	This Door Swings Both Ways	6/30/66	7/28/66	12	7
	Dandy	10/6/66	10/27/66	8	8
	East West	12/8/66	12/29/66	11	6
	There's A Kind Of Hush	2/16/67	3/9/67	3	8
	Don't Go Out Into The Rain (You're Going To Melt)	6/15/67	7/6/67	24	7
	Museum	9/7/67	9/7/67	28	2
	I Can Take Or Leave Your Loving	1/25/68	2/8/68	16	4
	Sleepy Joe	4/18/68	4/18/68	pr	1
Hillside Singers					
	I'd Like To Teach The World To Sing (In Perfect Harmony)	12/23/71	1/20/72	18	7
Hodge, Chris					
	We're On Our Way	5/25/72	7/6/72	21	10
Hollies					
	I Can't Let Go	3/10/66	4/14/66	10	8
	Bus Stop	7/21/66	9/1/66	1	10
	Stop Stop Stop	11/3/66	11/24/66	9	7
	On A Carousel	3/16/67	4/20/67	4	9
	Pay You Back With Interest	5/18/67	6/22/67	13	6
	Carrie-Anne	6/8/67	8/17/67	10	12
	King Midas In Reverse	9/28/67	9/28/67	pr	1
	Dear Eloise	11/16/67	11/16/67	pr	1
	Jennifer Eccles	2/29/68	5/16/68	14	6
	Sorry Suzanne	4/23/69	4/30/69	28	4

Artist	Title	Debut	Peak	Pos	Wks
	He Ain't Heavy, He's My Brother	1/19/70	2/23/70	6	11
	Long Cool Woman (In A Black Dress)	7/6/72	8/19/72	2	11
	The Air That I Breathe	7/20/74	8/24/74	2	12
	also see Crosby, Stills & Nash				

Holm, Michael
	When A Child Is Born	12/14/74	1/18/75	19	8

Holman, Eddie
	Hey There Lonely Girl	1/12/70	2/9/70	2	10

Holmes, Clint
	Playground In My Mind	7/7/73	7/28/73	2	10

Holmes, Richard "Groove"
	Misty	8/4/66	8/4/66	xx	2

Hombres
	Let It Out (Let It All Hang Out)	9/28/67	10/26/67	3	9

Hondells
	Younger Girl	4/28/66	4/28/66	pr	1
	Kissin' My Life Away	8/18/66	8/18/66	pr	1
	also see Campbell, Glen and Sagittarius				

Honey Cone
	Want Ads	4/29/71	6/10/71	1	11
	Stick-Up	9/9/71	10/14/71	9	8

Hopkin, Mary
	Those Were The Days	10/3/68	10/31/68	1	10
	Goodbye	5/14/69	6/4/69	22	4
	Temma Harbour	3/23/70	3/30/70	30	3

Hot Butter
	Popcorn	9/2/72	10/14/72	8	11

Hot Chocolate
	Emma	1/25/75	4/5/75	9	15
	Disco Queen	7/5/75	8/2/75	16	10
	You Sexy Thing	11/1/75	1/17/76	9	15

Artist	Title	Debut	Peak	Pos	Wks

Hotlegs
	Neanderthal Man	8/17/70	8/31/70	5	8

also see 10cc

Houston, Thelma
	Save The Country	1/26/70	2/9/70	23	4

Hudson Brothers
	So You Are A Star	11/9/74	12/7/74	16	8
	Rendezvous	8/2/75	9/6/75	14	9

Hues Corporation
	Rock The Boat	6/1/74	7/20/74	1	15

Human Beinz
	Nobody But Me	1/18/68	2/15/68	3	8

Humperdinck, Engelbert
	Release Me (And Let Me Love Again)	5/11/67	5/25/67	13	6
	There Goes My Everything	7/27/67	8/3/67	26	2
	The Last Waltz	10/19/67	11/9/67	23	3
	Am I That Easy To Forget	1/4/68	2/8/68	26	5
	A Man Without Love (Quando M'innamoro)	5/2/68	6/13/68	19	5
	Winter World Of Love	1/12/70	1/19/70	15	6
	My Marie	6/22/70	7/6/70	31	4
	When There's No You	4/8/71	4/29/71	28	4

Humphrey, Paul & his Cool Aid Chemists
	Cool Aid	4/15/71	6/3/71	10	11

Hutton, Danny
	Big Bright Eyes	12/23/65	2/10/66	xx	2

also see Three Dog Night

Hyland, Brian
	The Joker Went Wild	9/1/66	9/29/66	6	7
	Gypsy Woman	9/28/70	11/9/70	2	15

Ian, Janis
	Society's Child (Baby I've Been Thinking)	7/20/67	8/17/67	12	7
	Younger Generation Blues	9/14/67	9/14/67	pr	1
	At Seventeen	8/2/75	9/27/75	2	16

Artist	Title	Debut	Peak	Pos	Wks

Ides Of March
	You Wouldn't Listen	5/12/66	6/23/66	10	8
	Roller Coaster	8/18/66	9/15/66	xx	3
	Vehicle	3/9/70	4/20/70	3	13
	L.A. Goodbye	2/22/71	4/15/71	2	12

Illusion
	Did You See Her Eyes	8/6/69	9/3/69	11	6

Impressions
	We're A Winner	1/18/68	2/22/68	21	6
	Fool For You	10/10/68	11/7/68	16	5
	Check Out Your Mind	6/15/70	7/6/70	14	7
	Finally Got Myself Together (I'm A Changed Man)	6/15/74	7/20/74	25	9

also see Butler, Jerry and Mayfield, Curtis

Ingram, Luther
	(If Loving You Is Wrong) I Don't Want To Be Right	6/29/72	8/26/72	2	13

Innocence
	There's Got To Be A Word	1/5/67	1/5/67	xx	2
	Mairzy Doats	3/9/67	3/9/67	30	2

Intruders
	Cowboys To Girls	4/18/68	5/23/68	11	6

Irish Rovers
	The Unicorn	4/4/68	5/16/68	7	8
	The Marvelous Toy	12/14/70	12/14/70	xx	2

Iron Butterfly
	In-A-Gadda-Da-Vida	10/3/68	10/17/68	17	3

also see Blues Image

Isley Brothers
	It's Your Thing	3/12/69	4/2/69	3	10
	Pop That Thang	8/26/72	9/23/72	15	8
	That Lady (Part 1)	9/8/73	10/20/73	10	10
	Fight The Power Part 1	8/16/75	9/13/75	5	11

Artist	Title	Debut	Peak	Pos	Wks
Ivy League					
	Running Round In Circles	4/14/66	4/14/66	pr	1
Jacks, Terry					
	Seasons In The Sun	1/12/74	3/2/74	1	16
also see the Poppy Family					
Jackson, Deon					
	Love Makes The World Go Round	2/24/66	3/10/66	19	3
Jackson, J.J.					
	But It's Alright	5/28/69	6/25/69	21	5
Jackson, Jermaine					
	Daddy's Home	1/27/73	3/10/73	14	11
also see the Jackson 5					
Jackson, Michael					
	Got To Be There	10/28/71	12/9/71	4	10
	Rockin' Robin	3/2/72	4/13/72	2	12
	I Wanna Be Where You Are	6/1/72	7/22/72	6	11
	Ben	9/2/72	10/21/72	2	12
also see the Jackson 5					
Jackson, Millie					
	Ask Me What You Want	5/25/72	6/29/72	17	9
Jackson 5					
	Big Boy	4/4/68	4/25/68	27	2
	I Want You Back	1/12/70	1/12/70	8	3
	ABC	3/9/70	4/6/70	1	11
	The Love You Save	5/25/70	6/29/70	1	14
	I'll Be There	9/7/70	10/5/70	1	14
	Santa Claus Is Comin' To Town	12/14/70	12/14/70	xx	2
	Mama's Pearl	1/11/71	2/22/71	1	11
	Never Can Say Goodbye	3/25/71	5/13/71	2	12
	Maybe Tomorrow	7/22/71	8/26/71	2	10
	Sugar Daddy	12/9/71	1/20/72	2	10
	Little Bitty Pretty One	4/13/72	6/1/72	10	12
	Corner Of The Sky	11/11/72	12/16/72	8	8
	Dancing Machine	4/6/74	6/8/74	6	15

Artist	Title	Debut	Peak	Pos	Wks
	I Am Love (Parts I & II)	2/8/75	4/12/75	5	14
	also see Jackson, Jermaine and Jackson, Michael				

Jaggerz
	The Rapper	1/19/70	2/23/70	2	12

James, Etta
	Tell Mama	12/21/67	1/11/68	18	4

James, Tommy & the Shondells
	Hanky Panky	6/2/66	6/23/66	1	10
	Say I Am (What I Am)	7/14/66	8/18/66	3	9
	It's Only Love	10/20/66	12/15/66	10	8
	I Think We're Alone Now	1/26/67	3/2/67	1	12
	Mirage	4/13/67	5/18/67	1	7
	I Like The Way	6/15/67	7/27/67	14	7
	Gettin' Together	8/17/67	9/14/67	12	6
	Out Of The Blue	11/9/67	11/30/67	19	4
	Get Out Now	1/18/68	2/22/68	22	4
	Mony Mony	3/21/68	5/9/68	1	11
	Somebody Cares	7/11/68	8/8/68	20	4
	Crimson And Clover	12/26/68	1/15/69	3	10
	Sweet Cherry Wine	4/9/69	5/14/69	21	5
	Crystal Blue Persuasion	6/4/69	7/9/69	2	11
	Ball Of Fire	10/8/69	10/8/69	29	1
	She	1/12/70	1/12/70	30	2
	Gotta Get Back To You	2/9/70	3/2/70	27	5

James, Tommy
	Adrienne	3/1/71	3/11/71	35	3
	Draggin' The Line	6/3/71	7/22/71	2	13
	I'm Comin' Home	9/16/71	11/4/71	4	11
	Nothing To Hide	11/18/71	1/13/72	2	11
	Tell 'Em Willie Boy's A'Comin'	2/10/72	3/9/72	25	7

James Gang
	Walk Away	7/1/71	7/29/71	17	7
	also see Walsh, Joe				

Jamestown Massacre
	Summer Sun	7/22/72	8/26/72	20	7

Artist	Title	Debut	Peak	Pos	Wks

Jan & Dean
	Batman	3/3/66	3/3/66	xx	1
	Popsicle	5/26/66	7/21/66	20	5

Jane Avenue Bus Stop
	The Chant	12/14/70	12/14/70	xx	2

Jay & the Americans
	Sunday And Me	12/16/65	12/16/65	15	2
	Why Can't You Bring Me Home	2/10/66	2/10/66	pr	1
	Crying	5/19/66	5/19/66	pr	1
	This Magic Moment	1/22/69	2/26/69	3	7
	Walkin' In The Rain	1/12/70	2/9/70	11	7
	Capture The Moment	3/2/70	3/23/70	26	6

Jay & the Techniques
	Apples, Peaches, Pumpkin Pie	9/7/67	10/12/67	4	7
	Keep The Ball Rollin'	12/14/67	12/21/67	27	2

Jaye, Jerry
	My Girl Josephine	5/18/67	6/1/67	22	3

Jefferson
	Baby Take Me In Your Arms	1/26/70	2/16/70	15	7

Jefferson Airplane
	Somebody To Love	4/27/67	5/25/67	1	9
	White Rabbit	6/8/67	7/27/67	4	9
	Ballad Of You & Me & Pooneil	8/24/67	9/7/67	26	3

Jefferson Starship
	Miracles	10/11/75	11/22/75	2	15

Jeffrey, Joe, Group
	My Pledge Of Love	6/25/69	7/16/69	15	5

Jethro Tull
	Living In The Past	12/9/72	1/27/73	2	12
	Bungle In The Jungle	1/11/75	2/15/75	6	9

Artist	Title	Debut	Peak	Pos	Wks

Jigsaw
	Sky High	10/25/75	12/20/75	2	16

Jo Jo Gunne
	Run Run Run	3/9/72	5/11/72	2	14

also see Spirit

John, Elton
	Your Song	12/7/70	2/1/71	7	11
	Honky Cat	9/2/72	10/7/72	18	8
	Crocodile Rock	12/23/72	2/10/73	1	14
	Daniel	4/28/73	6/16/73	4	11
	Saturday Night's Alright For Fighting	7/28/73	9/22/73	4	13
	Goodbye Yellow Brick Road	10/27/73	12/15/73	3	14
	Bennie And The Jets	2/16/74	4/13/74	2	16
	Don't Let The Sun Go Down On Me	6/22/74	8/17/74	1	16
	The Bitch Is Back	9/28/74	11/9/74	1	13
	Lucy In The Sky With Diamonds	11/30/74	1/11/75	1	14
	Philadelphia Freedom	3/15/75	4/26/75	1	17
	Someone Saved My Life Tonight	7/5/75	8/30/75	1	16
	Island Girl	10/11/75	11/22/75	1	15

John, Robert
	When The Party Is Over	11/9/70	11/30/70	19	6
	The Lion Sleeps Tonight	1/13/72	3/9/72	2	12

Johns, Sammy
	Chevy Van	3/8/75	5/10/75	1	17

Johnson, Kevin
	Rock 'N Roll (I Gave You The Best Years Of My Life)	10/20/73	11/17/73	24	7

Jon & Robin & the In Crowd
	Do It Again A Little Bit Slower	6/15/67	7/13/67	8	6

Jones, Davy
	Rainy Jane	6/10/71	7/22/71	7	11

also see the Monkees

Artist	Title	Debut	Peak	Pos	Wks

Jones, Tom

	Green, Green Grass Of Home	1/26/67	2/16/67	12	5
	Detroit City	3/2/67	3/30/67	27	4
	Funny Familiar Forgotten Feelings	5/11/67	5/11/67	pr	1
	I'm Coming Home	12/21/67	12/21/67	pr	1
	Delilah	3/21/68	5/16/68	21	6
	Love Me Tonight	5/28/69	7/2/69	11	8
	I'll Never Fall In Love Again	7/2/69	8/13/69	11	11
	Without Love (There Is Nothing)	1/12/70	1/26/70	5	7
	Daughter Of Darkness	4/27/70	5/25/70	4	10
	I (Who Have Nothing)	8/17/70	9/14/70	11	10
	She's A Lady	2/8/71	4/1/71	1	14
	Puppet Man	5/20/71	6/17/71	8	8

Joplin, Janis

	Me And Bobby McGee	2/1/71	4/1/71	5	11

also see Big Brother & the Holding Company

Kallmann, Gunter, Chorus

	Wish Me A Rainbow	1/26/67	1/26/67	xx	1

Kasenetz-Katz Singing Orchestral Circus

	Quick Joey Small (Run Joey Run)	11/7/68	12/5/68	10	6

also see Crazy Elephant, 1910 Fruitgum Co., Ohio Express, Reunion and the Third Rail

KC & the Sunshine Band

	Get Down Tonight	8/16/75	9/20/75	1	16
	That's The Way (I Like It)	11/8/75	12/13/75	1	15

Keith

	Ain't Gonna Lie	9/29/66	10/27/66	15	6
	98.6	12/22/66	1/19/67	14	7
	Daylight Savin' Time	6/1/67	6/1/67	pr	1

Kendricks, Eddie

	Keep On Truckin' (Part 1)	9/15/73	11/10/73	3	14
	Boogie Down	1/19/74	3/9/74	5	13
	Son Of Sagittarius	5/11/74	6/15/74	21	9
	Shoeshine Boy	5/10/75	5/24/75	29	5

also see the Temptations

Artist	Title	Debut	Peak	Pos	Wks
Kent, Al					
	You've Got To Pay The Price	9/28/67	9/28/67	26	2
	also see Coffey, Dennis				
Kim, Andy					
	How'd We Ever Get This Way	5/16/68	6/27/68	6	8
	Baby, I Love You	6/18/69	7/23/69	3	9
	It's Your Life	7/6/70	8/3/70	25	6
	Be My Baby	11/2/70	12/7/70	7	10
	Rock Me Gently	8/10/74	9/14/74	2	12
	Fire, Baby I'm On Fire	11/2/74	12/7/74	17	9
	also see the Archies				
King, B.B.					
	Why I Sing The Blues	7/16/69	7/16/69	27	2
	The Thrill Is Gone	1/12/70	2/2/70	14	6
	I Like To Live The Love	2/16/74	3/23/74	20	8
King, Ben E.					
	Supernatural Thing—Part I	3/22/75	4/12/75	29	5
	also see the Drifters				
King, Carole					
	It's Too Late	5/20/71	6/24/71	1	14
	Jazzman	10/19/74	11/23/74	3	13
King, Jonathan					
	Round Round	5/4/67	5/4/67	pr	1
King Harvest					
	Dancing In The Moonlight	1/13/73	2/24/73	1	12
Kingsmen					
	Killer Joe	5/5/66	5/5/66	xx	2
	also see Ely, Jack				
Kinks					
	A Well Respected Man	1/6/66	1/20/66	15	4
	Till The End Of The Day	3/31/66	5/5/66	16	4
	Sunny Afternoon	6/16/66	9/15/66	16	7
	Lola	9/7/70	10/26/70	2	13
	Apeman	1/11/71	2/15/71	8	7

Artist	Title	Debut	Peak	Pos	Wks
Kiss					
	Rock And Roll All Nite	11/29/75	2/14/76	2	13
Kissoon, Mac & Katie					
	Chirpy Chirpy Cheep Cheep	9/30/71	11/11/71	4	10
Knickerbockers					
	Lies	1/20/66	2/10/66	4	5
	One Track Mind	3/10/66	4/7/66	xx	2
	High On Love	6/9/66	6/9/66	pr	1
Knight, Frederick					
	I've Been Lonely For So Long	6/15/72	7/6/72	25	5
Knight, Gladys & the Pips					
	I Heard It Through The Grapevine	11/9/67	1/4/68	8	9
	The End Of Our Road	2/22/68	3/7/68	23	4
	The Nitty Gritty	8/6/69	8/27/69	21	4
	You Need Love Like I Do (Don't You)	4/6/70	4/20/70	19	5
	If I Were Your Woman	12/14/70	1/4/71	10	7
	Neither One Of Us (Wants To Be The First To Say Goodbye)	3/10/73	4/14/73	13	9
	Daddy Could Swear, I Declare	6/16/73	7/21/73	27	7
	Midnight Train To Georgia	9/22/73	11/17/73	1	14
	I've Got To Use My Imagination	12/29/73	2/16/74	6	12
	Best Thing That Ever Happened To Me	3/16/74	5/25/74	4	16
	On And On	7/13/74	8/24/74	7	12
	I Feel A Song (In My Heart)	11/23/74	12/28/74	16	10
	The Way We Were/Try To Remember	5/24/75	7/12/75	8	14
Knight, Jean					
	Mr. Big Stuff	6/24/71	8/5/71	3	11
Knight, Robert					
	Everlasting Love	10/26/67	11/30/67	5	7
	Blessed Are The Lonely	12/28/67	12/28/67	pr	1
Kool & the Gang					
	Jungle Boogie	2/2/74	3/23/74	6	12
	Hollywood Swinging	6/8/74	7/6/74	15	10

Artist	Title	Debut	Peak	Pos	Wks
Kraftwerk					
	Autobahn	4/5/75	5/17/75	12	12
Kuban, Bob & the In-Men					
	The Cheater	3/3/66	3/3/66	xx	2
Kulis, Charlie					
	Runaway	3/1/75	4/26/75	8	13
Labelle					
	Lady Marmalade	3/8/75	4/19/75	1	14
Lai, Francis					
	Theme From Love Story	1/25/71	1/25/71	19	2
Laine, Frankie					
	I'll Take Care Of Your Cares	3/9/67	3/9/67	26	3
	Making Memories	5/18/67	5/18/67	30	2
	You Gave Me A Mountain	3/12/69	3/26/69	26	3
Lawrence, Vicki					
	The Night The Lights Went Out In Georgia	3/24/73	4/21/73	1	11
Leaves					
	Hey Joe	6/9/66	6/23/66	9	4
Led Zeppelin					
	Whole Lotta Love	1/12/70	1/12/70	5	5
	Immigrant Song	11/30/70	1/11/71	2	10
	Black Dog	12/16/71	2/3/72	2	13
	Over The Hills And Far Away	6/9/73	7/14/73	17	7
	D'yer Mak'er	10/13/73	12/15/73	4	14
	also see the Yardbirds				
Lee, Brenda					
	Coming On Strong	11/24/66	11/24/66	xx	3
	Ride, Ride, Ride	1/12/67	1/12/67	pr	1
Lee, Dickey					
	Red, Green, Yellow And Blue	1/4/68	1/4/68	pr	1

Artist	Title	Debut	Peak	Pos	Wks

Lee, Peggy
	Is That All There Is	10/8/69	10/8/69	30	1

Left Banke
	Pretty Ballerina	2/9/67	3/2/67	14	5

also see the Stories

Legend
	Raining In My Heart	8/25/66	8/25/66	pr	1

Lemon Pipers
	Green Tambourine	12/14/67	1/25/68	2	10
	Jelly Jungle (Of Orange Marmalade)	6/6/68	6/13/68	21	2

Lennon, John
	Instant Karma (We All Shine On)	2/23/70	3/23/70	3	10
	Mother	1/25/71	2/1/71	22	3
	Power To The People	5/6/71	6/3/71	8	8
	Imagine	10/7/71	11/18/71	2	11
	Mind Games	11/10/73	12/29/73	1	14
	Whatever Gets You Thru The Night	10/26/74	12/7/74	6	10
	#9 Dream	1/11/75	3/1/75	13	10
	Stand By Me	4/5/75	5/3/75	24	6

Lennon, John & Yoko Ono
	Happy Xmas (War Is Over)	12/23/71	12/30/71	32	2

also see the Beatles and the Plastic Ono Band

Lettermen
	Goin' Out Of My Head/Can't Take My Eyes Off You	12/21/67	2/1/68	6	10
	Sherry Don't Go	3/7/68	5/9/68	27	3
	Hurt So Bad	7/23/69	8/6/69	2	11
	Love	9/30/71	11/4/71	12	10

Lewis, Barbara
	Only All The Time	6/15/67	6/15/67	pr	1

Lewis, Gary & the Playboys
	She's Just My Style	12/30/65	1/20/66	9	5
	Sure Gonna Miss Her	3/3/66	3/31/66	13	5
	Green Grass	5/12/66	6/9/66	8	6

Artist	Title	Debut	Peak	Pos	Wks
	My Heart's Symphony	7/28/66	8/18/66	xx	3
	(You Don't Have To) Paint Me A Picture	9/29/66	11/17/66	18	6
	Where Will The Words Come From	1/5/67	2/9/67	17	7
	The Loser (With A Broken Heart)	2/23/67	4/6/67	26	2
	Girls In Love	5/4/67	6/1/67	28	3
	Sealed With A Kiss	7/11/68	8/8/68	7	8

Lewis, Jerry Lee
| | Me And Bobby McGee | 12/9/71 | 1/13/72 | 25 | 7 |
| | Drinking Wine Spo-Dee O'Dee | 4/14/73 | 4/28/73 | 28 | 5 |

Lewis, Ramsey
| | A Hard Day's Night | 1/13/66 | 1/13/66 | pr | 1 |
| | Wade In The Water | 8/4/66 | 8/4/66 | xx | 5 |

also see Young-Holt Unlimited

Lightfoot, Gordon
| | If You Could Read My Mind | 1/4/71 | 2/15/71 | 1 | 11 |
| | Sundown | 5/4/74 | 6/29/74 | 1 | 17 |

Lighthouse
| | One Fine Morning | 10/14/71 | 10/28/71 | 23 | 5 |

Lind, Bob
| | Elusive Butterfly | 2/17/66 | 3/24/66 | 7 | 7 |
| | Remember The Rain | 4/7/66 | 4/7/66 | pr | 1 |

Lindsay, Mark
| | Arizona | 1/12/70 | 2/2/70 | 4 | 11 |
| | Silver Bird | 7/13/70 | 8/10/70 | 19 | 9 |

also see Revere, Paul & the Raiders

Little Boy Blues
| | I'm Ready | 3/10/66 | 3/10/66 | xx | 1 |

Little Sister
| | You're The One-Part 1 | 4/6/70 | 4/13/70 | 28 | 3 |

Lobo
	Me And You And A Dog Named Boo	3/18/71	4/29/71	6	10
	I'd Love You To Want Me	9/23/72	11/25/72	1	15
	Don't Expect Me To Be Your Friend	1/13/73	2/17/73	2	11

Artist	Title	Debut	Peak	Pos	Wks
	It Sure Took A Long, Long Time	4/14/73	5/19/73	14	9
	How Can I Tell Her	7/14/73	9/1/73	13	11
	Standing At The End Of The Line	3/30/74	5/25/74	12	13
	Don't Tell Me Goodnight	3/29/75	5/10/75	23	10

Loggins & Messina
	Vahevala	3/23/72	5/18/72	3	11
	Your Mama Don't Dance	12/16/72	2/10/73	8	14
	Thinking Of You	5/12/73	6/23/73	10	9

also see Buffalo Springfield and Poco

Long, Shorty
	Here Comes The Judge	6/13/68	7/11/68	11	5

Looking Glass
	Brandy (You're A Fine Girl)	6/29/72	8/19/72	1	14
	Jimmy Loves Mary-Anne	9/1/73	10/13/73	5	12

Lopez, Trini
	I'm Comin' Home, Cindy	4/28/66	4/28/66	xx	1

Los Bravos
	Black Is Black	8/11/66	10/6/66	3	9
	Going Nowhere	11/24/66	11/24/66	pr	1
	Bring A Little Lovin'	5/16/68	5/16/68	pr	1

Lost Generation
	The Sly, Slick, And The Wicked	6/22/70	7/20/70	19	8

Love
	My Little Red Book	5/5/66	6/2/66	xx	3

Love Unlimited
	Walkin' In The Rain With The One I Love	5/11/72	6/15/72	16	8

also see the Love Unlimited Orchestra and White, Barry

Love Unlimited Orchestra
	Love's Theme	12/15/73	2/9/74	2	15

also see Love Unlimited and White, Barry

Artist	Title	Debut	Peak	Pos	Wks
Lovin' Spoonful					
	You Didn't Have To Be So Nice	12/30/65	1/27/66	9	7
	Daydream	2/24/66	3/31/66	5	8
	Did You Ever Have To Make Up Your Mind	5/5/66	6/2/66	5	7
	Summer In The City	7/7/66	8/4/66	1	11
	Rain On The Roof	10/27/66	11/3/66	13	6
	Nashville Cats	12/22/66	1/5/67	16	5
	Darling Be Home Soon	2/9/67	3/23/67	24	5
	Six O'Clock	4/20/67	6/1/67	17	5
	She Is Still A Mystery	11/16/67	11/23/67	22	2
also see the Mugwumps					
Lujack, Larry, "Superjock"					
	The Ballad Of The Mad Streaker	4/27/74	4/27/74	xx	4
Lulu					
	To Sir With Love	9/28/67	11/2/67	1	11
	Me, The Peaceful Heart	4/11/68	4/18/68	23	2
	Oh Me Oh My I'm A Fool For You Baby	2/9/70	3/2/70	15	8
	Hum A Song (From Your Heart)	4/27/70	5/11/70	23	4
Lundberg, Victor					
	An Open Letter To My Teenage Son	11/9/67	11/30/67	9	4
Lynn, Barbara					
	This Is The Thanks I Get	2/15/68	2/29/68	27	2
Lynyrd Skynyrd					
	Sweet Home Alabama	8/31/74	10/19/74	1	15
MacGregor, Byron					
	Americans	1/12/74	2/2/74	8	6
Magic Lanterns					
	Shame, Shame	10/31/68	11/28/68	4	6
Main Ingredient					
	Everybody Plays The Fool	9/9/72	10/28/72	1	12
	Just Don't Want To Be Lonely	3/2/74	5/4/74	3	15

Artist	Title	Debut	Peak	Pos	Wks
Malo					
	Suavecito	4/6/72	5/18/72	1	11
Mamas & the Papas					
	California Dreamin'	2/3/66	3/3/66	1	11
	Monday, Monday	3/31/66	5/5/66	1	10
	I Saw Her Again	6/23/66	7/28/66	4	10
	No Salt On Her Tail	9/15/66	9/15/66	pr	1
	Look Through My Window	10/13/66	11/10/66	18	4
	Words Of Love	12/8/66	1/19/67	5	8
	/Dancing In The Street	12/8/66	1/19/67	5	7
	Dedicated To The One I Love	2/16/67	3/30/67	5	8
	Creeque Alley	4/27/67	6/1/67	16	5
	Twelve Thirty (Young Girls Are Coming To The Canyon)	8/17/67	9/28/67	20	5
	Glad To Be Unhappy	10/19/67	11/23/67	16	6

also see Elliot, Mama Cass, the Mugwumps and Phillips, John

Artist	Title	Debut	Peak	Pos	Wks
Manchester, Melissa					
	Midnight Blue	6/28/75	8/9/75	6	13
Mancini, Henry					
	Love Theme From Romeo & Juliet	5/21/69	6/11/69	1	10
	Theme From Love Story	1/4/71	1/18/71	19	5
Manhattan Transfer					
	Operator	11/1/75	11/22/75	16	9
Manhattans					
	There's No Me Without You	6/9/73	7/14/73	26	7
Manilow, Barry					
	Mandy	12/28/74	2/8/75	1	13
	It's A Miracle	4/12/75	5/31/75	1	14
	I Write The Songs	11/15/75	2/7/76	1	15
Mann, Herbie					
	Hijack	4/26/75	5/24/75	27	8

Artist	Title	Debut	Peak	Pos	Wks
Mann, Manfred					
	Pretty Flamingo	7/7/66	7/14/66	15	4
	Mighty Quinn (Quinn The Eskimo)	3/7/68	4/11/68	12	8
Marketts					
	Batman Theme	2/10/66	2/24/66	18	4
Marmalade					
	Reflections Of My Life	3/16/70	4/20/70	7	13
Martha & the Vandellas					
	I'm Ready For Love	11/10/66	12/8/66	18	5
	Jimmy Mack	3/16/67	4/27/67	6	8
	Honey Chile	12/21/67	1/11/68	24	3
	Bless You	10/7/71	11/4/71	28	6
Martin, Bobbi					
	For The Love Of Him	3/23/70	4/27/70	5	10
Martin, Dean					
	Little Ole Wine Drinker, Me	8/10/67	8/10/67	pr	1
Martino, Al					
	Spanish Eyes	1/27/66	1/27/66	20	1
	Daddy's Little Girl	3/9/67	3/9/67	28	1
	Mary In The Morning	6/29/67	6/29/67	28	1
	To The Door Of The Sun (Alle Porte Del Sole)	2/8/75	3/8/75	25	8
Marvelettes					
	The Hunter Gets Captured By The Game	2/16/67	2/23/67	23	3
	Here I Am Baby	7/4/68	7/4/68	28	1
Masekela, Hugh					
	Grazing In The Grass	6/20/68	7/11/68	6	8
Mashmakhan					
	As The Years Go By	11/9/70	11/23/70	11	6
Matthews' Southern Comfort					
	Woodstock	2/22/71	4/8/71	12	11

Artist	Title	Debut	Peak	Pos	Wks

Mauds
| | Hold On | 6/22/67 | 7/20/67 | 11 | 6 |
| | Soul Drippin' | 8/22/68 | 10/10/68 | 16 | 8 |

Mauriat, Paul
| | Love Is Blue | 1/18/68 | 2/8/68 | 1 | 11 |

Mayfield, Curtis
| | Freddie's Dead (Theme From "Superfly") | 10/7/72 | 11/11/72 | 3 | 10 |
| | Superfly | 12/30/72 | 2/3/73 | 11 | 10 |

also see the Impressions

McCall, C.W.
| | Convoy | 12/6/75 | 1/17/76 | 1 | 12 |

McCartney, Paul
	Another Day	3/1/71	4/22/71	4	12
	/Oh Woman Oh Why	3/1/71	3/11/71	22	2
	My Love	5/5/73	6/23/73	1	14

McCartney, Paul & Linda
| | Uncle Albert/Admiral Halsey | 7/29/71 | 8/26/71 | 1 | 11 |

Wings
	Hi, Hi, Hi	1/20/73	2/3/73	30	5
	Live And Let Die	7/21/73	8/25/73	4	11
	Listen To What The Man Said	6/7/75	8/2/75	1	16
	Venus And Mars Rock Show	11/8/75	12/6/75	13	11

McCartney, Paul & Wings
	Helen Wheels	11/17/73	12/29/73	14	12
	Jet	2/16/74	4/6/74	5	13
	Band On The Run	4/27/74	6/15/74	1	16
	Junior's Farm	11/9/74	12/21/74	3	13

also see the Beatles

McCoy, Van with the Soul City Symphony
| | The Hustle | 5/31/75 | 7/19/75 | 3 | 18 |

McCoys
| | Up And Down | 2/3/66 | 2/3/66 | pr | 1 |
| | Come On Let's Go | 5/12/66 | 6/9/66 | 16 | 5 |

Artist	Title	Debut	Peak	Pos	Wks
	(You Make Me Feel) So Good	7/14/66	8/4/66	xx	2
also see Derringer, Rick					
McCrae, George					
	Rock Your Baby	6/22/74	7/27/74	1	13
McCrae, Gwen					
	Rockin' Chair	6/21/75	8/16/75	3	16
McGovern, Maureen					
	The Morning After	6/30/73	8/25/73	1	15
McKenzie, Scott					
	San Francisco (Be Sure To Wear Flowers In Your Hair)	6/15/67	7/13/67	4	9
	Like An Old Time Movie	10/12/67	10/12/67	pr	1
McLain, Tommy					
	Sweet Dreams	7/21/66	8/4/66	16	4
McLean, Don					
	American Pie—Parts I & II	12/2/71	1/13/72	1	14
McNamara, Robin					
	Lay A Little Lovin' On Me	6/8/70	7/13/70	9	13
Mead, Sister Janet					
	The Lord's Prayer	3/2/74	4/13/74	3	11
Mel & Tim					
	Starting All Over Again	9/23/72	10/21/72	19	8
Melanie					
	Lay Down (Candles In The Rain)	5/4/70	6/15/70	5	13
	Brand New Key	10/14/71	12/9/71	1	16
	Ring The Living Bell	2/10/72	3/30/72	3	11
Melvin, Harold & the Blue Notes					
	If You Don't Know Me By Now	11/25/72	1/13/73	7	11
Mendes, Sergio & Brasil '66					
	The Look Of Love	6/6/68	6/27/68	8	5
	The Fool On The Hill	8/22/68	9/19/68	8	8
	Scarborough Fair	11/28/68	12/12/68	21	5

Artist	Title	Debut	Peak	Pos	Wks
Mercy					
	Love (Can Make You Happy)	4/16/69	5/14/69	1	10
Meters					
	Sophisticated Cissy	2/5/69	2/19/69	27	3
MFSB featuring the Three Degrees					
	TSOP (The Sound Of Philadelphia)	3/23/74	5/11/74	5	13
also see the Three Degrees					
Michael & the Messengers					
	Midnight Hour	4/27/67	6/1/67	5	8
	Romeo And Juliet	7/6/67	8/3/67	14	6
Michaels, Lee					
	Do You Know What I Mean	9/2/71	10/14/71	2	10
Midler, Bette					
	Boogie Woogie Bugle Boy	6/16/73	7/21/73	1	12
	In The Mood	1/19/74	2/16/74	24	7
Miller, Roger					
	England Swings	12/16/65	12/23/65	19	2
	Husbands And Wives	2/3/66	2/3/66	pr	1
	Train Of Life	6/16/66	6/16/66	pr	1
Miller, Steve, Band					
	The Joker	11/17/73	1/12/74	1	15
Mills Brothers					
	Cab Driver	3/14/68	4/4/68	24	5
Mindbenders					
	A Groovy Kind Of Love	4/7/66	5/19/66	3	11
also see Fontana, Wayne and 10cc					
Miracles					
	Going To A Go-Go	12/30/65	12/30/65	pr	1
	(Come 'Round Here) I'm The One You Need	11/10/66	11/10/66	pr	1
	Do It Baby	9/21/74	10/12/74	21	6
	Love Machine (Part 1)	1/24/76	2/21/76	13	5

Artist	Title	Debut	Peak	Pos	Wks
Smokey Robinson & the Miracles					
	The Love I Saw In You Was Just A Mirage	3/23/67	3/23/67	28	1
	I Second That Emotion	11/23/67	12/28/67	10	8
	If You Can Want	3/14/68	4/4/68	19	5
	Special Occasion	8/29/68	9/26/68	21	4
	Baby, Baby Don't Cry	1/15/69	2/19/69	3	10
	Doggone Right	6/25/69	7/16/69	22	4
	The Tears Of A Clown	10/5/70	11/23/70	1	15
	I Don't Blame You At All	4/1/71	5/20/71	3	11
Mitchell, Joni					
	You Turn Me On, I'm A Radio	12/23/72	2/10/73	13	11
	Help Me	5/11/74	6/15/74	4	13
Mitchell, Willie					
	Soul Serenade	4/4/68	4/11/68	25	2
Mob					
	I Dig Everything About You	11/16/70	12/21/70	20	8
Mocedades					
	Eres Tu (Touch The Wind)	2/23/74	4/20/74	4	14
Moments					
	Love On A Two-Way Street	4/20/70	6/1/70	1	12
	Sexy Mama	2/9/74	3/16/74	11	10
Monkees					
	Last Train To Clarksville	9/8/66	10/20/66	3	11
	I'm A Believer	12/1/66	1/19/67	1	13
	/(I'm Not Your) Steppin' Stone	12/15/66	1/19/67	1	6
	A Little Bit Me, A Little Bit You	3/23/67	4/27/67	1	10
	Pleasant Valley Sunday	7/13/67	8/17/67	2	9
	/Words	7/20/67	8/17/67	2	8
	Daydream Believer	11/2/67	12/7/67	1	11
	Valleri	3/7/68	3/21/68	1	7
	/Tapioca Tundra	3/7/68	3/21/68	1	7
	It's Nice To Be With You	6/27/68	6/27/68	21	2
	/D.W. Washburn	7/4/68	7/4/68	23	1

also see Dolenz, Micky; Jones, Davy and Nesmith, Michael

Artist	Title	Debut	Peak	Pos	Wks
Montanas					
	You've Got To Be Loved	2/22/68	3/7/68	19	5
	Run To Me	10/17/68	11/21/68	9	6
Montenegro, Hugo					
	The Good, The Bad And The Ugly	3/21/68	4/25/68	3	10
Montez, Chris					
	Call Me	2/17/66	3/17/66	18	4
	The More I See You	6/2/66	6/30/66	13	7
	There Will Never Be Another You	8/25/66	8/25/66	xx	4
	Time After Time	11/17/66	12/8/66	17	5
	Because Of You	2/23/67	2/23/67	pr	1
Moody Blues					
	Tuesday Afternoon (Forever Afternoon)	8/15/68	9/19/68	7	7
	Question	5/11/70	6/15/70	8	12
	The Story In Your Eyes	8/26/71	10/7/71	3	10
	Isn't Life Strange	4/27/72	6/1/72	8	9
	Nights In White Satin	9/9/72	11/4/72	1	13
	I'm Just A Singer (In A Rock And Roll Band)	2/3/73	3/17/73	3	12
Moore, Bobby & the Rhythm Aces					
	Searching For My Love	8/18/66	8/18/66	xx	2
Moore, Jackie					
	Precious, Precious	1/25/71	2/1/71	35	2
	Sweet Charlie Babe	7/28/73	9/29/73	13	13
Morrison, Bob					
	I Fall To You	4/14/66	4/14/66	pr	1
Morrison, Van					
	Brown Eyed Girl	8/10/67	10/19/67	3	10
	Come Running	4/20/70	4/27/70	29	2
	Domino	11/16/70	12/14/70	13	8
	Blue Money	1/25/71	3/1/71	9	9
	Wild Night	10/7/71	12/2/71	7	12
Motherlode					
	When I Die	8/27/69	10/1/69	16	7

Artist	Title	Debut	Peak	Pos	Wks
Mountain					
	Mississippi Queen	6/29/70	8/3/70	7	10
Mouth & MacNeal					
	How Do You Do	6/29/72	8/5/72	4	9
Mugwumps					
	Jug Band Music	9/8/66	9/8/66	xx	2
also see Elliot, Mama Cass, the Lovin' Spoonful and the Mamas & the Papas					
Muldaur, Maria					
	Midnight At The Oasis	4/13/74	6/8/74	1	15
Mungo Jerry					
	In The Summertime	6/29/70	8/17/70	4	14
Murphey, Michael					
	Wildfire	5/24/75	7/5/75	1	16
	Renegade	1/31/76	2/21/76	27	4
Murray, Anne					
	Snowbird	9/21/70	10/5/70	17	6
	Talk It Over In The Morning	9/2/71	10/7/71	25	6
	Danny's Song	2/24/73	4/21/73	2	13
	Love Song	2/2/74	3/9/74	6	14
	You Won't See Me	5/25/74	7/13/74	2	15
Music Explosion					
	Little Bit O' Soul	5/18/67	6/8/67	2	11
Music Machine					
	Talk Talk	11/24/66	12/8/66	9	6
Napoleon XIV					
	They're Coming To Take Me Away, Ha-Haaa!	7/21/66	7/28/66	2	3
Nash, Johnny					
	Hold Me Tight	10/24/68	11/14/68	8	6
	Cupid	1/12/70	1/12/70	34	1
	I Can See Clearly Now	10/7/72	11/25/72	2	13
	Stir It Up	3/10/73	4/21/73	5	11

Artist	Title	Debut	Peak	Pos	Wks
Natural Four					
	Can This Be Real	2/2/74	3/2/74	18	8
Nazareth					
	Love Hurts	2/21/76	2/21/76	30	1
Nazz					
	Hello It's Me	2/5/69	2/12/69	24	2
	Hello It's Me	2/23/70	3/2/70	39	2
	also see Rundgren, Todd				
Neely, Sam					
	Loving You Just Crossed My Mind	8/26/72	10/14/72	14	11
Nelson, Rick & the Stone Canyon Band					
	Garden Party	9/23/72	11/11/72	2	13
Neon Philharmonic					
	Morning Girl	4/30/69	5/28/69	4	8
Nesmith, Michael & the First National Band					
	Joanne	9/14/70	10/12/70	13	9
	Silver Moon	1/4/71	1/11/71	31	3
	also see the Monkees				
Neville, Aaron					
	Tell It Like It Is	12/22/66	1/19/67	9	8
New Colony Six					
	I Confess	1/6/66	1/20/66	4	8
	I Lie Awake	4/7/66	4/21/66	19	3
	Cadillac	6/23/66	7/14/66	xx	4
	Love You So Much	12/29/66	1/26/67	4	9
	You're Gonna Be Mine	3/16/67	4/27/67	12	7
	I'm Just Waiting Anticipating For Her To Show Up	6/8/67	7/13/67	16	6
	Treat Her Groovy	9/21/67	11/23/67	12	8
	I Will Always Think About You	1/25/68	4/4/68	1	11
	Can't You See Me Cry	6/20/68	7/18/68	13	6
	Things I'd Like To Say	11/21/68	12/19/68	3	9
	I Could Never Lie To You	5/14/69	5/28/69	13	5

Artist	Title	Debut	Peak	Pos	Wks
	I Want You To Know	8/27/69	9/24/69	14	6
	Barbara, I Love You	1/12/70	1/12/70	29	3
	Roll On	7/29/71	9/16/71	10	12
	Long Time To Be Alone	11/18/71	1/13/72	13	11
	Someone, Sometime	3/9/72	4/20/72	19	9

New Seekers

	Look What They've Done To My Song Ma	9/7/70	10/19/70	8	11

also see the Seekers

New Vaudeville Band

	Winchester Cathedral	10/27/66	12/1/66	1	12

New York City

	I'm Doin' Fine Now	5/26/73	7/7/73	13	11

Newton, Wayne

	Daddy Don't You Walk So Fast	6/1/72	7/22/72	4	12

Newton-John, Olivia

	If Not For You	5/13/71	6/24/71	3	10
	Let Me Be There	12/8/73	2/2/74	2	14
	If You Love Me (Let Me Know)	6/8/74	7/6/74	1	12
	I Honestly Love You	8/24/74	9/28/74	1	18
	Have You Never Been Mellow	2/1/75	3/29/75	1	16
	Please Mr. Please	6/21/75	8/2/75	2	13

Nightingale, Maxine

	Right Back Where We Started From	2/21/76	2/21/76	37	1

Nilsson

	Everybody's Talkin'	9/10/69	10/8/69	8	5
	Without You	1/13/72	2/24/72	1	11

Nimoy, Leonard

	A Visit To A Sad Planet	10/12/67	10/12/67	27	1

1910 Fruitgum Co.

	Simon Says	2/15/68	3/14/68	2	7
	May I Take A Giant Step (Into Your Heart)	3/28/68	3/28/68	pr	1
	1, 2, 3, Red Light	7/25/68	9/5/68	1	10
	Goody Goody Gumdrops	11/7/68	12/12/68	11	6

Artist	Title	Debut	Peak	Pos	Wks
	Indian Giver	2/5/69	3/26/69	2	9
	Special Delivery	5/14/69	6/4/69	11	7
	The Train	8/27/69	9/10/69	3	7
also see Kasenetz-Katz Singing Orchestral Circus					

Nitty Gritty Dirt Band
	Buy For Me The Rain	5/11/67	5/18/67	25	2
	Mr. Bojangles	2/22/71	3/11/71	28	4

Nobles, Cliff, & Co.
	The Horse	6/13/68	7/11/68	8	7

Ocean
	Put Your Hand In The Hand	3/25/71	5/13/71	3	11

Odds & Ends
	Love Makes The World Go Round	2/8/71	2/22/71	25	5

O'Dell, Kenny
	Beautiful People	11/23/67	11/30/67	17	6

Ohio Express
	Beg, Borrow And Steal	11/30/67	12/14/67	24	4
	Yummy Yummy Yummy	5/2/68	6/6/68	1	9
	Down At Lulu's	8/15/68	9/12/68	5	8
	Chewy Chewy	10/24/68	11/21/68	3	8
	Mercy	4/2/69	4/30/69	5	8
also see Crazy Elephant, Kasenetz-Katz, Reunion and the Third Rail					

Ohio Players
	Funky Worm	4/21/73	5/26/73	14	8
	Skin Tight	9/21/74	10/26/74	15	10
	Fire	1/25/75	3/15/75	1	12
	Love Rollercoaster	11/29/75	1/31/76	1	13

O'Jays
	Back Stabbers	7/22/72	9/23/72	1	13
	Love Train	2/10/73	3/31/73	2	11
	For The Love Of Money	5/18/74	6/22/74	6	11
	I Love Music (Part 1)	12/20/75	2/7/76	7	10

Artist	Title	Debut	Peak	Pos	Wks
O'Kaysions					
	Girl Watcher	9/26/68	10/17/68	5	6
O'Keefe, Danny					
	Good Time Charlie's Got The Blues	9/9/72	11/11/72	6	13
Oldfield, Mike					
	Tubular Bells	3/16/74	5/4/74	2	14
Oliver					
	Good Morning Starshine	5/28/69	6/18/69	3	10
	Jean	9/3/69	10/1/69	4	6
	Angelica	3/16/70	3/16/70	42	1
100 Proof Aged In Soul					
	Somebody's Been Sleeping	9/21/70	10/26/70	10	10
Ones					
	You Haven't Seen My Love	12/21/67	12/21/67	pr	1
Orbison, Roy					
	Breakin' Up Is Breakin' My Heart	1/13/66	1/13/66	pr	1
	Twinkle Toes	5/5/66	5/5/66	xx	3
	Communication Breakdown	11/24/66	12/29/66	xx	3
Orleans					
	Dance With Me	8/23/75	10/4/75	2	15
Osmond, Donny					
	Sweet And Innocent	4/8/71	5/27/71	1	13
	Go Away Little Girl	8/5/71	9/23/71	1	12
	Hey Girl	11/18/71	12/30/71	2	12
	Puppy Love	2/17/72	3/30/72	1	12
	Too Young	6/8/72	7/15/72	3	10
	Why	9/30/72	11/18/72	7	11
	The Twelfth Of Never	3/31/73	5/19/73	3	11
	A Million To One	8/25/73	9/22/73	16	8
Osmond, Donny & Marie					
	I'm Leaving It (All) Up To You	7/20/74	9/7/74	9	14
	Morning Side Of The Mountain	12/28/74	2/1/75	7	10
	Deep Purple	2/21/76	2/21/76	34	1

also see the Osmonds

Artist	Title	Debut	Peak	Pos	Wks

Osmond, Marie
| | Paper Roses | 9/29/73 | 11/10/73 | 8 | 13 |
| | Who's Sorry Now | 3/15/75 | 4/12/75 | 26 | 7 |

also see Osmond, Donny & Marie and the Osmonds

Osmonds
	One Bad Apple	1/4/71	2/1/71	1	9
	Double Lovin'	5/20/71	6/24/71	4	9
	Yo-Yo	9/9/71	11/11/71	1	14
	Down By The Lazy River	1/13/72	3/9/72	1	14
	Hold Her Tight	6/22/72	8/19/72	8	12
	Crazy Horses	11/25/72	12/30/72	14	9
	Let Me In	9/15/73	11/3/73	14	11
	Love Me For A Reason	9/14/74	10/26/74	9	13

also see Osmond, Donny and Osmond, Marie

O'Sullivan, Gilbert
	Alone Again (Naturally)	6/22/72	8/5/72	1	14
	Clair	11/11/72	12/23/72	1	13
	Get Down	6/16/73	8/11/73	1	13
	Ooh Baby	10/6/73	12/1/73	6	13

Outsiders
	Time Won't Let Me	3/31/66	4/21/66	6	8
	Girl In Love	4/28/66	6/16/66	12	7
	Respectable	7/21/66	8/25/66	11	7
	Help Me Girl	10/20/66	12/1/66	16	5

also see Climax

Ozark Mountain Daredevils
| | Jackie Blue | 3/22/75 | 5/10/75 | 3 | 15 |

Pacific Gas & Electric
| | Are You Ready | 6/22/70 | 7/27/70 | 8 | 10 |

Paper Lace
| | The Night Chicago Died | 7/6/74 | 8/24/74 | 1 | 15 |

Parade
| | Sunshine Girl | 6/1/67 | 6/8/67 | 27 | 2 |

Artist	Title	Debut	Peak	Pos	Wks
Parker, Robert					
	Barefootin'	5/19/66	5/19/66	xx	4
Parks, Michael					
	Long Lonesome Highway	3/2/70	4/6/70	6	10
Partridge Family					
	I Think I Love You	10/12/70	11/2/70	1	14
	Doesn't Somebody Want To Be Wanted	1/25/71	3/11/71	1	12
	I'll Meet You Halfway	4/22/71	6/17/71	5	13
	I Woke Up In Love This Morning	8/5/71	9/23/71	3	11
	It's One Of Those Nights (Yes Love)	12/9/71	1/20/72	6	10
also see Cassidy, David					
Paul, Billy					
	Me And Mrs. Jones	12/2/72	1/13/73	1	12
Payne, Freda					
	Band Of Gold	6/1/70	6/29/70	3	12
	Cherish What Is Dear To You (While It's Near To You)	2/8/71	2/22/71	30	4
	Bring The Boys Home	6/3/71	7/8/71	23	7
Peaches & Herb					
	Close Your Eyes	4/27/67	5/11/67	24	3
	Love Is Strange	10/26/67	11/9/67	17	3
Peek, Paul					
	Pin The Tail On The Donkey	4/14/66	4/14/66	pr	1
People					
	I Love You	6/6/68	6/27/68	3	7
Pepper, Jim					
	Witchi-Tai-To	2/12/69	2/12/69	30	1
Peppermint Rainbow					
	Will You Be Staying After Sunday	4/2/69	4/16/69	15	5
Peter & Gordon					
	Woman	2/24/66	3/24/66	13	5
	Lady Godiva	10/6/66	12/1/66	5	9

Artist	Title	Debut	Peak	Pos	Wks
	Knight In Rusty Armour	12/15/66	1/26/67	16	6
	Sunday For Tea	3/9/67	4/20/67	27	3

Peter, Paul & Mary
	I Dig Rock And Roll Music	8/31/67	9/7/67	14	6
	Day Is Done	5/14/69	6/4/69	15	5
	Leaving On A Jet Plane	1/12/70	1/12/70	40	1

also see Stookey, Paul

Phillips, Esther
	What A Diff'rence A Day Makes	9/27/75	10/25/75	17	8

Phillips, John
	Mississippi	6/1/70	7/6/70	7	10

also see the Mamas & the Papas

Pickett, Bobby "Boris" & the Crypt-Kickers
	Monster Mash	6/2/73	7/14/73	2	14

Pickett, Wilson
	634-5789 (Soulsville, U.S.A.)	3/10/66	3/10/66	xx	3
	Land Of 1000 Dances	8/18/66	9/1/66	19	4
	Funky Broadway	8/17/67	9/21/67	6	10
	I'm In Love	12/14/67	1/18/68	14	5
	/Stag-O-Lee	10/26/67	11/23/67	23	6
	Jealous Love	2/8/68	2/8/68	pr	1
	She's Lookin' Good	3/28/68	5/23/68	16	8
	I'm A Midnight Mover	7/4/68	7/25/68	18	5
	Hey Jude	1/8/69	1/15/69	23	2
	Don't Let The Green Grass Fool You	2/8/71	3/11/71	24	6
	Don't Knock My Love—Pt. 1	5/20/71	7/1/71	3	11

Pieces Of Eight
	Lonely Drifter	6/22/67	8/3/67	24	4

Pilot
	Magic	5/17/75	7/19/75	2	17

Pink Floyd
	Money	5/26/73	7/21/73	8	14

Artist	Title	Debut	Peak	Pos	Wks

Pipkins
Gimme Dat Ding · 5/25/70 · 6/22/70 · 15 · 9

also see the Brotherhood Of Man, Edison Lighthouse, First Class and White Plains

Pitney, Gene
	Backstage	4/7/66	5/19/66	12	5
	Just One Smile	12/8/66	1/5/67	8	7
	She's A Heartbreaker	6/6/68	6/27/68	7	8

Plastic Ono Band
	Give Peace A Chance	7/30/69	8/13/69	16	3
	Cold Turkey	1/12/70	2/9/70	24	6

also see Lennon, John

P-Nut Gallery
Do You Know What Time It Is · 6/17/71 · 7/8/71 · 10 · 6

Poco
You Better Think Twice · 9/21/70 · 10/26/70 · 26 · 8

also see Buffalo Springfield, the Eagles and Loggins & Messina

Pointer Sisters
	Yes We Can Can	9/22/73	11/10/73	9	12
	Fairytale	11/16/74	12/28/74	13	11
	How Long (Betcha' Got A Chick On The Side)	8/30/75	10/4/75	11	11

Poppies
Lullaby Of Love · 3/3/66 · 3/3/66 · pr · 1

Poppy Family featuring Susan Jacks
	Which Way You Goin' Billy	3/23/70	4/20/70	9	12
	That's Where I Went Wrong	9/21/70	10/12/70	9	9

also see Jacks, Terry

Posey, Sandy
	Born A Woman	7/21/66	9/1/66	17	5
	Single Girl	12/8/66	12/8/66	xx	4

Post, Mike
The Rockford Files · 7/19/75 · 8/23/75 · 10 · 13

Artist	Title	Debut	Peak	Pos	Wks

Potliquor
	Cheer	3/16/72	4/27/72	9	9

Power Plant
	I Can't Happen Without You	9/21/67	10/26/67	29	2

Pozo-Seco Singers
	I Can Make It With You	10/20/66	10/20/66	xx	3

Prelude
	After The Goldrush	9/14/74	11/16/74	7	15

Presidents
	5-10-15-20 (25-30 Years Of Love)	11/16/70	12/7/70	22	5

Presley, Elvis
	Title	Debut	Peak	Pos	Wks
	Frankie And Johnny	3/17/66	4/21/66	xx	2
	Love Letters	7/21/66	8/4/66	19	4
	Spinout	10/27/66	10/27/66	xx	2
	If Every Day Was Like Christmas	12/22/66	12/22/66	pr	1
	Indescribably Blue	2/16/67	2/23/67	28	2
	There's Always Me	9/7/67	9/7/67	pr	1
	U.S. Male	4/11/68	5/9/68	15	6
	Let Yourself Go	6/27/68	7/4/68	25	2
	If I Can Dream	12/19/68	1/29/69	10	9
	Memories	4/2/69	4/23/69	22	4
	In The Ghetto	5/14/69	6/4/69	6	7
	Suspicious Minds	10/1/69	10/8/69	12	2
	Don't Cry Daddy	1/12/70	1/12/70	7	4
	Kentucky Rain	2/2/70	3/2/70	10	8
	The Wonder Of You	5/4/70	6/15/70	14	12
	You Don't Have To Say You Love Me	11/23/70	12/14/70	15	7
	I Really Don't Want To Know	1/18/71	1/25/71	36	3
	Burning Love	8/26/72	10/14/72	2	12
	Fool	5/26/73	6/30/73	23	7
	Promised Land	12/28/74	1/25/75	16	7

Preston, Billy
	Outa-Space	5/25/72	6/29/72	1	11
	Will It Go Round In Circles	5/26/73	7/14/73	4	13

Artist	Title	Debut	Peak	Pos	Wks
	Space Race	10/27/73	12/22/73	3	14
	Nothing From Nothing	8/17/74	10/5/74	2	16
Price, Ray					
	For The Good Times	12/7/70	1/4/71	20	7
Pride, Charley					
	Kiss An Angel Good Mornin'	12/23/71	2/10/72	9	12
Pride & Joy					
	Girl	5/25/67	6/1/67	26	2
also see the Del-Vetts					
Princetons					
	Georgianna	2/10/66	2/24/66	10	4
Procol Harum					
	A Whiter Shade Of Pale	7/6/67	8/10/67	15	7
	Conquistador	7/6/72	8/19/72	3	11
Puckett, Gary & the Union Gap					
	Woman, Woman	12/7/67	12/28/67	4	10
	Young Girl	2/22/68	4/18/68	2	10
	Lady Willpower	6/20/68	7/18/68	4	7
	Over You	9/19/68	10/24/68	2	8
	Don't Give In To Him	3/26/69	4/23/69	5	7
	This Girl Is A Woman Now	8/27/69	9/10/69	2	7
Pure Prairie League					
	Amie	4/5/75	5/10/75	20	11
Purify, James & Bobby					
	I'm Your Puppet	10/13/66	10/20/66	20	5
	Shake A Tail Feather	4/13/67	4/13/67	pr	1
Python Lee Jackson					
	In A Broken Dream	6/1/72	7/6/72	26	7
also see Stewart, Rod					
Quatro, Suzi					
	Can The Can	1/24/76	2/14/76	30	4

Artist	Title	Debut	Peak	Pos	Wks
Queen					
	Killer Queen	4/12/75	6/7/75	1	18
	Bohemian Rhapsody	2/14/76	2/21/76	31	2
? & the Mysterians					
	96 Tears	9/15/66	10/20/66	1	10
	I Need Somebody	12/22/66	12/22/66	xx	3
Rafferty, Gerry					
	Make You, Break You	3/30/72	4/27/72	25	7
also see Stealers Wheel					
Rare Earth					
	Get Ready	4/6/70	5/18/70	2	16
	(I Know) I'm Losing You	8/24/70	9/28/70	5	13
	Born To Wander	1/11/71	2/8/71	5	8
	I Just Want To Celebrate	8/5/71	9/23/71	4	10
	Hey Big Brother	12/9/71	12/30/71	27	4
Raspberries					
	Go All The Way	8/12/72	10/7/72	2	13
	I Wanna Be With You	11/18/72	12/30/72	6	11
	Let's Pretend	4/28/73	6/23/73	4	12
also see Carmen, Eric					
Rattles					
	The Witch	6/1/70	7/6/70	20	9
Rawls, Lou					
	Love Is A Hurtin' Thing	10/13/66	10/27/66	17	3
	Dead End Street	4/20/67	5/18/67	19	5
	Hard To Get Thing Called Love	10/5/67	10/5/67	pr	1
	Your Good Thing (Is About To End)	7/30/69	9/10/69	22	10
Razor's Edge					
	Let's Call It A Day Girl	9/15/66	9/15/66	xx	2
Redbone					
	The Witch Queen Of New Orleans	12/30/71	2/17/72	3	12
	Come And Get Your Love	3/30/74	4/27/74	1	12

Artist	Title	Debut	Peak	Pos	Wks

Redding, Gene
| | This Heart | 6/15/74 | 7/20/74 | 17 | 10 |

Redding, Otis
	(Sittin' On) The Dock Of The Bay	2/15/68	3/7/68	3	8
	The Happy Song (Dum-Dum)	4/25/68	5/23/68	28	3
	Papa's Got A Brand New Bag	1/8/69	1/8/69	27	2

Reddy, Helen
	I Am Woman	10/14/72	12/2/72	1	14
	Peaceful	3/3/73	4/14/73	2	12
	Delta Dawn	7/14/73	9/8/73	1	14
	Leave Me Alone (Ruby Red Dress)	11/3/73	1/12/74	8	14
	Keep On Singing	3/30/74	5/11/74	12	11
	You And Me Against The World	7/13/74	8/24/74	8	13
	Angie Baby	10/26/74	12/21/74	7	15
	Ain't No Way To Treat A Lady	8/23/75	10/11/75	4	14

Redeye
| | Games | 12/21/70 | 1/25/71 | 3 | 9 |

Reed, Jerry
| | Amos Moses | 1/18/71 | 3/1/71 | 3 | 11 |

Reed, Lou
| | Walk On The Wild Side | 4/21/73 | 6/9/73 | 3 | 11 |

Rene & Rene
| | Lo Mucho Que Te Quiero (The More I Love You) | 12/19/68 | 1/8/69 | 18 | 5 |

Reunion
| | Life Is A Rock (But The Radio Rolled Me) | 10/12/74 | 11/23/74 | 4 | 12 |

also see Crazy Elephant, Kasenetz-Katz, the Third Rail and Ohio Express

Revere, Paul & the Raiders
	Just Like Me	12/16/65	1/6/66	8	5
	Kicks	3/10/66	4/21/66	1	14
	Hungry	6/16/66	7/21/66	4	12
	The Great Airplane Strike	10/6/66	10/27/66	12	6
	Good Thing	12/1/66	1/12/67	3	9

Artist	Title	Debut	Peak	Pos	Wks
	Ups And Downs	2/23/67	3/23/67	7	6
	Him Or Me—What's It Gonna Be	4/20/67	5/25/67	4	8
	I Had A Dream	8/10/67	9/21/67	10	7
	Peace Of Mind	11/9/67	12/14/67	23	4
	Too Much Talk	2/1/68	3/14/68	11	7
	Don't Take It So Hard	6/27/68	8/1/68	12	6
	Mr. Sun, Mr. Moon	3/5/69	4/23/69	3	10
	Let Me	5/14/69	6/11/69	8	9

Raiders
	Indian Reservation (The Lament Of The Cherokee Reservation Indian)	7/8/71	8/5/71	1	9
	Birds Of A Feather	9/16/71	11/4/71	6	10
	Country Wine	1/27/72	3/2/72	13	7

also see Lindsay, Mark

Reynolds, Lawrence
	Jesus Is A Soul Man	10/8/69	10/8/69	23	1

Rhythm Heritage
	Theme From S.W.A.T.	1/24/76	2/21/76	10	5

Rich, Charlie
	Behind Closed Doors	7/7/73	9/1/73	12	11
	The Most Beautiful Girl	11/24/73	1/26/74	5	15

Riddles
	Sweets For My Sweet	3/16/67	4/6/67	22	6

Righteous Brothers
	Ebb Tide	12/30/65	12/30/65	19	2
	Georgia On My Mind	2/10/66	2/10/66	pr	1
	(You're My) Soul And Inspiration	3/10/66	5/5/66	8	12
	Rock And Roll Heaven	6/1/74	7/13/74	12	12
	Give It To The People	10/5/74	10/26/74	23	7

Riley, Jeannie C.
	Harper Valley P.T.A.	8/29/68	9/19/68	1	6

Rios, Miguel
	A Song Of Joy (Himno A La Alegria)	5/25/70	6/29/70	12	11

Artist	Title	Debut	Peak	Pos	Wks
Riperton, Minnie					
	Lovin' You	2/22/75	4/5/75	1	13
Ritchie Family					
	Brazil	9/13/75	10/18/75	13	11
Rivers, Johnny					
	Secret Agent Man	3/31/66	4/21/66	2	8
	(I Washed My Hands In) Muddy Water	7/14/66	7/14/66	xx	1
	Poor Side Of Town	9/8/66	11/17/66	4	12
	Baby I Need Your Lovin'	1/26/67	3/23/67	8	8
	The Tracks Of My Tears	5/25/67	7/6/67	13	6
	Summer Rain	12/21/67	1/18/68	9	7
	Look To Your Soul	4/25/68	5/9/68	21	3
	Rockin' Pneumonia—Boogie Woogie Flu	10/21/72	12/23/72	2	15
Road					
	She's Not There	1/29/69	2/5/69	22	2
Robbs					
	Race With The Wind	5/19/66	6/9/66	xx	5
	Next Time You See Me	9/15/66	9/15/66	pr	1
Roberts, Austin					
	Something's Wrong With Me	10/28/72	12/16/72	12	12
Rodgers, Jimmie					
	Child Of Clay	10/12/67	11/2/67	17	5
Roe, Tommy					
	Sweet Pea	6/30/66	8/4/66	10	8
	Hooray For Hazel	9/1/66	11/10/66	3	10
	It's Now Winters Day	1/5/67	2/9/67	11	7
	Dottie I Like It	2/1/68	2/1/68	pr	1
	Dizzy	2/12/69	3/12/69	1	10
	Jack And Jill	9/24/69	10/8/69	26	3
	Jam Up Jelly Tight	1/12/70	1/12/70	3	5
	Stir It Up And Serve It	2/23/70	3/16/70	22	6
	Pearl	6/8/70	7/13/70	17	10
	We Can Make Music	8/31/70	9/21/70	18	8
	Stagger Lee	8/12/71	9/30/71	9	11

Artist	Title	Debut	Peak	Pos	Wks

Rolling Stones

	As Tears Go By	1/13/66	1/27/66	17	3
	19th Nervous Breakdown	2/24/66	3/10/66	6	7
	Paint It, Black	5/19/66	6/2/66	1	8
	Mothers Little Helper	7/14/66	8/4/66	11	5
	/Lady Jane	7/28/66	8/4/66	11	3
	Have You Seen Your Mother, Baby, Standing In The Shadow	10/13/66	10/27/66	10	4
	Ruby Tuesday	1/19/67	2/16/67	1	10
	My Girl	7/13/67	7/13/67	pr	1
	Dandelion	8/31/67	9/28/67	17	5
	Jumpin' Jack Flash	6/13/68	7/11/68	1	8
	Honky Tonk Women	7/16/69	7/30/69	1	11
	/You Can't Always Get What You Want	7/16/69	7/30/69	1	7
	Brown Sugar	4/22/71	6/3/71	2	10
	Wild Horses	7/1/71	7/29/71	22	6
	Tumbling Dice	4/20/72	6/22/72	1	14
	Happy	7/15/72	8/19/72	7	9
	You Can't Always Get What You Want	4/21/73	5/19/73	19	7
	Angie	9/8/73	10/27/73	1	14
	Doo Doo Doo Doo Doo (Heartbreaker)	1/12/74	2/23/74	16	11
	It's Only Rock 'N Roll (But I Like It)	8/10/74	9/14/74	10	11
	Ain't Too Proud To Beg	11/23/74	12/21/74	22	6

Ronny & the Daytonas

	Sandy	1/13/66	2/3/66	8	5

Ronstadt, Linda

	Rock Me On The Water	2/24/72	3/30/72	21	7
	You're No Good	1/11/75	3/1/75	4	14
	When Will I Be Loved	5/10/75	6/21/75	2	15
	Heat Wave	10/4/75	11/15/75	9	13

also see the Stone Poneys

Rose Colored Glass

	Can't Find The Time	3/18/71	5/13/71	15	11
	If It's Alright With You	10/21/71	11/25/71	16	8

Ross, Diana

	Reach Out And Touch (Somebody's Hand)	4/27/70	5/11/70	29	8
	Ain't No Mountain High Enough	7/27/70	8/17/70	2	13

Artist	Title	Debut	Peak	Pos	Wks
	Remember Me	12/21/70	2/8/71	4	10
	Reach Out I'll Be There	4/22/71	6/10/71	8	10
	Touch Me In The Morning	7/7/73	8/18/73	5	11
	Last Time I Saw Him	2/9/74	3/23/74	13	10
	Theme From Mahogany (Do You Know Where You're Going To)	11/29/75	1/31/76	3	13

Ross, Diana & Marvin Gaye

Artist	Title	Debut	Peak	Pos	Wks
	You're A Special Part Of Me	10/6/73	11/3/73	28	6

also see Gaye, Marvin and the Supremes

Rosso, Nini

Artist	Title	Debut	Peak	Pos	Wks
	Il Silenzio	12/16/65	12/23/65	10	3

Roxy Music

Artist	Title	Debut	Peak	Pos	Wks
	Love Is The Drug	2/7/76	2/21/76	25	3

Royal, Billy Joe

Artist	Title	Debut	Peak	Pos	Wks
	Hush	10/12/67	11/9/67	10	7

Royal Guardsmen

Artist	Title	Debut	Peak	Pos	Wks
	Snoopy vs. The Red Baron	12/15/66	12/29/66	1	9
	The Return Of The Red Baron	3/2/67	3/23/67	21	4
	Snoopy's Christmas	12/7/67	12/21/67	6	5
	Baby Let's Wait	1/8/69	1/29/69	15	6

Royal Scots Dragoon Guards

Artist	Title	Debut	Peak	Pos	Wks
	Amazing Grace	5/18/72	6/15/72	10	9

Ruffin, David

Artist	Title	Debut	Peak	Pos	Wks
	My Whole World Ended (The Moment You Left Me)	2/26/69	3/19/69	9	5
	Walk Away From Love	12/6/75	1/24/76	13	12

also see the Temptations

Ruffin, Jimmy

Artist	Title	Debut	Peak	Pos	Wks
	What Becomes Of The Brokenhearted	9/1/66	11/24/66	10	13
	I've Passed This Way Before	12/8/66	2/9/67	23	4

Rufus

Artist	Title	Debut	Peak	Pos	Wks
	Tell Me Something Good	7/20/74	9/7/74	3	13

Rufus featuring Chaka Khan

Artist	Title	Debut	Peak	Pos	Wks
	You Got The Love	12/14/74	1/18/75	10	10
	Once You Get Started	3/1/75	4/12/75	17	9

Artist	Title	Debut	Peak	Pos	Wks
	Sweet Thing	2/21/76	2/21/76	36	1
also see the American Breed					
Rugbys					
	You, I	8/27/69	10/1/69	7	7
Runt					
	We Gotta Get You A Woman	1/11/71	1/25/71	32	3
Rundgren, Todd					
	I Saw The Light	4/13/72	6/1/72	25	9
	Hello It's Me	10/20/73	12/8/73	1	14
also see Nazz					
Rush, Merrilee & the Turnabouts					
	Angel Of The Morning	6/6/68	6/27/68	2	6
Russell, Leon					
	Tight Rope	9/9/72	10/14/72	11	10
	Lady Blue	9/13/75	11/8/75	5	14
Ryder, Mitch & the Detroit Wheels					
	Jenny Take A Ride	2/3/66	2/10/66	12	2
	Little Latin Lupe Lu	2/24/66	3/17/66	xx	3
	Devil With A Blue Dress On & Good Golly Miss Molly	10/6/66	12/15/66	5	11
	Sock It To Me-Baby	2/2/67	3/9/67	9	8
	Too Many Fish In The Sea & Three Little Fishes	5/18/67	5/25/67	26	2
Ryder, Mitch					
	What Now My Love	9/14/67	9/14/67	pr	1
Detroit featuring Mitch Ryder					
	Rock 'N Roll	1/13/72	2/3/72	29	4
Sadler, S/Sgt. Barry					
	The Ballad Of The Green Berets	2/10/66	3/10/66	4	9
	The "A" Team	5/12/66	5/12/66	xx	1
Sagittarius					
	My World Fell Down	7/13/67	7/27/67	19	4
also see Campbell, Glen and the Hondells					

Artist	Title	Debut	Peak	Pos	Wks
Sailcat					
	Motorcycle Mama	7/22/72	9/16/72	8	12
Sainte-Marie, Buffy					
	Mister Can't You See	3/23/72	5/11/72	9	10
Sam & Dave					
	Hold On! I'm A Comin'	5/26/66	5/26/66	xx	2
	Soul Man	9/28/67	11/2/67	12	8
	I Thank You	2/8/68	2/29/68	16	7
	Soul Sister, Brown Sugar	1/22/69	1/22/69	27	1
Sam the Sham & the Pharaohs					
	Lil' Red Riding Hood	6/30/66	8/11/66	3	11
	The Hair On My Chinny Chin Chin	9/22/66	11/24/66	18	4
	How Do You Catch A Girl	12/15/66	12/15/66	pr	1
	Oh That's Good, No That's Bad	3/16/67	3/16/67	pr	1
Sami Jo					
	It Could Have Been Me	8/31/74	9/21/74	20	7
Sandpipers					
	Guantanamera	8/25/66	9/29/66	8	8
	Louie, Louie	10/13/66	12/1/66	20	5
	Come Saturday Morning	4/27/70	5/25/70	15	9
Santana					
	Evil Ways	2/16/70	3/16/70	6	9
	Black Magic Woman	11/23/70	1/18/71	4	11
	Oye Como Va	3/1/71	4/8/71	10	8
Satisfactions					
	Daddy You Gotta Let Him In	4/28/66	4/28/66	pr	1
Sayer, Leo					
	Long Tall Glasses (I Can Dance)	4/26/75	6/7/75	2	13
Schifrin, Lalo					
	Mission-Impossible	2/22/68	2/29/68	22	2

Artist	Title	Debut	Peak	Pos	Wks
Scott, Freddie					
	Are You Lonely For Me	2/2/67	2/2/67	xx	1
Scott, Peggy & Jo Jo Benson					
	Lover's Holiday	7/11/68	7/25/68	25	4
	Soulshake	2/12/69	2/19/69	25	2
Sea, Johnny					
	Day For Decision	6/2/66	6/16/66	16	3
Seals & Crofts					
	Summer Breeze	11/4/72	12/16/72	2	12
	Hummingbird	3/3/73	4/14/73	4	10
	Diamond Girl	7/21/73	8/25/73	2	10
	We May Never Pass This Way (Again)	9/29/73	11/17/73	9	12
Searchers					
	Take Me For What I'm Worth	1/6/66	1/6/66	pr	1
Seatrain					
	13 Questions	3/25/71	5/13/71	14	9
Sedaka, Neil					
	The Answer To My Prayer	1/6/66	2/10/66	xx	4
	Laughter In The Rain	12/7/74	1/25/75	1	14
	Bad Blood	9/20/75	11/8/75	1	19
	Breaking Up Is Hard To Do	12/20/75	2/21/76	2	10
Seeds					
	Pushin' Too Hard	1/12/67	2/9/67	2	9
	Mr. Farmer	2/2/67	2/2/67	pr	1
	Can't Seem To Make You Mine	4/27/67	5/18/67	15	7
Seekers					
	Georgy Girl	1/5/67	2/2/67	1	10
	Morningtown Ride	3/30/67	3/30/67	25	1
	also see the New Seekers				
Seger, Bob, System					
	Ramblin' Gamblin' Man	1/8/69	2/19/69	1	11

Artist	Title	Debut	Peak	Pos	Wks
Senator Bobby					
	Wild Thing	1/12/67	1/19/67	20	2
Shades Of Blue					
	Oh How Happy	6/9/66	6/30/66	18	5
Shadows Of Knight					
	Gloria	2/17/66	3/31/66	1	11
	Oh Yeah	5/26/66	6/16/66	15	6
	Bad Little Woman	8/18/66	9/29/66	19	4
	I'm Gonna Make You Mine	11/3/66	12/1/66	xx	3
	Willie Jean	3/30/67	3/30/67	26	2
	Shake	10/31/68	12/19/68	10	9
Shangri-Las					
	Long Live Our Love	1/27/66	2/10/66	xx	4
Shannon					
	Abergavenny	7/30/69	8/6/69	22	3
Shepstone & Dibbens					
	Shady Lady	8/25/73	10/6/73	19	8
Sherman, Bobby					
	Little Woman	9/10/69	10/1/69	1	5
	La La La (If I Had You)	1/12/70	1/12/70	6	3
	Easy Come, Easy Go	2/2/70	3/30/70	8	12
	Hey, Mister Sun	5/11/70	6/15/70	15	8
	Julie, Do Ya Love Me	7/20/70	8/24/70	7	13
	Goin' Home (Sing A Song Of Christmas Cheer)	12/14/70	12/14/70	xx	2
	Cried Like A Baby	2/1/71	3/1/71	20	9
	The Drum	5/27/71	7/8/71	7	10
Shirley (And Company)					
	Shame, Shame, Shame	3/29/75	5/3/75	4	11
Shocking Blue					
	Venus	1/12/70	1/12/70	1	7
	Mighty Joe	3/16/70	4/6/70	28	4

Artist	Title	Debut	Peak	Pos	Wks

Silver Convention
	Fly, Robin, Fly	11/1/75	12/6/75	4	16

Simmons, "Jumpin'" Gene
	Bossy Boss	2/17/66	2/17/66	pr	1

Simon, Carly
	That's The Way I've Always Heard It Should Be	5/6/71	6/10/71	3	10
	Anticipation	1/13/72	2/24/72	6	11
	You're So Vain	12/16/72	1/20/73	1	17
	The Right Thing To Do	4/21/73	6/16/73	1	13

Simon, Carly & James Taylor
	Mockingbird	2/9/74	3/23/74	1	13

also see Taylor, James

Simon, Joe
	The Chokin' Kind	4/9/69	5/7/69	12	7
	Drowning In The Sea Of Love	1/13/72	2/3/72	27	4
	Power Of Love	8/5/72	9/16/72	15	8
	Theme From Cleopatra Jones	9/15/73	10/6/73	26	4

Simon, Paul
	Mother And Child Reunion	2/10/72	3/30/72	2	12
	Kodachrome	5/19/73	7/14/73	1	15
	Loves Me Like A Rock	8/11/73	9/22/73	1	13
	50 Ways To Leave Your Lover	1/17/76	2/14/76	1	6

also see Simon & Garfunkel

Simon & Garfunkel
	The Sounds Of Silence	12/16/65	1/6/66	1	10
	Homeward Bound	1/27/66	3/3/66	9	8
	I Am A Rock	5/12/66	6/9/66	2	9
	The Dangling Conversation	7/28/66	8/25/66	xx	3
	A Hazy Shade Of Winter	10/27/66	12/8/66	15	5
	At The Zoo	3/16/67	4/20/67	12	6
	Fakin' It	7/20/67	8/24/67	20	3
	Scarborough Fair (/Canticle)	2/15/68	4/11/68	20	4
	Mrs. Robinson	4/18/68	6/6/68	2	11
	The Boxer	4/2/69	4/30/69	2	9
	Bridge Over Troubled Water	2/2/70	2/16/70	1	13

Artist	Title	Debut	Peak	Pos	Wks
	Cecilia	3/16/70	5/4/70	1	12
	El Condor Pasa	10/19/70	10/19/70	35	4
	My Little Town	11/29/75	1/24/76	6	13
	also see Garfunkel, Art and Simon, Paul				
Sinatra, Frank					
	It Was A Very Good Year	2/17/66	2/17/66	18	1
	Strangers In The Night	5/26/66	6/16/66	3	8
	Summer Wind	9/29/66	9/29/66	xx	2
	That's Life	12/1/66	1/5/67	15	6
	The World We Knew (Over And Over)	7/27/67	8/24/67	27	2
	Cycles	11/14/68	11/21/68	21	2
	also see Sinatra, Nancy & Frank Sinatra				
Sinatra, Nancy					
	These Boots Are Made For Walkin'	2/10/66	3/10/66	2	9
	How Does That Grab You, Darlin'	4/21/66	5/26/66	15	6
	Friday's Child	7/21/66	7/21/66	xx	1
	Sugar Town	11/24/66	12/15/66	8	9
	Love Eyes	3/9/67	4/20/67	25	5
	Lightning's Girl	9/14/67	11/2/67	22	5
Sinatra, Nancy & Frank Sinatra					
	Somethin' Stupid	3/23/67	5/11/67	1	10
Sinatra, Nancy & Lee Hazlewood					
	Jackson	7/13/67	7/20/67	27	4
	also see Sinatra, Frank				
Sir Douglas Quintet					
	Mendocino	3/5/69	3/19/69	16	4
Skylark					
	Wildflower	3/10/73	5/19/73	4	15
Sledge, Percy					
	When A Man Loves A Woman	5/12/66	6/23/66	8	7
	Take Time To Know Her	4/11/68	4/18/68	24	4
Sly & the Family Stone					
	Dance To The Music	2/22/68	3/28/68	13	6
	Everyday People	1/8/69	1/29/69	1	10
	Hot Fun In The Summertime	10/8/69	10/8/69	22	1

Artist	Title	Debut	Peak	Pos	Wks
	Thank You Falettinme Be Mice Elf Agin	1/12/70	1/26/70	1	10
	Family Affair	11/11/71	12/16/71	3	10
Small Faces					
	Itchycoo Park	11/2/67	2/15/68	4	6
	Tin Soldier	2/22/68	2/22/68	pr	1
also see Faces					
Smith					
	Baby It's You	9/24/69	10/8/69	14	3
	Take A Look Around	2/23/70	3/9/70	24	4
Smith, Adrian					
	Wild About My Lovin'	4/28/73	6/23/73	13	12
Smith, Hurricane					
	Oh, Babe, What Would You Say	12/16/72	2/10/73	17	11
Smith, Jimmy					
	Got My Mojo Working (Part 1)	3/31/66	4/28/66	xx	2
Smith, O.C.					
	Little Green Apples	9/5/68	10/24/68	1	10
	Daddy's Little Man	8/27/69	9/10/69	23	6
Smith, Whistling Jack					
	I Was Kaiser Bill's Batman	5/4/67	5/11/67	19	3
Snow, Phoebe					
	Poetry Man	2/22/75	3/29/75	16	10
Sonny & Cher					
	What Now My Love	2/10/66	3/3/66	20	5
	Little Man	9/22/66	10/20/66	xx	4
	The Beat Goes On	1/19/67	3/9/67	6	10
	A Beautiful Story	4/20/67	5/25/67	27	2
	Plastic Man	5/25/67	5/25/67	pr	1
	It's The Little Things	7/20/67	7/20/67	pr	1
	Good Combination	12/14/67	12/14/67	pr	1
	All I Ever Need Is You	10/28/71	12/23/71	2	14
	A Cowboy's Work Is Never Done	2/24/72	4/27/72	1	14
also see Cher					

Artist	Title	Debut	Peak	Pos	Wks
Sopwith Camel					
	Hello Hello	2/2/67	2/9/67	19	3
Soul Survivors					
	Expressway To Your Heart	10/5/67	11/30/67	7	9
	Explosion In Your Soul	12/28/67	1/11/68	25	4
Soulful Strings					
	Burning Spear	1/25/68	2/8/68	22	4
South, Joe					
	Games People Play	1/29/69	2/26/69	10	6
	Don't It Make You Want To Go Home	9/10/69	10/8/69	18	5
	Walk A Mile In My Shoes	1/12/70	2/2/70	8	6
	Fool Me	11/11/71	12/9/71	27	6
Spanky & Our Gang					
	Sunday Will Never Be The Same	6/8/67	7/6/67	16	7
	Making Every Minute Count	8/17/67	8/17/67	pr	1
	Lazy Day	11/2/67	11/2/67	29	1
	Like To Get To Know You	5/9/68	6/13/68	6	7
Spector, Ronnie					
	Try Some, Buy Some	5/27/71	6/10/71	31	3
Spinners					
	It's A Shame	10/5/70	10/19/70	30	5
	I'll Be Around	9/16/72	11/11/72	1	13
	Could It Be I'm Falling In Love	1/20/73	3/10/73	3	13
	One Of A Kind (Love Affair)	5/5/73	7/7/73	9	12
	They Just Can't Stop It The (Games People Play)	8/30/75	11/1/75	3	18
	also see Warwick, Dionne & Spinners				
Spiral Starecase					
	More Today Than Yesterday	5/21/69	5/21/69	30	1
Spirit					
	I Got A Line On You	1/22/69	2/26/69	7	8
	also see Jo Jo Gunne				

Artist	Title	Debut	Peak	Pos	Wks

Springfield, Dusty
	You Don't Have To Say You Love Me	6/9/66	7/7/66	8	8
	Goin' Back	7/28/66	7/28/66	pr	1
	All I See Is You	9/29/66	9/29/66	xx	3
	I'll Try Anything	3/9/67	4/6/67	29	2
	The Look Of Love	10/19/67	11/16/67	7	7
	/Give Me Time	6/22/67	6/22/67	pr	1
	Son-Of-A Preacher Man	12/12/68	1/22/69	9	8

Springfield, Rick
	Speak To The Sky	8/5/72	8/26/72	30	5

Springsteen, Bruce
	Born To Run	10/4/75	10/18/75	28	6

St. Peters, Crispian
	The Pied Piper	6/16/66	7/14/66	3	10
	Changes	9/8/66	10/6/66	xx	4

Stafford, Jim
	Spiders & Snakes	3/2/74	4/20/74	3	11
	My Girl Bill	5/4/74	6/22/74	8	13
	Wildwood Weed	7/6/74	8/24/74	5	11
	Your Bulldog Drinks Champagne	1/11/75	2/1/75	29	5
	I Got Stoned And I Missed It	9/20/75	10/4/75	28	5

Stampeders
	Sweet City Woman	8/26/71	10/7/71	2	11

Standells
	Dirty Water	5/5/66	6/30/66	3	11

Staple Singers
	Heavy Makes You Happy (Sha-Na-Boom Boom)	1/18/71	3/11/71	6	12
	Respect Yourself	11/18/71	1/13/72	5	12
	I'll Take You There	5/4/72	6/8/72	12	11
	If You're Ready (Come Go With Me)	11/17/73	1/12/74	11	12
	Touch A Hand, Make A Friend	4/13/74	5/4/74	25	6
	Let's Do It Again	11/15/75	12/20/75	6	12

Artist	Title	Debut	Peak	Pos	Wks
Starcher, Buddy					
	History Repeats Itself	4/14/66	4/28/66	19	3
Starr, Edwin					
	Twenty-Five Miles	3/19/69	4/9/69	12	5
	War	7/20/70	8/10/70	1	16
	Stop The War Now	12/7/70	1/4/71	19	6
Starr, Ringo					
	It Don't Come Easy	4/29/71	6/10/71	2	10
	Back Off Boogaloo	3/30/72	5/25/72	1	12
	Photograph	10/13/73	12/1/73	1	12
	You're Sixteen	12/15/73	2/2/74	1	14
	Oh My My	3/9/74	4/13/74	13	12
	Only You	12/14/74	1/25/75	6	10
	No No Song	2/22/75	4/26/75	3	15
	also see the Beatles				
Staton, Candi					
	Stand By Your Man	10/19/70	11/16/70	20	7
Status Quo					
	Pictures Of Matchstick Men	6/13/68	7/4/68	2	8
Stealers Wheel					
	Stuck In The Middle With You	3/10/73	4/28/73	2	12
	also see Rafferty, Gerry				
Steam					
	Na Na Hey Hey Kiss Him Goodbye	1/12/70	1/12/70	19	2
Steely Dan					
	Do It Again	12/23/72	2/17/73	8	14
	Reeling In The Years	4/7/73	5/26/73	3	12
	Rikki Don't Lose That Number	6/8/74	7/27/74	4	14
	Black Friday	6/7/75	6/21/75	28	8
Steppenwolf					
	Born To Be Wild	7/11/68	8/15/68	1	10
	Magic Carpet Ride	10/10/68	11/7/68	2	9
	Rock Me	3/12/69	4/9/69	6	6

Artist	Title	Debut	Peak	Pos	Wks
	Hey Lawdy Mama	3/30/70	4/20/70	14	7
	Straight Shootin' Woman	10/5/74	11/2/74	20	7

Stevens, Cat
	Wild World	3/25/71	5/13/71	8	10
	Moon Shadow	6/17/71	8/12/71	7	12
	Peace Train	9/23/71	11/18/71	1	13
	Morning Has Broken	4/13/72	6/1/72	1	11
	Sitting	11/25/72	1/27/73	6	14
	The Hurt	8/18/73	10/6/73	1	11
	Oh Very Young	5/4/74	6/1/74	17	11
	Another Saturday Night	9/21/74	11/2/74	2	13

Stevens, Ray
	Gitarzan	4/9/69	4/30/69	1	8
	Along Came Jones	7/23/69	7/23/69	24	1
	Everything Is Beautiful	5/11/70	5/25/70	11	7
	Bridget The Midget (The Queen Of The Blues)	1/25/71	2/8/71	35	4
	The Streak	4/20/74	5/18/74	1	12
	Misty	7/12/75	8/2/75	19	8

Stevenson, B.W.
	My Maria	8/11/73	10/6/73	3	13

Stewart, Billy
	Summertime	8/4/66	8/25/66	15	5
	Secret Love	9/29/66	11/17/66	20	3

Stewart, Rod
	Maggie May	9/9/71	9/30/71	1	10
	You Wear It Well	9/30/72	11/4/72	16	9

also see Faces and Python Lee Jackson

Stills, Stephen
	Love The One You're With	12/7/70	1/18/71	3	9
	Marianne	8/19/71	9/30/71	4	11

also see Buffalo Springfield and Crosby, Stills & Nash

Stokes, Simon
	Captain Howdy	7/27/74	8/24/74	20	9

Artist	Title	Debut	Peak	Pos	Wks

Stone Poneys featuring Linda Ronstadt
	Different Drum	10/19/67	2/8/68	4	8

also see the Eagles and Ronstadt, Linda

Stookey, Paul
	Wedding Song (There Is Love)	7/15/71	9/9/71	2	13

also see Peter, Paul & Mary

Stories
	I'm Coming Home	7/22/72	8/12/72	22	5
	Brother Louie	6/23/73	8/18/73	1	13
	Mammy Blue	10/27/73	12/15/73	7	12

also see the Left Banke

Strangeloves
	Night Time	1/20/66	1/20/66	pr	1

Strawberry Alarm Clock
	Incense And Peppermints	10/19/67	11/9/67	2	9
	Tomorrow	1/18/68	2/15/68	14	6
	Sit With The Guru	3/7/68	3/7/68	pr	1

Street People
	Jennifer Tomkins	3/9/70	3/23/70	15	6

Streisand, Barbra
	Second Hand Rose	2/10/66	2/10/66	20	1
	Sleep In Heavenly Peace (Silent Night)	12/22/66	12/22/66	pr	1
	Stoney End	1/4/71	1/25/71	2	6
	The Way We Were	12/22/73	2/9/74	1	16

Stylistics
	I'm Stone In Love With You	11/18/72	1/20/73	9	13
	Break Up To Make Up	3/3/73	4/7/73	18	8
	Rockin' Roll Baby	12/1/73	1/26/74	12	13
	You Make Me Feel Brand New	4/20/74	5/25/74	16	11
	Let's Put It All Together	9/7/74	10/5/74	10	10

Styx
	Lady	1/11/75	2/15/75	3	11

Artist	Title	Debut	Peak	Pos	Wks

Sugar Bears
	You Are The One	2/17/72	4/13/72	6	12

Sugarloaf
	Green-Eyed Lady	9/14/70	10/12/70	5	12

Jerry Corbetta & Sugarloaf
	Don't Call Us, We'll Call You	2/22/75	4/19/75	4	14

Summer, Donna
	Love To Love You Baby	12/27/75	2/7/76	2	9

Summers, Bob
	When I'm Dead And Gone	1/11/71	2/8/71	15	5

Sunrays
	Andrea	2/3/66	2/24/66	12	4

also see Heaven Bound

Supremes
	My World Is Empty Without You	1/13/66	2/17/66	17	5
	Love Is Like An Itching In My Heart	5/12/66	5/12/66	xx	2
	You Can't Hurry Love	8/4/66	9/22/66	2	11
	You Keep Me Hangin' On	10/20/66	11/24/66	3	10
	Love Is Here And Now You're Gone	1/19/67	2/23/67	7	9
	The Happening	3/30/67	4/27/67	9	8
	Up The Ladder To The Roof	3/2/70	4/6/70	3	11
	Stoned Love	11/23/70	1/4/71	2	10
	Nathan Jones	5/20/71	7/1/71	5	11
	Floy Joy	1/27/72	3/23/72	2	11
	Automatically Sunshine	5/4/72	6/22/72	6	12

Diana Ross & the Supremes
	Reflections	8/3/67	9/7/67	5	11
	In And Out Of Love	11/9/67	12/28/67	16	7
	Forever Came Today	3/14/68	4/18/68	19	6
	Some Things You Never Get Used To	7/4/68	7/4/68	26	1
	Love Child	10/24/68	11/21/68	1	10
	I'm Livin' In Shame	1/22/69	2/12/69	13	7
	The Composer	4/16/69	5/7/69	18	4
	No Matter What Sign You Are	6/4/69	6/11/69	21	4
	Someday We'll Be Together	1/12/70	1/12/70	10	5

Artist	Title	Debut	Peak	Pos	Wks
Diana Ross & the Supremes & the Temptations					
	I'm Gonna Make You Love Me	12/5/68	1/15/69	1	11
	I'll Try Something New	3/26/69	4/2/69	26	2
Supremes & the Four Tops					
	River Deep—Mountain High	12/7/70	1/11/71	11	8
also see the Four Tops; Ross, Diana and the Temptations					
Surfaris					
	Wipe Out	8/25/66	9/29/66	3	9
Sutherland Brothers & Quiver					
	(I Don't Want To Love You But) You Got Me Anyway	9/15/73	10/20/73	14	9
Swan, Billy					
	I Can Help	11/23/74	12/28/74	1	14
Sweathog					
	Hallelujah	11/4/71	12/9/71	21	7
Sweet					
	Little Willy	2/10/73	4/14/73	1	15
	Blockbuster	6/30/73	7/28/73	22	7
	Ballroom Blitz	8/16/75	10/4/75	1	16
	Fox On The Run	11/15/75	12/27/75	1	15
	Action	2/14/76	2/21/76	33	2
Sweet Inspirations					
	Sweet Inspiration	3/21/68	4/18/68	11	6
Sylvia					
	Pillow Talk	4/14/73	6/2/73	1	12
Syndicate Of Sound					
	Little Girl	6/23/66	7/21/66	19	5
Tanega, Norma					
	Walkin' My Cat Named Dog	3/3/66	3/31/66	xx	3
Tavares					
	Remember What I Told You To Forget	4/19/75	5/31/75	19	9
	It Only Takes A Minute	9/13/75	10/25/75	7	14

Artist	Title	Debut	Peak	Pos	Wks
Taylor, Bobby & the Vancouvers					
	Does Your Mama Know About Me	5/2/68	5/23/68	22	4
also see Cheech & Chong					
Taylor, James					
	Fire And Rain	10/5/70	11/2/70	3	10
	Country Road	1/25/71	3/1/71	11	8
	You've Got A Friend	5/27/71	7/15/71	1	12
	Don't Let Me Be Lonely Tonight	12/9/72	2/17/73	5	14
also see Simon, Carly & James Taylor					
Taylor, Johnnie					
	Who's Making Love	10/31/68	11/28/68	10	9
	Jody's Got Your Girl And Gone	2/15/71	3/11/71	25	4
	I Believe In You (You Believe In Me)	7/14/73	9/1/73	10	11
Taylor, R. Dean					
	Indiana Wants Me	8/24/70	10/19/70	1	15
T-Bones					
	No Matter What Shape (Your Stomach's In)	1/13/66	1/27/66	5	5
also see Hamilton, Joe Frank & Reynolds					
Tee Set					
	Ma Belle Amie	1/12/70	2/9/70	7	9
Teegarden & Van Winkle					
	God, Love And Rock & Roll	9/21/70	10/19/70	18	8
Temptations					
	Get Ready	3/24/66	3/24/66	xx	1
	Ain't Too Proud To Beg	6/16/66	6/16/66	xx	2
	Beauty Is Only Skin Deep	8/25/66	10/6/66	15	9
	(I Know) I'm Losing You	12/1/66	12/1/66	xx	4
	All I Need	4/27/67	4/27/67	pr	1
	You're My Everything	8/17/67	9/14/67	17	5
	(Loneliness Made Me Realize) It's You That I Need	10/19/67	11/2/67	21	4
	I Wish It Would Rain	1/11/68	2/29/68	9	8
	I Could Never Love Another (After Loving You)	5/16/68	6/13/68	18	6
	Please Return Your Love To Me	8/15/68	9/5/68	19	5

Artist	Title	Debut	Peak	Pos	Wks
	Cloud Nine	11/28/68	1/8/69	6	10
	Run Away Child, Running Wild	3/12/69	3/26/69	10	4
	I Can't Get Next To You	8/27/69	10/8/69	3	7
	Psychedelic Shack	1/12/70	2/9/70	3	11
	Ball Of Confusion (That's What The World Is Today)	5/18/70	6/22/70	3	14
	Just My Imagination (Running Away With Me)	2/1/71	3/25/71	1	15
	Superstar (Remember How You Got Where You Are)	11/25/71	12/23/71	14	8
	Papa Was A Rollin' Stone	10/28/72	12/9/72	1	14
	Masterpiece	3/17/73	4/28/73	20	9

also see Kendricks, Eddie; Ruffin, David and the Supremes & the Temptations

10cc

	Rubber Bullets	9/15/73	11/3/73	7	13
	I'm Not In Love	6/14/75	8/2/75	4	16

also see Hotlegs and the Mindbenders

Ten Wheel Drive with Genya Ravan

	Morning Much Better	7/13/70	8/17/70	16	8

Terrell, Tammi

	Come On And See Me	7/28/66	7/28/66	xx	1

also see Gaye, Marvin & Tammi Terrell

Tex, Joe

	S.Y.S.L.J.F.M. (The Letter Song)	5/26/66	5/26/66	xx	1
	I've Got To Do A Little Bit Better	10/6/66	10/6/66	pr	1
	Skinny Legs And All	11/9/67	12/7/67	10	7
	Men Are Gettin' Scarce	2/1/68	2/22/68	30	3

Third Booth

	I Need Love	6/13/68	6/27/68	9	7

Third Rail

	Run, Run, Run	8/17/67	8/31/67	23	3

also see Crazy Elephant, Kasenetz-Katz, the Ohio Express and Reunion

Thomas, B.J.

	I'm So Lonesome I Could Cry	3/17/66	4/21/66	9	7
	Mama	5/5/66	6/2/66	xx	4
	The Eyes Of A New York Woman	8/22/68	9/12/68	7	6

Artist	Title	Debut	Peak	Pos	Wks
	Hooked On A Feeling	12/12/68	1/29/69	6	10
	It's Only Love	4/16/69	4/30/69	23	4
	Raindrops Keep Fallin' On My Head	1/12/70	1/12/70	2	9
	Everybody's Out Of Town	4/6/70	5/4/70	29	6
	I Just Can't Help Believing	7/13/70	8/17/70	6	11
	Most Of All	1/11/71	1/25/71	30	3
	No Love At All	2/15/71	4/22/71	15	11
	Mighty Clouds Of Joy	6/24/71	7/29/71	16	9
	Rock And Roll Lullaby	2/3/72	4/6/72	6	12
	(Hey Won't You Play) Another Somebody Done Somebody Wrong Song	3/15/75	5/17/75	1	17

Thomas, Carla

	Pick Up The Pieces	1/11/68	1/11/68	pr	1

Thomas, Ian

	Painted Ladies	11/3/73	12/29/73	4	13

Thomas, Rufus

	Do The Funky Chicken	3/16/70	3/23/70	27	2

Thomas, Timmy

	Why Can't We Live Together	12/9/72	1/20/73	2	12

Three Degrees

	When Will I See You Again	11/30/74	1/11/75	4	13

also see MFSB

Three Dog Night

	Nobody	12/5/68	12/5/68	28	1
	One	5/28/69	7/2/69	1	10
	Easy To Be Hard	8/13/69	9/17/69	4	9
	Celebrate	2/9/70	3/9/70	7	10
	Mama Told Me (Not To Come)	5/18/70	6/22/70	1	14
	Out In The Country	8/24/70	9/28/70	10	11
	One Man Band	11/9/70	12/7/70	19	7
	Joy To The World	4/1/71	4/29/71	1	12
	Liar	7/22/71	8/26/71	11	11
	An Old Fashioned Love Song	10/14/71	12/9/71	3	12
	The Family Of Man	3/30/72	5/11/72	14	9
	Black & White	8/19/72	9/30/72	1	11
	Pieces Of April	12/9/72	2/3/73	2	12

Artist	Title	Debut	Peak	Pos	Wks
	Shambala	5/26/73	7/21/73	7	15
	Let Me Serenade You	11/3/73	12/15/73	8	12
	The Show Must Go On	3/16/74	5/18/74	3	15
	Sure As I'm Sittin' Here	7/27/74	8/31/74	11	11
	Play Something Sweet (Brickyard Blues)	11/23/74	12/21/74	20	8
	Til The World Ends	7/12/75	8/16/75	14	10
also see Hutton, Danny					
Tim Tam & the Turn-Ons					
	Wait A Minute	3/24/66	3/24/66	xx	1
Tin Tin					
	Toast And Marmalade For Tea	3/25/71	4/29/71	23	8
Tiny Tim					
	Tip-Toe Thru' The Tulips With Me	6/6/68	6/20/68	20	3
Tokens					
	I Hear Trumpets Blow	4/14/66	4/14/66	xx	4
	Greatest Moments In A Girl's Life	5/26/66	5/26/66	pr	1
also see Cross Country					
Tower Of Power					
	You're Still A Young Man	8/19/72	10/7/72	11	11
	So Very Hard To Go	6/2/73	7/14/73	24	9
Tremeloes					
	Here Comes My Baby	4/6/67	5/18/67	4	8
	Silence Is Golden	7/20/67	8/24/67	11	7
Trend, Bobby					
	Good Day	10/12/70	11/9/70	19	6
T. Rex					
	Hot Love	4/22/71	5/27/71	15	8
	Bang A Gong (Get It On)	1/13/72	2/17/72	19	7
Troggs					
	Wild Thing	6/23/66	7/14/66	1	9
	/With A Girl Like You	7/21/66	9/1/66	15	7
	I Can't Control Myself	9/29/66	10/20/66	xx	3

Artist	Title	Debut	Peak	Pos	Wks
	Love Is All Around	2/29/68	4/4/68	17	6
	Surprise, Surprise (I Need You)	4/25/68	4/25/68	pr	1
Trolls					
	Every Day And Every Night	9/8/66	10/6/66	12	6
	There Was A Time	4/6/67	4/6/67	pr	1
Turner, Ike & Tina					
	I'll Never Need More Than This	6/29/67	6/29/67	pr	1
	I Want To Take You Higher	7/27/70	8/24/70	13	11
	Proud Mary	1/25/71	3/11/71	2	10
Turner, Spyder					
	Stand By Me	1/26/67	1/26/67	xx	1
Turtles					
	You Baby	3/3/66	4/7/66	4	8
	Outside Chance	7/14/66	7/14/66	pr	1
	Happy Together	1/26/67	3/16/67	1	14
	She'd Rather Be With Me	5/11/67	6/22/67	4	7
	You Know What I Mean	8/17/67	9/14/67	15	9
	She's My Girl	10/26/67	12/21/67	11	9
	Sound Asleep	2/29/68	4/4/68	20	3
	The Story Of Rock And Roll	7/4/68	7/4/68	29	1
	Elenore	10/3/68	11/7/68	4	8
	You Showed Me	1/15/69	2/12/69	3	9
	You Don't Have To Walk In The Rain	7/2/69	7/2/69	29	1
Twilley, Dwight, Band					
	I'm On Fire	6/7/75	6/28/75	23	9
2 Of Clubs					
	Walk Tall	3/2/67	4/13/67	10	7
Tymes					
	You Little Trustmaker	9/14/74	11/2/74	4	14
Uncle Dog					
	River Road	2/24/73	3/24/73	29	6

Artist	Title	Debut	Peak	Pos	Wks
Underground Sunshine					
	Birthday	7/23/69	8/13/69	4	7
Undisputed Truth					
	Smiling Faces Sometimes	7/8/71	8/19/71	1	11
Unifics					
	Court Of Love	10/31/68	11/14/68	23	3
Valli, Frankie					
	You're Ready Now	4/21/66	4/21/66	pr	1
	Can't Take My Eyes Off You	6/1/67	7/27/67	1	13
	I Make A Fool Of Myself	8/24/67	9/28/67	12	8
	To Give (The Reason I Live)	12/21/67	1/25/68	11	7
	My Eyes Adored You	1/18/75	3/22/75	1	17
	Swearin' To God	6/28/75	8/2/75	11	11
also see the Four Seasons					
Vanilla Fudge					
	You Keep Me Hangin' On	8/8/68	9/5/68	6	6
	Take Me For A Little While	11/7/68	11/14/68	26	2
Vanity Fare					
	Early In The Morning	1/12/70	1/12/70	25	2
	Hitchin' A Ride	4/13/70	5/18/70	1	16
Vee, Bobby					
	Come Back When You Grow Up	8/10/67	9/14/67	2	9
	My Girl/Hey Girl	4/11/68	5/23/68	6	7
Ventures					
	Hawaii Five-O	4/9/69	5/7/69	10	6
Vera, Billy					
	With Pen In Hand	7/18/68	7/18/68	30	1
Vinton, Bobby					
	Coming Home Soldier	12/22/66	1/12/67	19	3
	Please Love Me Forever	10/26/67	11/23/67	6	7
	Just As Much As Ever	12/14/67	1/18/68	23	6
	Take Good Care Of My Baby	4/18/68	5/9/68	17	5

Artist	Title	Debut	Peak	Pos	Wks
	Halfway To Paradise	8/8/68	8/22/68	20	3
	I Love How You Love Me	11/14/68	12/26/68	3	10
	To Know You Is To Love You	4/9/69	5/7/69	21	5
	Every Day Of My Life	2/17/72	3/23/72	13	7
	My Melody Of Love	10/19/74	11/30/74	1	15

Viscounts
	Harlem Nocturne	12/23/65	1/6/66	16	3

Vogues
	Five O'Clock World	12/16/65	12/30/65	1	8
	Magic Town	2/24/66	3/17/66	9	6
	The Land Of Milk And Honey	6/9/66	7/7/66	16	6
	Turn Around, Look At Me	6/27/68	8/15/68	2	9
	My Special Angel	9/5/68	10/3/68	8	7
	Till	11/21/68	12/12/68	18	6
	No, Not Much	3/5/69	3/12/69	11	3

Wadsworth Mansion
	Sweet Mary	1/18/71	3/1/71	2	11

Wainwright III, Loudon
	Dead Skunk	3/3/73	4/14/73	8	12

Wakelin, Johnny & the Kinshasa Band
	Black Superman—"Muhammad Ali"	7/26/75	9/13/75	6	12

Walker, Gary
	You Don't Love Me	5/19/66	5/19/66	xx	1

also see the Walker Brothers

Walker, Jr. & the All Stars
	Come See About Me	12/28/67	1/25/68	22	3
	Hip City—Pt. 2	9/12/68	9/19/68	25	2
	What Does It Take (To Win Your Love)	6/11/69	7/23/69	5	9
	Gotta Hold On To This Feeling	2/23/70	3/16/70	23	6
	Take Me Girl, I'm Ready	8/19/71	9/23/71	15	8
	Walk In The Night	4/6/72	5/18/72	15	9

Walker Brothers
	The Sun Ain't Gonna Shine (Anymore)	5/5/66	5/26/66	14	4

also see Walker, Gary

Artist	Title	Debut	Peak	Pos	Wks

Walsh, Joe
	Rocky Mountain Way	9/22/73	10/27/73	22	8
	also see the Eagles and James Gang				

Wanderley, Walter
	Summer Samba (So Nice)	9/22/66	9/29/66	20	3

War
	The World Is A Ghetto	2/3/73	3/10/73	5	9
	The Cisco Kid	3/24/73	5/5/73	5	10
	Gypsy Man	7/21/73	9/15/73	13	11
	Why Can't We Be Friends	6/21/75	8/16/75	1	17
	also see Burdon, Eric & War				

Warwick, Dionne
	Message To Michael	5/5/66	5/26/66	17	5
	Trains And Boats And Planes	7/21/66	7/21/66	xx	3
	Alfie	8/4/66	8/18/66	20	3
	The Windows Of The World	9/28/67	9/28/67	30	2
	(Theme From) Valley Of The Dolls	2/8/68	2/22/68	7	6
	/I Say A Little Prayer	11/16/67	12/7/67	7	5
	Do You Know The Way To San José	5/2/68	5/23/68	13	6
	Promises, Promises	11/21/68	12/5/68	20	5
	This Girl's In Love With You	2/19/69	3/19/69	7	6
	I'll Never Fall In Love Again	1/12/70	1/26/70	6	7

Warwick, Dionne & Spinners
	Then Came You	8/17/74	10/12/74	3	14

Watts 103rd Street Rhythm Band
	Do Your Thing	3/5/69	4/2/69	6	6

Charles Wright & the Watts 103rd Street Rhythm Band
	Love Land	5/18/70	6/15/70	2	11

Weatherly, Jim
	The Need To Be	8/24/74	10/5/74	12	11
	I'll Still Love You	2/1/75	2/15/75	32	3

Wednesday
	Last Kiss	1/26/74	3/16/74	5	13

Artist	Title	Debut	Peak	Pos	Wks

Weissberg, Eric & Steve Mandell
Dueling Banjos — 2/3/73 — 3/10/73 — 2 — 12

Welch, Lenny
Breaking Up Is Hard To Do — 1/12/70 — 2/9/70 — 29 — 3

West, Keith
Excerpt From "A Teenage Opera" (Grocer Jack) — 10/12/67 — 10/12/67 — pr — 1

Wet Willie
Keep On Smilin' — 7/20/74 — 8/24/74 — 14 — 11

White, Barry
I'm Gonna Love You Just A Little More Baby — 4/28/73 — 6/30/73 — 4 — 13
Never, Never Gonna Give Ya Up — 12/15/73 — 2/9/74 — 5 — 13
Can't Get Enough Of Your Love, Babe — 8/3/74 — 9/14/74 — 5 — 12
You're The First, The Last, My Everything — 11/30/74 — 1/11/75 — 3 — 12
What Am I Gonna Do With You — 3/29/75 — 5/3/75 — 14 — 9
also see Love Unlimited and the Love Unlimited Orchestra

White, Tony Joe
Polk Salad Annie — 7/2/69 — 7/30/69 — 4 — 7

White Plains
My Baby Loves Lovin' — 4/20/70 — 6/8/70 — 1 — 15
also see the Brotherhood Of Man, Edison Lighthouse, First Class and the Pipkins

Whittaker, Roger
The Last Farewell — 5/31/75 — 6/28/75 — 15 — 10

Whittington's, Dick, Cats
In The Midnight Hour — 2/9/67 — 2/9/67 — pr — 1

Who
My Generation — 1/20/66 — 1/20/66 — pr — 1
I Can See For Miles — 11/23/67 — 12/21/67 — 8 — 6
Call Me Lightning — 4/18/68 — 5/2/68 — 17 — 3
Magic Bus — 8/29/68 — 9/19/68 — 9 — 4
Pinball Wizard — 4/2/69 — 5/14/69 — 5 — 9
The Seeker — 4/13/70 — 5/11/70 — 16 — 7
See Me, Feel Me — 11/2/70 — 11/30/70 — 3 — 10

Artist	Title	Debut	Peak	Pos	Wks
	Won't Get Fooled Again	7/8/71	9/9/71	4	12
	Join Together	8/5/72	9/16/72	18	9
	Squeeze Box	1/17/76	2/21/76	9	6
Williams, Andy					
	Music To Watch Girls By	4/20/67	5/11/67	17	4
Williams, John					
	Main Title (Theme From "Jaws")	8/30/75	9/27/75	16	10
Williams, Mason					
	Classical Gas	7/11/68	8/15/68	4	8
Williams, Roger					
	Lara's Theme From "Dr. Zhivago"	4/14/66	5/5/66	17	4
	Born Free	10/13/66	10/13/66	xx	1
Wilson, Al					
	The Snake	10/3/68	10/3/68	24	1
	Show And Tell	11/10/73	1/12/74	5	14
Wilson, Brian					
	Caroline, No	3/24/66	4/7/66	16	5
also see the Beach Boys					
Wilson, Jackie					
	(Your Love Keeps Lifting Me) Higher And Higher	9/14/67	10/19/67	16	6
	I Get The Sweetest Feeling	8/8/68	8/15/68	26	2
Wilson, Nancy					
	Face It Girl, It's Over	6/6/68	7/11/68	16	7
Wind					
	Make Believe	9/17/69	10/8/69	13	4
also see Dawn					
Wingfield, Pete					
	Eighteen With A Bullet	9/13/75	11/8/75	3	15
Winstons					
	Color Him Father	6/4/69	7/9/69	5	8

Artist	Title	Debut	Peak	Pos	Wks
Winter, Edgar, Group					
	Frankenstein	3/31/73	5/19/73	1	13
	Free Ride	9/1/73	10/27/73	3	15
Winters, Ruby					
	I Want Action	10/19/67	10/19/67	pr	1
Withers, Bill					
	Ain't No Sunshine	8/5/71	9/9/71	5	9
	Lean On Me	6/15/72	7/15/72	1	11
	Use Me	9/23/72	10/28/72	6	9
	Kissing My Love	2/17/73	4/7/73	1	11
Womack, Bobby					
	Lookin' For A Love	3/30/74	5/4/74	22	9
Wonder, Stevie					
	Uptight (Everything's Alright)	2/17/66	2/17/66	xx	2
	A Place In The Sun	11/17/66	11/17/66	pr	1
	I Was Made To Love Her	7/6/67	8/24/67	5	9
	I'm Wondering	10/5/67	11/2/67	23	4
	Shoo-Be-Doo-Be-Doo-Da-Day	4/18/68	6/6/68	8	8
	You Met Your Match	8/1/68	8/1/68	28	2
	For Once In My Life	11/14/68	12/19/68	2	7
	My Cherie Amour	6/11/69	8/6/69	5	10
	Yester-Me, Yester-You, Yesterday	1/12/70	1/12/70	23	2
	Signed, Sealed, Delivered I'm Yours	7/6/70	8/10/70	4	12
	Heaven Help Us All	10/19/70	11/30/70	7	10
	We Can Work It Out	3/1/71	4/29/71	8	12
	If You Really Love Me	8/26/71	10/14/71	6	11
	Superstition	12/16/72	2/3/73	3	12
	You Are The Sunshine Of My Life	4/7/73	5/12/73	10	10
	Higher Ground	8/18/73	10/13/73	8	13
	Living For The City	11/24/73	1/19/74	10	12
	Don't You Worry 'Bout A Thing	4/27/74	6/15/74	11	12
	You Haven't Done Nothin'	8/24/74	9/28/74	12	10
	Boogie On Reggae Woman	12/21/74	2/8/75	4	12
Eivets Rednow					
	Alfie	10/17/68	10/31/68	25	3

Artist	Title	Debut	Peak	Pos	Wks
Wood, Brenton					
	The Oogum Boogum Song	5/18/67	6/1/67	19	4
	Gimme Little Sign	9/7/67	10/12/67	5	7
	Baby You Got It	11/16/67	12/14/67	22	4
Wright, Gary					
	Dream Weaver	1/31/76	2/21/76	15	4
Yardbirds					
	I'm A Man	12/16/65	12/16/65	10	5
	Shapes Of Things	3/10/66	3/31/66	3	9
	Over Under Sideways Down	7/14/66	8/4/66	15	7
	Happenings Ten Years Time Ago	12/15/66	12/15/66	xx	1
	Little Games	4/6/67	4/6/67	pr	1
	Ha Ha Said The Clown	7/27/67	8/31/67	28	2
	also see Clapton, Eric and Led Zeppelin				
Yellow Balloon					
	Yellow Balloon	3/23/67	6/8/67	12	7
Yes					
	Your Move	9/30/71	11/25/71	4	12
	Roundabout	2/3/72	3/23/72	4	11
	America	8/19/72	9/2/72	25	5
Young, Don					
	She Let Her Hair Down (Early In The Morning)	1/26/70	2/23/70	17	7
Young, John Paul					
	Yesterday's Hero	1/17/76	1/17/76	32	3
Young, Neil					
	Sugar Mountain	2/1/71	2/8/71	34	3
	Heart Of Gold	1/27/72	3/23/72	1	14
	also see Buffalo Springfield and Crosby, Stills, Nash & Young				
Young Rascals					
	I Ain't Gonna Eat Out My Heart Anymore	1/20/66	1/20/66	17	1
	Good Lovin'	3/24/66	5/5/66	3	11
	You Better Run	6/9/66	6/23/66	xx	6

Artist	Title	Debut	Peak	Pos	Wks
	I've Been Lonely Too Long	2/23/67	3/9/67	23	5
	Groovin'	5/11/67	6/22/67	3	10
	A Girl Like You	7/6/67	8/24/67	15	6
	How Can I Be Sure	8/31/67	10/19/67	4	11
	It's Wonderful	11/30/67	1/18/68	10	7
Rascals					
	A Beautiful Morning	4/4/68	5/9/68	3	10
	People Got To Be Free	7/18/68	8/29/68	1	10
	A Ray Of Hope	12/12/68	12/19/68	25	3
	Heaven	2/19/69	2/26/69	26	2
	See	5/28/69	6/4/69	19	4
	Carry Me Back	8/27/69	9/17/69	22	7
also see Bulldog					
Youngbloods					
	Grizzly Bear	12/15/66	1/5/67	17	5
	Get Together	8/6/69	9/3/69	6	9
Young-Holt Unlimited					
	Soulful Strut	12/12/68	1/22/69	3	9
also see Lewis, Ramsey					
Zager & Evans					
	In The Year 2525 (Exordium & Terminus)	6/25/69	7/16/69	1	8
Zombies					
	Indication	8/18/66	8/18/66	xx	3
	Time Of The Season	2/5/69	3/19/69	1	10
also see Argent					
ZZ Top					
	La Grange	5/18/74	6/29/74	2	15
	Tush	7/26/75	9/13/75	2	14

ALPHABETICAL LISTING BY TITLE

Debut	Peak	Title	Artist	Pos	Wks
8/31/67	8/31/67	A Banda	Herb Alpert & the Tijuana Brass	pr	1
5/12/66	5/12/66	"A" Team, The	S/Sgt. Barry Sadler	xx	1
3/9/70	4/6/70	ABC	Jackson 5	1	11
7/30/69	8/6/69	Abergavenny	Shannon	22	3
12/29/73	2/23/74	Abra-Ca-Dabra	DeFranco Family featuring Tony DeFranco	3	13
11/7/68	11/28/68	Abraham, Martin And John	Dion	1	8
10/7/71	11/25/71	Absolutely Right	Five Man Electrical Band	2	12
2/14/76	2/21/76	Action	Sweet	33	2
3/1/71	3/11/71	Adrienne	Tommy James	35	3
5/25/72	6/8/72	After Midnight	J.J. Cale	26	4
11/9/70	12/21/70	After Midnight	Eric Clapton	6	10
9/14/74	11/16/74	After The Goldrush	Prelude	7	15
9/29/66	10/27/66	Ain't Gonna Lie	Keith	15	6
8/10/67	8/10/67	Ain't No Mountain High Enough	Marvin Gaye & Tammi Terrell	25	1
7/27/70	8/17/70	Ain't No Mountain High Enough	Diana Ross	2	13
8/5/71	9/9/71	Ain't No Sunshine	Bill Withers	5	9
4/4/68	5/9/68	Ain't No Way	Aretha Franklin	19	4
8/23/75	10/11/75	Ain't No Way To Treat A Lady	Helen Reddy	4	14
2/24/73	4/7/73	Ain't No Woman (Like The One I've Got)	Four Tops	4	11
5/9/68	6/13/68	Ain't Nothing Like The Real Thing	Marvin Gaye & Tammi Terrell	15	6
11/23/74	12/21/74	Ain't Too Proud To Beg	Rolling Stones	22	6
6/16/66	6/16/66	Ain't Too Proud To Beg	Temptations	xx	2
7/20/74	8/24/74	Air That I Breathe, The	Hollies	2	12

Debut	Peak	Title	Artist	Pos	Wks
3/30/70	4/20/70	Airport Love Theme (Gwen And Vern)	Vincent Bell	26	7
3/30/67	4/6/67	Al Sleet, Your Hippy-Dippy Weatherman	George Carlin	20	2
10/17/68	10/31/68	Alfie	Eivets Rednow	25	3
8/4/66	8/18/66	Alfie	Dionne Warwick	20	3
7/25/68	8/29/68	Alice Long (You're Still My Favorite Girlfriend)	Tommy Boyce & Bobby Hart	7	8
1/5/67	2/2/67	All	James Darren	15	6
10/17/68	11/7/68	All Along The Watchtower	Jimi Hendrix Experience	19	4
12/20/75	2/21/76	All By Myself	Eric Carmen	6	10
10/28/71	12/23/71	All I Ever Need Is You	Sonny & Cher	2	14
9/22/73	11/3/73	All I Know	Art Garfunkel	4	12
4/27/67	4/27/67	All I Need	Temptations	pr	1
9/29/66	9/29/66	All I See Is You	Dusty Springfield	xx	3
8/24/70	10/5/70	All Right Now	Free	3	14
7/13/67	8/31/67	All You Need Is Love	Beatles	4	9
6/22/72	8/5/72	Alone Again (Naturally)	Gilbert O'Sullivan	1	14
7/23/69	7/23/69	Along Came Jones	Ray Stevens	24	1
6/23/66	7/14/66	Along Comes Mary	Association	10	6
6/22/74	7/13/74	Already Gone	Eagles	14	9
2/24/73	3/24/73	Also Sprach Zarathustra (2001)	Deodato	1	9
1/19/70	2/16/70	Always Something There To Remind Me	R.B. Greaves	17	7
11/14/68	11/14/68	Always Together	Dells	20	2
1/4/68	2/8/68	Am I That Easy To Forget	Engelbert Humperdinck	26	5
12/14/70	2/8/71	Amazing Grace	Judy Collins	20	7
5/18/72	6/15/72	Amazing Grace	Royal Scots Dragoon Guards	10	9
8/19/72	9/2/72	America	Yes	25	5
12/2/71	1/13/72	American Pie—Parts I & II	Don McLean	1	14
3/23/70	4/20/70	American Woman	Guess Who	1	12
1/12/74	2/2/74	Americans	Byron MacGregor	8	6
4/5/75	5/10/75	Amie	Pure Prairie League	20	11
1/18/71	3/1/71	Amos Moses	Jerry Reed	3	11
2/3/66	2/24/66	Andrea	Sunrays	12	4

Debut	Peak	Title	Artist	Pos	Wks
8/4/73	9/8/73	Angel	Aretha Franklin	24	8
1/18/71	2/8/71	Angel Baby	Dusk	27	5
6/6/68	6/27/68	Angel Of The Morning	Merrilee Rush & the Turnabouts	2	6
3/16/70	3/16/70	Angelica	Oliver	42	1
9/8/73	10/27/73	Angie	Rolling Stones	1	14
10/26/74	12/21/74	Angie Baby	Helen Reddy	7	15
6/15/74	8/3/74	Annie's Song	John Denver	1	16
3/1/71	4/22/71	Another Day	Paul McCartney	4	12
4/13/67	4/13/67	Another Day, Another Heartache	5th Dimension	pr	1
5/11/74	6/22/74	Another Park, Another Sunday	Doobie Brothers	10	11
9/21/74	11/2/74	Another Saturday Night	Cat Stevens	2	13
3/15/75	5/17/75	(Hey Won't You Play) Another Somebody Done Somebody Wrong Song	B.J. Thomas	1	17
1/6/66	2/10/66	Answer To My Prayer, The	Neil Sedaka	xx	4
1/13/72	2/24/72	Anticipation	Carly Simon	6	11
9/7/67	9/28/67	Anything Goes	Harpers Bizarre	19	5
2/22/71	3/18/71	Anytime Sunshine	Crazy Paving	30	4
1/11/71	2/15/71	Apeman	Kinks	8	7
2/22/71	3/11/71	Apple Scruffs	George Harrison	18	3
9/7/67	10/12/67	Apples, Peaches, Pumpkin Pie	Jay & the Techniques	4	7
3/19/69	4/23/69	Aquarius/Let The Sunshine In (The Flesh Failures)	5th Dimension	1	10
2/2/67	2/2/67	Are You Lonely For Me	Freddie Scott	xx	1
7/28/73	9/15/73	Are You Man Enough	Four Tops	9	11
6/22/70	7/27/70	Are You Ready	Pacific Gas & Electric	8	10
1/12/70	2/2/70	Arizona	Mark Lindsay	4	11
1/13/66	1/27/66	As Tears Go By	Rolling Stones	17	3
11/9/70	11/23/70	As The Years Go By	Mashmakhan	11	6
5/25/72	6/29/72	Ask Me What You Want	Millie Jackson	17	9
8/2/75	9/27/75	At Seventeen	Janis Ian	2	16
1/27/66	3/10/66	At The Scene	Dave Clark Five	13	6

Debut	Peak	Title	Artist	Pos	Wks
3/16/67	4/20/67	At The Zoo	Simon & Garfunkel	12	6
4/23/69	5/21/69	Atlantis	Donovan	6	6
4/5/75	5/17/75	Autobahn	Kraftwerk	12	12
5/4/72	6/22/72	Automatically Sunshine	Supremes	6	12
7/4/68	8/8/68	Autumn Of My Life	Bobby Goldsboro	16	6
1/15/69	2/19/69	Baby, Baby Don't Cry	Smokey Robinson & the Miracles	3	10
3/16/72	5/4/72	Baby Blue	Badfinger	4	12
9/26/68	10/17/68	Baby, Come Back	Equals	12	4
8/12/72	9/23/72	Baby Don't Get Hooked On Me	Mac Davis	4	12
7/20/67	9/7/67	Baby I Love You	Aretha Franklin	15	8
6/18/69	7/23/69	Baby, I Love You	Andy Kim	3	9
1/26/67	3/23/67	Baby I Need Your Lovin'	Johnny Rivers	8	8
10/21/71	12/9/71	Baby I'm-A Want You	Bread	2	11
9/24/69	10/8/69	Baby It's You	Smith	14	3
8/12/72	9/16/72	Baby Let Me Take You (In My Arms)	Detroit Emeralds	6	10
1/8/69	1/29/69	Baby Let's Wait	Royal Guardsmen	15	6
2/1/68	2/29/68	Baby, Now That I've Found You	Foundations	4	5
3/10/66	3/24/66	Baby Scratch My Back	Slim Harpo	18	3
1/26/70	2/16/70	Baby Take Me In Your Arms	Jefferson	15	7
12/1/66	12/1/66	Baby What I Mean	Drifters	pr	1
11/16/67	12/14/67	Baby You Got It	Brenton Wood	22	4
7/13/67	8/31/67	Baby You're A Rich Man	Beatles	4	8
3/12/69	3/19/69	Back Door Man	Derek	28	2
10/12/74	11/16/74	Back Home Again	John Denver	9	10
5/23/68	6/20/68	Back In Love Again	Buckinghams	21	4
3/30/72	5/25/72	Back Off Boogaloo	Ringo Starr	1	12
2/22/68	4/4/68	Back On My Feet Again	Foundations	26	3
7/22/72	9/23/72	Back Stabbers	O'Jays	1	13
4/28/73	6/9/73	Back When My Hair Was Short	Gunhill Road	13	10
4/7/66	5/19/66	Backstage	Gene Pitney	12	5
5/12/73	7/14/73	Bad, Bad Leroy Brown	Jim Croce	5	15

Debut	Peak	Title	Artist	Pos	Wks
9/20/75	11/8/75	Bad Blood	Neil Sedaka	1	19
8/18/66	9/29/66	Bad Little Woman	Shadows Of Knight	19	4
5/21/69	6/11/69	Bad Moon Rising	Creedence Clearwater Revival	2	8
4/19/75	6/14/75	Bad Time	Grand Funk	3	14
5/18/70	6/22/70	Ball Of Confusion (That's What The World Is Today)	Temptations	3	14
10/8/69	10/8/69	Ball Of Fire	Tommy James & the Shondells	29	1
2/22/68	3/21/68	Ballad Of Bonnie And Clyde, The	Georgie Fame	12	9
6/4/69	7/16/69	Ballad Of John And Yoko, The	Beatles	8	8
2/10/66	3/10/66	Ballad Of The Green Berets, The	S/Sgt. Barry Sadler	4	9
4/27/74	4/27/74	Ballad Of The Mad Streaker, The	Larry Lujack "Superjock"	xx	4
8/24/67	9/7/67	Ballad Of You & Me & Pooneil	Jefferson Airplane	26	3
8/16/75	10/4/75	Ballroom Blitz	Sweet	1	16
6/1/70	6/29/70	Band Of Gold	Freda Payne	3	12
4/27/74	6/15/74	Band On The Run	Paul McCartney & Wings	1	16
1/13/72	2/17/72	Bang A Gong (Get It On)	T. Rex	19	7
3/17/66	4/7/66	Bang Bang (My Baby Shot Me Down)	Cher	8	9
11/7/68	11/21/68	Bang-Shang-A-Lang	Archies	10	4
8/5/71	9/16/71	Bangla-Desh	George Harrison	15	8
1/6/66	2/17/66	Barbara Ann	Beach Boys	2	9
1/12/70	1/12/70	Barbara, I Love You	New Colony Six	29	3
5/19/66	5/19/66	Barefootin'	Robert Parker	xx	4
9/29/73	11/3/73	Basketball Jones Featuring Tyrone Shoelaces	Cheech & Chong	3	11
3/3/66	3/3/66	Batman	Jan & Dean	xx	1
5/19/66	5/26/66	Batman & His Grandmother	Dickie Goodman	10	4
2/10/66	2/24/66	Batman Theme	Marketts	18	4
10/20/73	11/24/73	Be	Neil Diamond	16	10
11/2/70	12/7/70	Be My Baby	Andy Kim	7	10
8/17/74	9/28/74	Beach Baby	First Class	2	15

Debut	Peak	Title	Artist	Pos	Wks
1/19/67	3/9/67	Beat Goes On, The	Sonny & Cher	6	10
4/4/68	5/9/68	Beautiful Morning, A	Rascals	3	10
11/23/67	11/30/67	Beautiful People	Kenny O'Dell	17	6
4/20/67	5/25/67	Beautiful Story, A	Sonny & Cher	27	2
8/26/72	10/21/72	Beautiful Sunday	Daniel Boone	1	13
8/25/66	10/6/66	Beauty Is Only Skin Deep	Temptations	15	9
2/23/67	2/23/67	Because Of You	Chris Montez	pr	1
4/12/75	5/31/75	Before The Next Teardrop Falls	Freddy Fender	3	12
11/30/67	12/14/67	Beg, Borrow And Steal	Ohio Express	24	4
2/23/67	4/27/67	Beggin'	Four Seasons	20	7
7/1/71	7/29/71	Beginnings	Chicago	6	9
7/7/73	9/1/73	Behind Closed Doors	Charlie Rich	12	11
10/27/66	10/27/66	Behind The Door	Cher	pr	1
12/5/68	1/15/69	Bella Linda	Grass Roots	15	7
9/2/72	10/21/72	Ben	Michael Jackson	2	12
11/30/67	1/18/68	Bend Me, Shape Me	American Breed	1	12
2/16/74	4/13/74	Bennie And The Jets	Elton John	2	16
3/2/67	4/6/67	Bernadette	Four Tops	15	6
3/15/75	4/19/75	Bertha Butt Boogie-Part 1, The	Jimmy Castor Bunch	19	9
12/14/74	2/15/75	Best Of My Love	Eagles	1	15
3/16/74	5/25/74	Best Thing That Ever Happened To Me	Gladys Knight & the Pips	4	16
4/4/68	4/25/68	Big Boy	Jackson 5	27	2
12/23/65	2/10/66	Big Bright Eyes	Danny Hutton	xx	2
2/17/73	4/7/73	Big City Miss Ruth Ann	Gallery	7	11
4/20/74	6/15/74	Billy, Don't Be A Hero	Bo Donaldson & the Heywoods	2	16
9/16/71	11/4/71	Birds Of A Feather	Raiders	6	10
7/23/69	8/13/69	Birthday	Underground Sunshine	4	7
9/28/74	11/9/74	Bitch Is Back, The	Elton John	1	13
8/19/72	9/30/72	Black & White	Three Dog Night	1	11
12/16/71	2/3/72	Black Dog	Led Zeppelin	2	13
6/7/75	6/21/75	Black Friday	Steely Dan	28	8
8/11/66	10/6/66	Black Is Black	Los Bravos	3	9

Debut	Peak	Title	Artist	Pos	Wks
11/23/70	1/18/71	Black Magic Woman	Santana	4	11
5/28/69	7/2/69	Black Pearl	Sonny Charles & the Checkmates, Ltd.	8	8
7/26/75	9/13/75	Black Superman— "Muhammad Ali"	Johnny Wakelin & the Kinshasa Band	6	12
2/1/75	3/1/75	Black Water	Doobie Brothers	1	12
10/7/71	11/4/71	Bless You	Martha Reeves & the Vandellas	28	6
12/28/67	12/28/67	Blessed Are The Lonely	Robert Knight	pr	1
6/30/73	7/28/73	Blockbuster	Sweet	22	7
1/12/70	1/26/70	Blowing Away	5th Dimension	16	6
11/24/73	12/22/73	Blue Collar	Bachman-Turner Overdrive	27	6
1/25/71	3/1/71	Blue Money	Van Morrison	9	9
6/29/67	6/29/67	Bluebird	Buffalo Springfield	pr	1
7/13/67	8/3/67	Blue's Theme	Davie Allan & the Arrows	3	8
2/14/76	2/21/76	Bohemian Rhapsody	Queen	31	2
11/30/67	12/21/67	Boogaloo Down Broadway	Fantastic Johnny C	9	7
1/19/74	3/9/74	Boogie Down	Eddie Kendricks	5	13
12/21/74	2/8/75	Boogie On Reggae Woman	Stevie Wonder	4	12
6/16/73	7/21/73	Boogie Woogie Bugle Boy	Bette Midler	1	12
7/21/66	9/1/66	Born A Woman	Sandy Posey	17	5
10/13/66	10/13/66	Born Free	Roger Williams	xx	1
7/11/68	8/15/68	Born To Be Wild	Steppenwolf	1	10
10/4/75	10/18/75	Born To Run	Bruce Springsteen	28	6
1/11/71	2/8/71	Born To Wander	Rare Earth	5	8
2/17/66	2/17/66	Bossy Boss	"Jumpin'" Gene Simmons	pr	1
11/14/68	12/19/68	Both Sides Now	Judy Collins	11	7
12/28/67	1/4/68	Bottle Of Wine	Fireballs	17	4
4/27/67	4/27/67	Bowling Green	Everly Brothers	pr	1
4/2/69	4/30/69	Boxer, The	Simon & Garfunkel	2	9
7/23/69	8/13/69	Boy Named Sue, A	Johnny Cash	6	8
6/22/70	7/20/70	(How Bout A Little Hand For) The Boys In The Band	Boys In The Band	20	7
10/14/71	12/9/71	Brand New Key	Melanie	1	16
6/29/72	8/19/72	Brandy (You're A Fine Girl)	Looking Glass	1	14

Debut	Peak	Title	Artist	Pos	Wks
9/13/75	10/18/75	Brazil	Ritchie Family	13	11
8/27/69	8/27/69	Break My Mind	Pat Boone	29	1
3/3/73	4/7/73	Break Up To Make Up	Stylistics	18	8
1/13/66	1/13/66	Breakin' Up Is Breakin' My Heart	Roy Orbison	pr	1
12/20/75	2/21/76	Breaking Up Is Hard To Do	Neil Sedaka	2	10
1/12/70	2/9/70	Breaking Up Is Hard To Do	Lenny Welch	29	3
5/6/71	6/3/71	Bridge Over Troubled Water	Aretha Franklin	15	7
2/2/70	2/16/70	Bridge Over Troubled Water	Simon & Garfunkel	1	13
1/25/71	2/8/71	Bridget The Midget (The Queen Of The Blues)	Ray Stevens	35	4
5/16/68	5/16/68	Bring A Little Lovin'	Los Bravos	pr	1
11/21/68	11/28/68	Bring It On Home To Me	Eddie Floyd	23	2
6/3/71	7/8/71	Bring The Boys Home	Freda Payne	23	7
5/23/68	6/6/68	Brooklyn Roads	Neil Diamond	18	3
6/23/73	8/18/73	Brother Louie	Stories	1	13
3/26/69	4/16/69	Brother Love's Travelling Salvation Show	Neil Diamond	12	6
8/10/67	10/19/67	Brown Eyed Girl	Van Morrison	3	10
4/22/71	6/3/71	Brown Sugar	Rolling Stones	2	10
1/22/69	2/26/69	Build Me Up Buttercup	Foundations	2	8
1/11/75	2/15/75	Bungle In The Jungle	Jethro Tull	6	9
1/4/71	2/1/71	Burning Bridges	Mike Curb Congregation	9	8
8/26/72	10/14/72	Burning Love	Elvis Presley	2	12
1/25/68	2/8/68	Burning Spear	Soulful Strings	22	4
7/21/66	9/1/66	Bus Stop	Hollies	1	10
5/28/69	6/25/69	But It's Alright	J.J. Jackson	21	5
2/5/69	2/26/69	But You Know I Love You	First Edition	18	4
5/11/67	5/18/67	Buy For Me The Rain	Nitty Gritty Dirt Band	25	2
12/21/67	12/28/67	By The Time I Get To Phoenix	Glen Campbell	18	2
3/14/68	4/4/68	Cab Driver	Mills Brothers	24	5
6/23/66	7/14/66	Cadillac	New Colony Six	xx	4
2/3/66	3/3/66	California Dreamin'	Mamas & the Papas	1	11

Debut	Peak	Title	Artist	Pos	Wks
3/30/67	4/27/67	California Nights	Lesley Gore	8	6
1/15/69	2/5/69	California Soul	5th Dimension	19	4
3/2/70	3/16/70	Call Me	Aretha Franklin	18	5
2/17/66	3/17/66	Call Me	Chris Montez	18	4
3/10/73	4/21/73	Call Me (Come Back Home)	Al Green	16	10
4/18/68	5/2/68	Call Me Lightning	Who	17	3
1/15/69	2/5/69	Can I Change My Mind	Tyrone Davis	16	4
6/30/66	6/30/66	Can I Trust You	Bachelors	pr	1
1/24/76	2/14/76	Can The Can	Suzi Quatro	30	4
2/2/74	3/2/74	Can This Be Real	Natural Four	18	8
8/10/70	9/21/70	Candida	Dawn	1	15
6/15/72	7/15/72	Candy Man, The	Sammy Davis, Jr.	2	9
3/18/71	5/13/71	Can't Find The Time	Rose Colored Glass	15	11
9/14/74	11/2/74	Can't Get Enough	Bad Company	1	14
8/3/74	9/14/74	Can't Get Enough Of Your Love, Babe	Barry White	5	12
2/15/75	3/29/75	Can't Get It Out Of My Head	Electric Light Orchestra	7	12
4/27/67	5/18/67	Can't Seem To Make You Mine	Seeds	15	7
6/1/67	7/27/67	Can't Take My Eyes Off You	Frankie Valli	1	13
1/19/67	1/19/67	Can't You See (That I Really Love Her)	Flock	xx	3
6/20/68	7/18/68	Can't You See Me Cry	New Colony Six	13	6
7/27/74	8/24/74	Captain Howdy	Simon Stokes	20	9
3/2/70	3/23/70	Capture The Moment	Jay & the Americans	26	6
1/4/68	1/4/68	Carmen	Herb Alpert & the Tijuana Brass	pr	1
3/24/66	4/7/66	Caroline, No	Brian Wilson	16	5
6/8/67	8/17/67	Carrie-Anne	Hollies	10	12
8/27/69	9/17/69	Carry Me Back	Rascals	22	7
4/6/67	6/8/67	Casino Royale	Herb Alpert & the Tijuana Brass	17	7
8/24/67	9/14/67	Cat In The Window (The Bird In The Sky), The	Petula Clark	29	4
11/2/74	12/14/74	Cat's In The Cradle	Harry Chapin	1	13
3/16/70	5/4/70	Cecilia	Simon & Garfunkel	1	12

Debut	Peak	Title	Artist	Pos	Wks
2/9/70	3/9/70	Celebrate	Three Dog Night	7	10
11/30/67	1/11/68	Chain Of Fools	Aretha Franklin	4	9
10/10/68	10/17/68	Chained	Marvin Gaye	26	2
9/8/66	10/6/66	Changes	Crispian St. Peters	xx	4
12/14/70	12/14/70	Chant, The	Jane Avenue Bus Stop	xx	2
9/9/71	10/28/71	Charity Ball	Fanny	3	11
3/3/66	3/3/66	Cheater, The	Bob Kuban & the In-Men	xx	2
6/15/70	7/6/70	Check Out Your Mind	Impressions	14	7
3/16/72	4/27/72	Cheer	Potliquor	9	9
8/4/66	9/15/66	Cherish	Association	1	12
11/11/71	12/23/71	Cherish	David Cassidy	3	11
2/8/71	2/22/71	Cherish What Is Dear To You (While It's Near To You)	Freda Payne	30	4
9/15/66	10/27/66	Cherry, Cherry	Neil Diamond	4	8
3/31/73	5/19/73	"Cherry Cherry" from Hot August Night	Neil Diamond	8	12
3/8/75	5/10/75	Chevy Van	Sammy Johns	1	17
10/24/68	11/21/68	Chewy Chewy	Ohio Express	3	8
2/22/71	4/29/71	Chick-A-Boom (Don't Ya Jes' Love It)	Daddy Dewdrop	7	15
10/12/67	11/2/67	Child Of Clay	Jimmie Rodgers	17	5
8/25/73	10/13/73	China Grove	Doobie Brothers	2	13
9/30/71	11/11/71	Chirpy Chirpy Cheep Cheep	Mac & Katie Kissoon	4	10
4/9/69	5/7/69	Chokin' Kind, The	Joe Simon	12	7
6/13/68	6/20/68	Choo Choo Train	Box Tops	26	3
10/3/68	11/28/68	Cinnamon	Derek	7	13
3/24/73	5/5/73	Cisco Kid, The	War	5	10
11/11/72	12/23/72	Clair	Gilbert O'Sullivan	1	13
9/21/74	11/2/74	Clap For The Wolfman	Guess Who	11	12
7/11/68	8/15/68	Classical Gas	Mason Williams	4	8
9/15/73	10/6/73	Cleopatra Jones, Theme From	Joe Simon featuring the Mainstreeters	26	4
6/22/70	7/13/70	(They Long To Be) Close To You	Carpenters	1	15
4/27/67	5/11/67	Close Your Eyes	Peaches & Herb	24	3

Debut	Peak	Title	Artist	Pos	Wks
9/21/70	10/19/70	Closer To Home	Grand Funk Railroad	16	9
11/28/68	1/8/69	Cloud Nine	Temptations	6	10
6/1/67	7/20/67	C'mon Marianne	Four Seasons	10	11
1/12/70	2/9/70	Cold Turkey	Plastic Ono Band	24	6
6/4/69	7/9/69	Color Him Father	Winstons	5	8
12/15/66	1/19/67	Color My World	Petula Clark	xx	3
2/23/70	3/30/70	Come And Get It	Badfinger	4	11
3/30/74	4/27/74	Come And Get Your Love	Redbone	1	12
8/10/67	9/14/67	Come Back When You Grow Up	Bobby Vee	2	9
7/28/66	7/28/66	Come On And See Me	Tammi Terrell	xx	1
6/8/67	7/20/67	Come On Down To My Boat	Every Mothers' Son	1	11
7/7/66	7/7/66	Come On Home	Wayne Fontana	pr	1
5/12/66	6/9/66	Come On Let's Go	McCoys	16	5
4/20/70	4/27/70	Come Running	Van Morrison	29	2
4/27/70	5/25/70	Come Saturday Morning	Sandpipers	15	9
12/28/67	1/25/68	Come See About Me	Jr. Walker & the All Stars	22	3
12/22/66	1/12/67	Coming Home Soldier	Bobby Vinton	19	3
11/24/66	11/24/66	Coming On Strong	Brenda Lee	xx	3
7/30/69	8/27/69	Commotion	Creedence Clearwater Revival	6	5
11/24/66	12/29/66	Communication Breakdown	Roy Orbison	xx	3
4/16/69	5/7/69	Composer, The	Diana Ross & the Supremes	18	4
1/8/69	1/22/69	Condition Red	Goodees	14	3
7/6/72	8/19/72	Conquistador	Procol Harum	3	11
10/28/72	11/11/72	Convention '72	Delegates	5	7
12/6/75	1/17/76	Convoy	C.W. McCall	1	12
4/15/71	6/3/71	Cool Aid	Paul Humphrey & his Cool Aid Chemists	10	11
5/26/66	6/23/66	Cool Jerk	Capitols	7	6
11/11/72	12/16/72	Corner Of The Sky	Jackson 5	8	8
7/13/70	8/24/70	Cottage Cheese	Crow	4	12
2/10/72	3/30/72	Could It Be Forever	David Cassidy	5	10
1/20/73	3/10/73	Could It Be I'm Falling In Love	Spinners	3	13

Debut	Peak	Title	Artist	Pos	Wks
12/6/75	1/17/76	Country Boy (You Got Your Feet In L.A.)	Glen Campbell	13	10
1/25/71	3/1/71	Country Road	James Taylor	11	8
1/27/72	3/2/72	Country Wine	Raiders	13	7
10/31/68	11/14/68	Court Of Love	Unifics	23	3
1/13/73	3/3/73	Cover Of "Rolling Stone", The	Dr. Hook & the Medicine Show	5	13
4/18/68	5/23/68	Cowboys To Girls	Intruders	11	6
2/24/72	4/27/72	Cowboy's Work Is Never Done, A	Sonny & Cher	1	14
8/10/70	9/28/70	Cracklin' Rosie	Neil Diamond	2	15
11/25/72	12/30/72	Crazy Horses	Osmonds	14	9
7/6/70	8/3/70	Crazy Love	Happenings	19	6
2/17/72	3/9/72	Crazy Mama	J.J. Cale	29	5
4/27/67	6/1/67	Creeque Alley	Mamas & the Papas	16	5
2/1/71	3/1/71	Cried Like A Baby	Bobby Sherman	20	9
12/26/68	1/15/69	Crimson And Clover	Tommy James & the Shondells	3	10
12/23/72	2/10/73	Crocodile Rock	Elton John	1	14
2/12/69	3/5/69	Crossroads	Cream	18	5
12/8/66	12/15/66	Cry	Ronnie Dove	18	4
3/21/68	4/25/68	Cry Like A Baby	Box Tops	2	9
10/26/70	11/23/70	Cry Me A River	Joe Cocker	10	9
5/19/66	5/19/66	Crying	Jay & the Americans	pr	1
12/30/65	2/17/66	Crying Time	Ray Charles	xx	2
6/4/69	7/9/69	Crystal Blue Persuasion	Tommy James & the Shondells	2	11
1/12/70	1/12/70	Cupid	Johnny Nash	34	1
11/14/68	11/21/68	Cycles	Frank Sinatra	21	2
6/16/73	7/21/73	Daddy Could Swear, I Declare	Gladys Knight & the Pips	27	7
6/1/72	7/22/72	Daddy Don't You Walk So Fast	Wayne Newton	4	12
4/28/66	4/28/66	Daddy You Gotta Let Him In	Satisfactions	pr	1
1/27/73	3/10/73	Daddy's Home	Jermaine Jackson	14	11
3/9/67	3/9/67	Daddy's Little Girl	Al Martino	28	1

Debut	Peak	Title	Artist	Pos	Wks
8/27/69	9/10/69	Daddy's Little Man	O.C. Smith	23	6
2/22/68	3/28/68	Dance To The Music	Sly & the Family Stone	13	6
8/23/75	10/4/75	Dance With Me	Orleans	2	15
1/13/73	2/24/73	Dancing In The Moonlight	King Harvest	1	12
12/8/66	1/19/67	Dancing In The Street	Mamas & the Papas	5	7
4/6/74	6/8/74	Dancing Machine	Jackson 5	6	15
8/31/67	9/28/67	Dandelion	Rolling Stones	17	5
10/6/66	10/27/66	Dandy	Herman's Hermits	8	8
7/28/66	8/25/66	Dangling Conversation, The	Simon & Garfunkel	xx	3
4/28/73	6/16/73	Daniel	Elton John	4	11
2/24/73	4/21/73	Danny's Song	Anne Murray	2	13
1/19/74	3/2/74	Dark Lady	Cher	2	13
12/7/67	2/8/68	Darlin'	Beach Boys	30	2
2/9/67	3/23/67	Darling Be Home Soon	Lovin' Spoonful	24	5
4/27/70	5/25/70	Daughter Of Darkness	Tom Jones	4	10
5/5/66	5/5/66	David's Mood	Jack Ely & the Courtmen	pr	1
11/25/71	1/27/72	Day After Day	Badfinger	2	13
6/1/72	7/22/72	Day By Day	Godspell	12	10
3/16/72	5/4/72	Day Dreaming	Aretha Franklin	2	11
6/2/66	6/16/66	Day For Decision	Johnny Sea	16	3
5/14/69	6/4/69	Day Is Done	Peter, Paul & Mary	15	5
12/30/65	1/13/66	Day Tripper	Beatles	1	9
2/24/66	3/31/66	Daydream	Lovin' Spoonful	5	8
11/2/67	12/7/67	Daydream Believer	Monkees	1	11
6/1/67	6/1/67	Daylight Savin' Time	Keith	pr	1
4/20/67	5/18/67	Dead End Street	Lou Rawls	19	5
3/3/73	4/14/73	Dead Skunk	Loudon Wainwright III	8	12
11/16/67	11/16/67	Dear Eloise	Hollies	pr	1
12/27/75	2/21/76	December, 1963 (Oh, What A Night)	Four Seasons	3	9
2/16/67	3/30/67	Dedicated To The One I Love	Mamas & the Papas	5	8
2/3/66	2/24/66	Dedication Song, The	Freddy Cannon	xx	3
2/21/76	2/21/76	Deep Purple	Donny & Marie Osmond	34	1
3/21/68	5/16/68	Delilah	Tom Jones	21	6
7/14/73	9/8/73	Delta Dawn	Helen Reddy	1	14

Debut	Peak	Title	Artist	Pos	Wks
3/2/67	3/30/67	Detroit City	Tom Jones	27	4
10/6/66	12/15/66	Devil With A Blue Dress On & Good Golly Miss Molly	Mitch Ryder & the Detroit Wheels	5	11
11/4/72	12/23/72	Dialogue (Parts I & II)	Chicago	8	11
7/21/73	8/25/73	Diamond Girl	Seals & Crofts	2	10
5/11/72	6/29/72	Diary	Bread	5	9
5/5/66	6/2/66	Did You Ever Have To Make Up Your Mind	Lovin' Spoonful	5	7
8/6/69	9/3/69	Did You See Her Eyes	Illusion	11	6
6/30/66	6/30/66	Diddy Wah Diddy	Captain Beefheart & his Magic Band	pr	1
2/9/70	3/2/70	Didn't I (Blow Your Mind This Time)	Delfonics	4	10
10/19/67	2/8/68	Different Drum	Stone Poneys featuring Linda Ronstadt	4	8
6/1/67	6/15/67	Ding Dong! The Witch Is Dead	Fifth Estate	16	5
5/5/66	6/30/66	Dirty Water	Standells	3	11
7/5/75	8/2/75	Disco Queen	Hot Chocolate	16	10
8/4/66	8/4/66	Distant Shores	Chad & Jeremy	xx	3
2/12/69	3/12/69	Dizzy	Tommy Roe	1	10
10/28/71	12/30/71	Do I Love You	Paul Anka	8	10
1/4/71	1/18/71	Do It	Neil Diamond	25	4
11/16/74	12/28/74	Do It ('Til You're Satisfied)	B.T. Express	5	12
8/8/68	9/12/68	Do It Again	Beach Boys	1	9
12/23/72	2/17/73	Do It Again	Steely Dan	8	14
6/15/67	7/13/67	Do It Again A Little Bit Slower	Jon & Robin & the In Crowd	8	6
9/21/74	10/12/74	Do It Baby	Miracles	21	6
4/1/71	4/15/71	Do Me Right	Detroit Emeralds	32	3
3/16/70	3/23/70	Do The Funky Chicken	Rufus Thomas	27	2
8/3/70	9/28/70	Do What You Wanna Do	Five Flights Up	9	14
5/2/68	5/23/68	Do You Know The Way To San José	Dionne Warwick	13	6
9/2/71	10/14/71	Do You Know What I Mean	Lee Michaels	2	10
6/17/71	7/8/71	Do You Know What Time It Is	P-Nut Gallery	10	6

Debut	Peak	Title	Artist	Pos	Wks
3/5/69	4/2/69	Do Your Thing	Watts 103rd Street Rhythm Band	6	6
2/15/68	3/7/68	(Sittin' On) The Dock Of The Bay	Otis Redding	3	8
3/2/72	5/11/72	Doctor My Eyes	Jackson Browne	1	15
12/28/74	2/15/75	Doctor's Orders	Carol Douglas	8	12
11/2/70	12/21/70	Does Anybody Really Know What Time It Is	Chicago	5	12
5/2/68	5/23/68	Does Your Mama Know About Me	Bobby Taylor & the Vancouvers	22	4
1/25/71	3/11/71	Doesn't Somebody Want To Be Wanted	Partridge Family	1	12
6/25/69	7/16/69	Doggone Right	Smokey Robinson & the Miracles	22	4
11/16/70	12/14/70	Domino	Van Morrison	13	8
5/20/71	6/24/71	Done Too Soon	Neil Diamond	21	7
5/19/66	6/2/66	Don't Bring Me Down	Animals	11	6
2/22/75	4/19/75	Don't Call Us, We'll Call You	Jerry Corbetta & Sugarloaf	4	14
1/27/73	2/17/73	Don't Cross The River	America	26	6
1/12/70	1/12/70	Don't Cry Daddy	Elvis Presley	7	4
2/2/67	2/2/67	Don't Do It	Micky Dolenz	pr	1
9/30/72	11/4/72	Don't Ever Be Lonely (A Poor Little Fool Like Me)	Cornelius Brothers & Sister Rose	25	8
1/13/73	2/17/73	Don't Expect Me To Be Your Friend	Lobo	2	11
3/26/69	4/23/69	Don't Give In To Him	Gary Puckett & the Union Gap	5	7
6/15/67	7/6/67	Don't Go Out Into The Rain (You're Going To Melt)	Herman's Hermits	24	7
9/10/69	10/8/69	Don't It Make You Want To Go Home	Joe South & the Believers	18	5
5/20/71	7/1/71	Don't Knock My Love	Wilson Pickett	3	11
12/9/72	2/17/73	Don't Let Me Be Lonely Tonight	James Taylor	5	14
4/30/69	5/21/69	Don't Let Me Down	Beatles with Billy Preston	1	6
2/8/71	3/11/71	Don't Let The Green Grass Fool You	Wilson Pickett	24	6

Debut	Peak	Title	Artist	Pos	Wks
8/24/67	8/24/67	Don't Let The Rain Fall Down On Me	Critters	26	2
6/22/74	8/17/74	Don't Let The Sun Go Down On Me	Elton John	1	16
6/10/71	7/22/71	Don't Pull Your Love	Hamilton, Joe Frank & Reynolds	1	13
2/24/66	3/17/66	Don't Push Me	Hedgehoppers Anonymous	xx	3
12/23/71	2/10/72	Don't Say You Don't Remember	Beverly Bremers	4	11
5/25/67	7/13/67	Don't Sleep In The Subway	Petula Clark	14	7
6/27/68	8/1/68	Don't Take It So Hard	Paul Revere & the Raiders featuring Mark Lindsay	12	6
3/29/75	5/10/75	Don't Tell Me Goodnight	Lobo	23	10
12/16/65	12/23/65	Don't Think Twice	Wonder Who	11	5
10/12/70	11/16/70	Don't Try To Lay No Boogie Woogie On The "King Of Rock & Roll"	Crow	13	8
10/14/71	11/25/71	Don't Wanna Live Inside Myself	Bee Gees	17	8
3/16/67	5/18/67	Don't You Care	Buckinghams	2	11
3/24/66	5/5/66	Don't You Know	Keith Everett	10	8
4/27/74	6/15/74	Don't You Worry 'Bout A Thing	Stevie Wonder	11	12
1/12/74	2/23/74	Doo Doo Doo Doo Doo (Heartbreaker)	Rolling Stones	16	11
2/1/68	2/1/68	Dottie I Like It	Tommy Roe	pr	1
5/20/71	6/24/71	Double Lovin'	Osmonds	4	9
8/15/68	9/12/68	Down At Lulu's	Ohio Express	5	8
1/13/72	3/9/72	Down By The Lazy River	Osmonds	1	14
9/5/68	9/26/68	Down On Me	Big Brother & the Holding Company	20	4
1/12/70	1/12/70	Down On The Corner	Creedence Clearwater Revival	22	2
6/3/71	7/22/71	Draggin' The Line	Tommy James	2	13
7/25/68	8/29/68	Dream A Little Dream Of Me	Mama Cass with the Mamas & the Papas	11	6
4/8/71	4/29/71	Dream Baby (How Long Must I Dream)	Glen Campbell	31	4
2/7/76	2/21/76	Dream On	Aerosmith	20	3

Debut	Peak	Title	Artist	Pos	Wks
1/31/76	2/21/76	Dream Weaver	Gary Wright	15	4
7/11/68	7/25/68	Dreams Of The Everyday Housewife	Glen Campbell	23	3
3/24/73	6/9/73	Drift Away	Dobie Gray	6	15
4/14/73	4/28/73	Drinking Wine Spo-Dee O'Dee	Jerry Lee Lewis	28	5
1/13/72	2/3/72	Drowning In The Sea Of Love	Joe Simon	27	4
5/27/71	7/8/71	Drum, The	Bobby Sherman	7	10
2/3/73	3/10/73	Dueling Banjos	Eric Weissberg & Steve Mandell	2	12
11/17/66	11/17/66	Dusty	Floyd & Jerry	pr	1
7/4/68	7/4/68	D.W. Washburn	Monkees	23	1
10/13/73	12/15/73	D'yer Mak'er	Led Zeppelin	4	14
7/5/75	8/23/75	Dynomite—Part I	Tony Camillo's Bazuka	4	12
8/31/74	9/28/74	Earache My Eye Featuring Alice Bowie	Cheech & Chong	6	12
1/12/70	1/12/70	Early In The Morning	Vanity Fare	25	2
12/8/66	12/29/66	East West	Herman's Hermits	11	6
2/2/70	3/30/70	Easy Come, Easy Go	Bobby Sherman	8	12
10/14/71	11/18/71	Easy Loving	Freddie Hart	13	8
5/4/70	5/25/70	Easy To Be Free	Happy Day	24	5
8/13/69	9/17/69	Easy To Be Hard	Three Dog Night	4	9
12/30/65	12/30/65	Ebb Tide	Righteous Brothers	19	2
4/14/66	5/19/66	Eight Miles High	Byrds	8	7
2/15/71	4/15/71	Eighteen	Alice Cooper	4	13
9/13/75	11/8/75	Eighteen With A Bullet	Pete Wingfield	3	15
10/19/70	10/19/70	El Condor Pasa	Simon & Garfunkel	35	4
8/11/66	9/8/66	Eleanor Rigby	Beatles	3	10
10/14/72	11/11/72	Elected	Alice Cooper	22	8
10/3/68	11/7/68	Elenore	Turtles	4	8
2/17/66	3/24/66	Elusive Butterfly	Bob Lind	7	7
1/25/75	4/5/75	Emma	Hot Chocolate	9	15
2/22/68	3/7/68	End Of Our Road, The	Gladys Knight & the Pips	23	4
2/16/74	3/9/74	Energy Crisis '74	Dickie Goodman	12	7
12/16/65	12/23/65	England Swings	Roger Miller	19	2
3/30/74	6/1/74	Entertainer, The	Marvin Hamlisch	2	16

Debut	Peak	Title	Artist	Pos	Wks
2/23/67	3/9/67	Epistle To Dippy	Donovan	24	3
2/23/74	4/20/74	Eres Tu (Touch The Wind)	Mocedades	4	14
3/23/72	4/27/72	Eve	Jim Capaldi	17	8
10/5/74	11/30/74	Everlasting Love	Carl Carlton	10	13
10/26/67	11/30/67	Everlasting Love	Robert Knight	5	7
9/8/66	10/6/66	Every Day And Every Night	Trolls	12	6
2/17/72	3/23/72	Every Day Of My Life	Bobby Vinton	13	7
11/2/70	11/30/70	Everybody I Love You	Happy Day	30	5
1/4/68	1/4/68	Everybody Knows	Dave Clark Five	28	3
7/30/69	8/6/69	Everybody Knows Matilda	Duke Baxter	27	3
9/9/72	10/28/72	Everybody Plays The Fool	Main Ingredient	1	12
4/6/70	5/4/70	Everybody's Out Of Town	B.J. Thomas	29	6
9/10/69	10/8/69	Everybody's Talkin'	Nilsson	8	5
1/8/69	1/29/69	Everyday People	Sly & the Family Stone	1	10
5/28/69	6/25/69	Everyday With You Girl	Classics IV featuring Dennis Yost	13	5
1/20/72	3/16/72	Everything I Own	Bread	2	12
5/11/70	5/25/70	Everything Is Beautiful	Ray Stevens	11	7
1/25/68	2/29/68	Everything That Touches You	Association	11	8
2/16/70	3/16/70	Evil Ways	Santana	6	9
12/20/75	2/14/76	Evil Woman	Electric Light Orchestra	4	10
1/12/70	1/12/70	Evil Woman Don't Play Your Games With Me	Crow	17	3
3/31/66	6/2/66	Evol-Not Love	Five Americans	7	8
12/28/67	1/11/68	Explosion In Your Soul	Soul Survivors	25	4
3/8/75	4/19/75	Express	B.T. Express	9	11
10/5/67	11/30/67	Expressway To Your Heart	Soul Survivors	7	9
8/22/68	9/12/68	Eyes Of A New York Woman, The	B.J. Thomas	7	6
6/6/68	7/11/68	Face It Girl, It's Over	Nancy Wilson	16	7
11/2/67	11/23/67	Face The Autumn	Family	13	5
11/16/74	12/28/74	Fairytale	Pointer Sisters	13	11
7/20/67	8/24/67	Fakin' It	Simon & Garfunkel	20	3
7/19/75	9/13/75	Fallin' In Love	Hamilton, Joe Frank & Reynolds	1	18
9/6/75	10/18/75	Fame	David Bowie	1	15

Debut	Peak	Title	Artist	Pos	Wks
11/11/71	12/16/71	Family Affair	Sly & the Family Stone	3	10
3/30/72	5/11/72	Family Of Man, The	Three Dog Night	14	9
12/27/75	2/21/76	Fanny (Be Tender With My Love)	Bee Gees	7	9
8/9/75	9/27/75	Feel Like Makin' Love	Bad Company	4	16
7/27/74	8/31/74	Feel Like Makin' Love	Roberta Flack	1	12
7/7/73	9/1/73	Feelin' Stronger Every Day	Chicago	2	12
11/22/75	12/20/75	Feelings	Morris Albert	1	13
11/23/67	11/30/67	Felicidad	Sally Field	22	2
12/14/70	12/14/70	Feliz Navidad	José Feliciano	xx	2
3/16/67	4/13/67	59th Street Bridge Song (Feelin' Groovy), The	Harpers Bizarre	16	7
1/17/76	2/14/76	50 Ways To Leave Your Lover	Paul Simon	1	6
8/16/75	9/13/75	Fight The Power Part 1	Isley Brothers	5	11
6/15/74	7/20/74	Finally Got Myself Together (I'm A Changed Man)	Impressions	25	9
9/12/68	9/26/68	Fire	Crazy World Of Arthur Brown	1	8
10/10/68	11/7/68	Fire	Five By Five	5	7
1/25/75	3/15/75	Fire	Ohio Players	1	12
3/30/70	4/20/70	Fire & Rain	R.B. Greaves	29	4
10/5/70	11/2/70	Fire And Rain	James Taylor	3	10
11/2/74	12/7/74	Fire, Baby I'm On Fire	Andy Kim	17	9
3/2/72	4/13/72	First Time Ever I Saw Your Face, The	Roberta Flack	1	12
2/26/69	3/5/69	First Train To California	Cryan' Shames	26	2
12/9/71	1/27/72	Five Hundred Miles	Heaven Bound with Tony Scotti	5	10
12/16/65	12/30/65	Five O'Clock World	Vogues	1	8
11/16/70	12/7/70	5-10-15-20 (25-30 Years Of Love)	Presidents	22	5
8/25/66	9/22/66	Flamingo	Herb Alpert & the Tijuana Brass	xx	4
1/27/72	3/23/72	Floy Joy	Supremes	2	11
1/17/76	1/24/76	Fly Away	John Denver	20	5
11/1/75	12/6/75	Fly, Robin, Fly	Silver Convention	4	16
3/28/68	3/28/68	Foggy Mountain Breakdown	Lester Flatt & Earl Scruggs	pr	1

Debut	Peak	Title	Artist	Pos	Wks
5/26/73	6/30/73	Fool	Elvis Presley	23	7
11/10/66	11/10/66	Fool Am I, A	Cilla Black	pr	1
10/10/68	11/7/68	Fool For You	Impressions	16	5
11/11/71	12/9/71	Fool Me	Joe South	27	6
8/22/68	9/19/68	Fool On The Hill, The	Sergio Mendes & Brasil '66	8	8
2/1/71	4/8/71	For All We Know	Carpenters	3	13
11/14/68	12/19/68	For Once In My Life	Stevie Wonder	2	7
12/7/70	1/4/71	For The Good Times	Ray Price	20	7
3/23/70	4/27/70	For The Love Of Him	Bobbi Martin	5	10
5/18/74	6/22/74	For The Love Of Money	O'Jays	6	11
2/16/67	3/23/67	For What It's Worth (Stop, Hey What's That Sound)	Buffalo Springfield	3	10
5/18/70	6/22/70	For You Blue	Beatles	9	10
3/14/68	4/18/68	Forever Came Today	Diana Ross & the Supremes	19	6
11/15/75	12/27/75	Fox On The Run	Sweet	1	15
11/30/67	11/30/67	Foxey Lady	Jimi Hendrix Experience	pr	1
3/31/73	5/19/73	Frankenstein	Edgar Winter Group	1	13
3/17/66	4/21/66	Frankie And Johnny	Elvis Presley	xx	2
10/7/72	11/11/72	Freddie's Dead (Theme From "Superfly")	Curtis Mayfield	3	10
2/15/71	3/18/71	Free	Chicago	15	8
9/1/73	10/27/73	Free Ride	Edgar Winter Group	3	15
7/21/66	7/21/66	Friday's Child	Nancy Sinatra	xx	1
4/11/68	4/11/68	Friends	Beach Boys	pr	1
5/4/70	6/8/70	Friends	Feather	29	6
10/21/72	11/25/72	From The Beginning	Emerson, Lake & Palmer	14	8
8/17/67	9/21/67	Funky Broadway	Wilson Pickett	6	10
6/17/71	7/22/71	Funky Nassau-Part 1	Beginning Of The End	4	11
2/29/68	2/29/68	Funky North Philly	Bill Cosby	pr	1
4/4/68	5/9/68	Funky Street	Arthur Conley	10	8
4/21/73	5/26/73	Funky Worm	Ohio Players	14	8
12/2/72	1/27/73	Funny Face	Donna Fargo	14	12
5/11/67	5/11/67	Funny Familiar Forgotten Feelings	Tom Jones	pr	1
12/29/66	12/29/66	Gallant Men	Senator Everett McKinley Dirksen	xx	3
3/19/69	4/16/69	Galveston	Glen Campbell	4	6

Debut	Peak	Title	Artist	Pos	Wks
12/21/70	1/25/71	Games	Redeye	3	9
1/29/69	2/26/69	Games People Play	Joe South	10	6
9/23/72	11/11/72	Garden Party	Rick Nelson & the Stone Canyon Band	2	13
10/17/68	10/24/68	Gentle On My Mind	Glen Campbell	28	2
2/10/66	2/10/66	Georgia On My Mind	Righteous Brothers	pr	1
2/10/66	2/24/66	Georgianna	Princetons	10	4
1/5/67	2/2/67	Georgy Girl	Seekers	1	10
9/29/66	9/29/66	Get Away	Georgie Fame & the Blue Flames	xx	2
4/30/69	5/21/69	Get Back	Beatles with Billy Preston	1	9
12/21/74	2/8/75	Get Dancin'	Disco Tex & the Sex-O-Lettes	15	12
6/16/73	8/11/73	Get Down	Gilbert O'Sullivan	1	13
8/16/75	9/20/75	Get Down Tonight	KC & the Sunshine Band	1	16
3/2/67	3/2/67	Get Me To The World On Time	Electric Prunes	pr	1
9/14/67	10/19/67	Get On Up	Esquires	21	6
1/18/68	2/22/68	Get Out Now	Tommy James & the Shondells	22	4
4/6/70	5/18/70	Get Ready	Rare Earth	2	16
3/24/66	3/24/66	Get Ready	Temptations	xx	1
8/6/69	9/3/69	Get Together	Youngbloods	6	9
8/17/67	9/14/67	Gettin' Together	Tommy James & the Shondells	12	6
5/25/70	6/22/70	Gimme Dat Ding	Pipkins	15	9
3/26/69	5/7/69	Gimme Gimme Good Lovin'	Crazy Elephant	3	9
9/7/67	10/12/67	Gimme Little Sign	Brenton Wood	5	7
1/19/67	2/16/67	Gimme Some Lovin'	Spencer Davis Group	6	6
5/25/67	6/1/67	Girl	Pride & Joy	26	2
4/28/66	6/16/66	Girl In Love	Outsiders	12	7
7/6/67	8/24/67	Girl Like You, A	Young Rascals	15	6
9/1/66	10/20/66	Girl On A Swing	Gerry & the Pacemakers	11	7
11/24/66	11/24/66	Girl That Stood Beside Me, The	Bobby Darin	pr	1
9/26/68	10/17/68	Girl Watcher	O'Kaysions	5	6
3/30/67	5/11/67	Girl, You'll Be A Woman Soon	Neil Diamond	8	7

Debut	Peak	Title	Artist	Pos	Wks
5/4/67	6/1/67	Girls In Love	Gary Lewis & the Playboys	28	3
4/9/69	4/30/69	Gitarzan	Ray Stevens	1	8
4/14/73	6/16/73	Give It To Me	J. Geils Band	7	13
10/5/74	10/26/74	Give It To The People	Righteous Brothers	23	7
2/19/69	2/26/69	Give It Up Or Turnit A Loose	James Brown	21	2
1/26/70	2/23/70	Give Me Just A Little More Time	Chairmen Of The Board	3	11
5/19/73	6/30/73	Give Me Love—(Give Me Peace On Earth)	George Harrison	1	13
6/22/67	6/22/67	Give Me Time	Dusty Springfield	pr	1
7/30/69	8/13/69	Give Peace A Chance	Plastic Ono Band	16	3
6/16/73	7/28/73	Give Your Baby A Standing Ovation	Dells	14	10
10/19/67	11/23/67	Glad To Be Unhappy	Mamas & the Papas	16	6
2/17/66	3/31/66	Gloria	Shadows Of Knight	1	11
2/10/72	3/30/72	Glory Bound	Grass Roots	7	11
2/8/71	2/15/71	Glory Of Love, The	Dells	32	2
8/12/72	10/7/72	Go All The Way	Raspberries	2	13
9/22/66	10/27/66	Go Away Little Girl	Happenings	16	4
8/5/71	9/23/71	Go Away Little Girl	Donny Osmond	1	12
8/17/70	9/14/70	Go Back	Crabby Appleton	12	9
12/29/66	3/16/67	Go Where You Wanna Go	5th Dimension	17	5
9/21/70	10/19/70	God, Love And Rock & Roll	Teegarden & Van Winkle	18	8
7/21/66	8/25/66	God Only Knows	Beach Boys	4	8
7/28/66	7/28/66	Goin' Back	Dusty Springfield	pr	1
2/3/72	3/16/72	Goin' Down (On The Road To L.A.)	Terry Black & Laurel Ward	20	9
12/14/70	12/14/70	Goin' Home (Sing A Song Of Christmas Cheer)	Bobby Sherman	xx	2
12/21/67	2/1/68	Goin' Out Of My Head/ Can't Take My Eyes Off You	Lettermen	6	10
1/12/70	1/12/70	Going In Circles	Friends Of Distinction	14	3
11/24/66	11/24/66	Going Nowhere	Los Bravos	pr	1
12/30/65	12/30/65	Going To A Go-Go	Miracles	pr	1
12/19/68	1/29/69	Going Up The Country	Canned Heat	7	6
12/14/67	12/14/67	Good Combination	Sonny & Cher	pr	1

Debut	Peak	Title	Artist	Pos	Wks
10/12/70	11/9/70	Good Day	Bobby Trend	19	6
3/24/66	5/5/66	Good Lovin'	Young Rascals	3	11
2/26/69	2/26/69	Good Lovin' Ain't Easy To Come By	Marvin Gaye & Tammi Terrell	29	1
5/18/70	6/15/70	Good Morning Freedom	Daybreak	25	5
5/28/69	6/18/69	Good Morning Starshine	Oliver	3	10
7/2/69	7/23/69	Good Old Rock 'N Roll	Cat Mother & the All Night News Boys	20	4
3/21/68	4/25/68	Good, The Bad And The Ugly, The	Hugo Montenegro	3	10
12/1/66	1/12/67	Good Thing	Paul Revere & the Raiders featuring Mark Lindsay	3	9
9/9/72	11/11/72	Good Time Charlie's Got The Blues	Danny O'Keefe	6	13
10/27/66	11/17/66	Good Vibrations	Beach Boys	1	10
5/14/69	6/4/69	Goodbye	Mary Hopkin	22	4
7/15/72	9/9/72	Goodbye To Love	Carpenters	2	13
10/27/73	12/15/73	Goodbye Yellow Brick Road	Elton John	3	14
1/8/69	1/22/69	Goodnight My Love	Paul Anka	17	3
11/7/68	12/12/68	Goody Goody Gumdrops	1910 Fruitgum Co.	11	6
3/31/66	4/28/66	Got My Mojo Working (Part 1)	Jimmy Smith	xx	2
10/28/71	12/9/71	Got To Be There	Michael Jackson	4	10
2/9/70	3/2/70	Gotta Get Back To You	Tommy James & the Shondells	27	5
2/23/70	3/16/70	Gotta Hold On To This Feeling	Jr. Walker & the All Stars	23	6
5/7/69	6/4/69	Grazing In The Grass	Friends Of Distinction	1	7
6/20/68	7/11/68	Grazing In The Grass	Hugh Masekela	6	8
10/6/66	10/27/66	Great Airplane Strike, The	Paul Revere & the Raiders featuring Mark Lindsay	12	6
5/26/66	5/26/66	Greatest Moments In A Girl's Life	Tokens	pr	1
9/14/70	10/12/70	Green-Eyed Lady	Sugarloaf	5	12
5/12/66	6/9/66	Green Grass	Gary Lewis & the Playboys	8	6
1/26/67	2/16/67	Green, Green Grass Of Home	Tom Jones	12	5
1/25/68	3/21/68	Green Light	American Breed	18	5

Debut	Peak	Title	Artist	Pos	Wks
7/30/69	8/27/69	Green River	Creedence Clearwater Revival	6	10
12/14/67	1/25/68	Green Tambourine	Lemon Pipers	2	10
9/26/68	10/10/68	Greenburg, Glickstein, Charles, David Smith & Jones	Cryan' Shames	9	6
12/15/66	1/5/67	Grizzly Bear	Youngbloods	17	5
1/11/71	2/8/71	Groove Me	King Floyd	26	6
9/21/67	9/21/67	Groovin'	Booker T. & the MG's	26	2
5/11/67	6/22/67	Groovin'	Young Rascals	3	10
4/7/66	5/19/66	Groovy Kind Of Love, A	Mindbenders	3	11
8/10/70	9/14/70	Groovy Situation	Gene Chandler	2	10
4/13/70	4/13/70	Grover Henson Feels Forgotten	Bill Cosby	43	1
8/25/66	9/29/66	Guantanamera	Sandpipers	8	8
7/29/72	9/16/72	Guitar Man, The	Bread	10	11
7/21/73	9/15/73	Gypsy Man	War	13	11
9/28/70	11/9/70	Gypsy Woman	Brian Hyland	2	15
9/23/71	10/28/71	Gypsys, Tramps & Thieves	Cher	1	11
7/27/67	8/31/67	Ha Ha Said The Clown	Yardbirds	28	2
3/19/69	4/2/69	Hair	Cowsills	1	10
9/22/66	11/24/66	Hair On My Chinny Chin Chin, The	Sam the Sham & the Pharaohs	18	4
8/18/73	10/13/73	Half-Breed	Cher	1	15
8/8/68	8/22/68	Halfway To Paradise	Bobby Vinton	20	3
11/4/71	12/9/71	Hallelujah	Sweathog	21	7
7/6/70	8/17/70	Hand Me Down World	Guess Who	30	6
11/28/68	1/15/69	Hang 'Em High	Booker T. & the MG's	6	10
6/29/74	8/10/74	Hang On In There Baby	Johnny Bristol	13	11
1/11/71	2/15/71	Hang On To Your Life	Guess Who	4	8
2/8/68	2/8/68	Hang Up City	Berkeley Kites	pr	1
6/2/66	6/23/66	Hanky Panky	Tommy James & the Shondells	1	10
7/6/67	8/3/67	Happening, The	Herb Alpert & the Tijuana Brass	30	2
3/30/67	4/27/67	Happening, The	Supremes	9	8
12/15/66	12/15/66	Happenings Ten Years Time Ago	Yardbirds	xx	1

Debut	Peak	Title	Artist	Pos	Wks
6/22/72	8/5/72	Happiest Girl In The Whole U.S.A., The	Donna Fargo	16	9
7/15/72	8/19/72	Happy	Rolling Stones	7	9
4/25/68	5/23/68	Happy Song (Dum-Dum), The	Otis Redding	28	3
7/7/66	7/7/66	Happy Summer Days	Ronnie Dove	xx	1
1/26/67	3/16/67	Happy Together	Turtles	1	14
12/23/71	12/30/71	Happy Xmas (War Is Over)	John Lennon & Yoko Ono & the Plastic Ono Band	32	2
1/13/66	1/13/66	Hard Day's Night, A	Ramsey Lewis Trio	pr	1
10/5/67	10/5/67	Hard To Get Thing Called Love	Lou Rawls	pr	1
12/23/65	1/6/66	Harlem Nocturne	Viscounts	16	3
8/29/68	9/19/68	Harper Valley P.T.A.	Jeannie C. Riley	1	6
3/1/75	4/12/75	Harry Truman	Chicago	14	10
1/18/71	3/1/71	Have You Ever Seen The Rain	Creedence Clearwater Revival	4	11
2/1/75	3/29/75	Have You Never Been Mellow	Olivia Newton-John	1	16
11/4/71	12/16/71	Have You Seen Her	Chi-Lites	2	11
10/13/66	10/27/66	Have You Seen Your Mother, Baby, Standing In The Shadow	Rolling Stones	10	4
8/3/74	9/7/74	(You're) Having My Baby	Paul Anka with Odia Coates	1	14
4/9/69	5/7/69	Hawaii Five-O	Ventures	10	6
10/27/66	12/8/66	Hazy Shade Of Winter	Simon & Garfunkel	15	5
12/7/70	12/21/70	He Ain't Heavy … He's My Brother	Neil Diamond	26	3
1/19/70	2/23/70	He Ain't Heavy, He's My Brother	Hollies	6	11
3/15/75	5/17/75	He Don't Love You (Like I Love You)	Tony Orlando & Dawn	2	15
1/27/72	3/23/72	Heart Of Gold	Neil Young	1	14
9/8/73	11/10/73	Heartbeat—It's A Lovebeat	DeFranco Family featuring Tony DeFranco	1	16
10/4/75	11/15/75	Heat Wave	Linda Ronstadt	9	13
2/19/69	2/26/69	Heaven	Rascals	26	2
10/19/70	11/30/70	Heaven Help Us All	Stevie Wonder	7	10
1/12/70	1/12/70	Heaven Knows	Grass Roots	27	1

Debut	Peak	Title	Artist	Pos	Wks
1/18/71	3/11/71	Heavy Makes You Happy (Sha-Na-Boom Boom)	Staple Singers	6	12
8/26/71	9/30/71	He'd Rather Have The Rain	Heaven Bound with Tony Scotti	16	8
6/15/70	7/13/70	Heighty-Hi	Happy Day	24	5
11/17/73	12/29/73	Helen Wheels	Paul McCartney & Wings	14	12
11/23/67	12/21/67	Hello Goodbye	Beatles	1	9
2/2/67	2/9/67	Hello Hello	Sopwith Camel	19	3
7/11/68	8/8/68	Hello, I Love You	Doors	1	8
2/5/69	2/12/69	Hello It's Me	Nazz	24	2
2/23/70	3/2/70	Hello It's Me	Nazz	39	2
10/20/73	12/8/73	Hello It's Me	Todd Rundgren	1	14
5/11/74	6/15/74	Help Me	Joni Mitchell	4	13
12/15/66	12/15/66	Help Me Girl	Eric Burdon & the Animals	xx	2
10/20/66	12/1/66	Help Me Girl	Outsiders	16	5
4/6/67	5/18/67	Here Comes My Baby	Tremeloes	4	8
5/6/71	7/8/71	Here Comes That Rainy Day Feeling Again	Fortunes	4	13
6/13/68	7/11/68	Here Comes The Judge	Shorty Long	11	5
5/6/71	7/1/71	Here Comes The Sun	Richie Havens	7	12
8/4/73	8/25/73	Here I Am (Come And Take Me)	Al Green	25	6
7/4/68	7/4/68	Here I Am Baby	Marvelettes	28	1
6/22/67	7/6/67	Here We Go Again	Ray Charles	21	4
7/27/67	8/31/67	Heroes And Villians	Beach Boys	14	6
9/7/67	10/19/67	Hey Baby (They're Playing Our Song)	Buckinghams	6	8
12/9/71	12/30/71	Hey Big Brother	Rare Earth	27	4
11/18/71	12/30/71	Hey Girl	Donny Osmond	2	12
6/9/66	6/23/66	Hey Joe	Leaves	9	4
9/5/68	9/26/68	Hey Jude	Beatles	2	11
1/8/69	1/15/69	Hey Jude	Wilson Pickett	23	2
3/30/70	4/20/70	Hey Lawdy Mama	Steppenwolf	14	7
1/26/67	1/26/67	Hey Leroy, Your Mama's Callin' You	Jimmy Castor	xx	1
5/11/70	6/15/70	Hey, Mister Sun	Bobby Sherman	15	8
1/12/70	2/9/70	Hey There Lonely Girl	Eddie Holman	2	10

Debut	Peak	Title	Artist	Pos	Wks
1/18/71	2/1/71	Hey Tonight	Creedence Clearwater Revival	19	3
10/10/68	11/7/68	Hey, Western Union Man	Jerry Butler	14	5
5/17/75	6/28/75	Hey You	Bachman-Turner Overdrive	7	15
7/20/70	8/17/70	Hi-De-Ho	Blood, Sweat & Tears	22	11
10/17/68	10/31/68	Hi-Heel Sneakers	José Feliciano	17	4
11/3/66	11/3/66	Hi Hi Hazel	Gary & the Hornets	pr	1
1/20/73	2/3/73	Hi, Hi, Hi	Wings	30	5
6/9/66	6/9/66	High On Love	Knickerbockers	pr	1
6/17/71	7/22/71	High Time We Went	Joe Cocker	10	9
9/14/67	10/19/67	(Your Love Keeps Lifting Me) Higher And Higher	Jackie Wilson	16	6
8/18/73	10/13/73	Higher Ground	Stevie Wonder	8	13
4/26/75	5/24/75	Hijack	Herbie Mann	27	8
4/20/67	5/25/67	Him Or Me—What's It Gonna Be	Paul Revere & the Raiders	4	8
9/12/68	9/19/68	Hip City—Pt. 2	Jr. Walker & the All Stars	25	2
4/14/66	4/28/66	History Repeats Itself	Buddy Starcher	19	3
4/13/70	5/18/70	Hitchin' A Ride	Vanity Fare	1	16
4/7/73	5/26/73	Hocus Pocus	Focus	1	13
6/22/72	8/19/72	Hold Her Tight	Osmonds	8	12
10/24/68	11/14/68	Hold Me Tight	Johnny Nash	8	6
6/22/67	7/20/67	Hold On	Mauds	11	6
5/26/66	5/26/66	Hold On! I'm A Comin'	Sam & Dave	xx	2
7/22/72	9/16/72	Hold Your Head Up	Argent	2	13
1/12/70	1/12/70	Holly Holy	Neil Diamond	39	1
6/8/74	7/6/74	Hollywood Swinging	Kool & the Gang	15	10
1/27/66	3/3/66	Homeward Bound	Simon & Garfunkel	9	8
3/14/68	4/18/68	Honey	Bobby Goldsboro	1	10
12/21/67	1/11/68	Honey Chile	Martha & the Vandellas	24	3
2/2/70	2/9/70	Honey Come Back	Glen Campbell	25	2
9/2/72	10/7/72	Honky Cat	Elton John	18	8
7/16/69	7/30/69	Honky Tonk Women	Rolling Stones	1	11
2/16/74	4/13/74	Hooked On A Feeling	Blue Swede	1	16
12/12/68	1/29/69	Hooked On A Feeling	B.J. Thomas	6	10

Debut	Peak	Title	Artist	Pos	Wks
9/1/66	11/10/66	Hooray For Hazel	Tommy Roe	3	10
6/13/68	7/11/68	Horse, The	Cliff Nobles & Co.	8	7
2/17/72	4/6/72	Horse With No Name, A	America	1	13
10/8/69	10/8/69	Hot Fun In The Summertime	Sly & the Family Stone	22	1
4/22/71	5/27/71	Hot Love	T. Rex	15	8
3/16/72	4/27/72	Hot Rod Lincoln	Commander Cody & his Lost Planet Airmen	2	10
2/26/69	3/26/69	Hot Smoke & Sasafrass	Bubble Puppy	8	6
2/16/70	3/9/70	House Of The Rising Sun	Frijid Pink	2	9
8/15/68	9/12/68	House That Jack Built, The	Aretha Franklin	6	7
5/11/72	6/15/72	How Can I Be Sure	David Cassidy	15	7
8/31/67	10/19/67	How Can I Be Sure	Young Rascals	4	11
7/14/73	9/1/73	How Can I Tell Her	Lobo	13	11
6/17/71	7/29/71	How Can You Mend A Broken Heart	Bee Gees	1	12
12/15/66	12/15/66	How Do You Catch A Girl	Sam the Sham & the Pharaohs	pr	1
6/29/72	8/5/72	How Do You Do	Mouth & MacNeal	4	9
4/21/66	5/26/66	How Does That Grab You, Darlin'	Nancy Sinatra	15	6
3/22/75	5/24/75	How Long	Ace	5	17
8/30/75	10/4/75	How Long (Betcha' Got A Chick On The Side)	Pointer Sisters	11	11
5/16/68	6/27/68	How'd We Ever Get This Way	Andy Kim	6	8
4/27/70	5/11/70	Hum A Song (From Your Heart)	Lulu with the Dixie Flyers	23	4
3/3/73	4/14/73	Hummingbird	Seals & Crofts	4	10
6/16/66	7/21/66	Hungry	Paul Revere & the Raiders featuring Mark Lindsay	4	12
2/16/67	2/23/67	Hunter Gets Captured By The Game, The	Marvelettes	23	3
7/4/68	8/1/68	Hurdy Gurdy Man	Donovan	7	7
8/18/73	10/6/73	Hurt, The	Cat Stevens	1	11
7/23/69	8/6/69	Hurt So Bad	Lettermen	2	11
1/13/72	2/17/72	Hurting Each Other	Carpenters	1	11
2/3/66	2/3/66	Husbands And Wives	Roger Miller	pr	1
9/5/68	9/26/68	Hush	Deep Purple	6	6

Debut	Peak	Title	Artist	Pos	Wks
10/12/67	11/9/67	Hush	Billy Joe Royal	10	7
5/31/75	7/19/75	Hustle, The	Van McCoy with the Soul City Symphony	3	18
8/17/70	9/14/70	I (Who Have Nothing)	Tom Jones	11	10
1/20/66	1/20/66	I Ain't Gonna Eat Out My Heart Anymore	Young Rascals	17	1
8/12/71	9/16/71	I Ain't Got Time Anymore	Glass Bottle	17	9
5/12/66	6/9/66	I Am A Rock	Simon & Garfunkel	2	9
3/18/71	4/29/71	I Am … I Said	Neil Diamond	16	9
2/8/75	4/12/75	I Am Love (Parts I & II)	Jackson 5	5	14
11/23/67	12/21/67	I Am The Walrus	Beatles	1	8
3/23/74	5/4/74	I Am What I Am	Lois Fletcher	14	12
10/14/72	12/2/72	I Am Woman	Helen Reddy	1	14
10/14/72	12/2/72	I Believe In Music	Gallery	7	12
7/14/73	9/1/73	I Believe In You (You Believe In Me)	Johnnie Taylor	10	11
6/16/66	7/7/66	I Call Your Name	Buckinghams	17	4
5/18/72	6/22/72	I Can Feel You	Addrisi Brothers	20	7
3/26/69	4/16/69	I Can Hear Music	Beach Boys	7	7
11/23/74	12/28/74	I Can Help	Billy Swan	1	14
9/1/66	9/1/66	I Can Make It With You	Jackie DeShannon	pr	1
10/20/66	10/20/66	I Can Make It With You	Pozo-Seco Singers	xx	3
10/7/72	11/25/72	I Can See Clearly Now	Johnny Nash	2	13
11/23/67	12/21/67	I Can See For Miles	Who	8	6
1/25/68	2/8/68	I Can Take Or Leave Your Loving	Herman's Hermits	16	4
9/29/66	10/20/66	I Can't Control Myself	Troggs	xx	3
8/27/69	10/8/69	I Can't Get Next To You	Temptations	3	7
9/21/67	10/26/67	I Can't Happen Without You	Power Plant	29	2
3/10/66	4/14/66	I Can't Let Go	Hollies	10	8
8/1/68	9/5/68	I Can't Stop Dancing	Archie Bell & the Drells	10	6
11/28/68	12/19/68	I Can't Turn You Loose	Chambers Brothers	15	5
1/6/66	1/20/66	I Confess	New Colony Six	4	8
5/14/69	5/28/69	I Could Never Lie To You	New Colony Six	13	5
5/16/68	6/13/68	I Could Never Love Another (After Loving You)	Temptations	18	6

Debut	Peak	Title	Artist	Pos	Wks
7/7/66	8/18/66	I Couldn't Live Without Your Love	Petula Clark	5	9
5/11/72	6/29/72	(Last Night) I Didn't Get To Sleep At All	5th Dimension	2	12
10/28/72	12/9/72	I Didn't Know I Loved You (Till I Saw You Rock And Roll)	Gary Glitter	19	10
11/16/70	12/21/70	I Dig Everything About You	Mob	20	8
8/31/67	9/7/67	I Dig Rock And Roll Music	Peter, Paul & Mary	14	6
2/21/76	2/21/76	I Do, I Do, I Do, I Do, I Do	ABBA	38	1
4/1/71	5/20/71	I Don't Blame You At All	Smokey Robinson & the Miracles	3	11
4/15/71	6/10/71	I Don't Know How To Love Him	Yvonne Elliman	4	12
3/29/75	5/17/75	I Don't Like To Sleep Alone	Paul Anka with Odia Coates	9	14
6/29/72	8/26/72	(If Loving You Is Wrong) I Don't Want To Be Right	Luther Ingram	2	13
4/14/66	4/14/66	I Fall To You	Bob Morrison	pr	1
11/23/74	12/28/74	I Feel A Song (In My Heart)	Gladys Knight & the Pips	16	10
1/27/66	2/17/66	I Fought The Law	Bobby Fuller Four	6	7
8/8/68	8/15/68	I Get The Sweetest Feeling	Jackie Wilson	26	2
1/22/69	2/26/69	I Got A Line On You	Spirit	7	8
10/13/73	12/1/73	I Got A Name	Jim Croce	2	14
5/4/67	5/25/67	I Got Rhythm	Happenings	2	8
9/20/75	10/4/75	I Got Stoned And I Missed It	Jim Stafford	28	5
3/14/68	4/25/68	I Got The Feelin'	James Brown	10	9
10/27/66	11/24/66	I Got The Feelin' (Oh No No)	Neil Diamond	xx	7
8/10/67	9/21/67	I Had A Dream	Paul Revere & the Raiders featuring Mark Lindsay	10	7
1/5/67	2/16/67	I Had Too Much To Dream (Last Night)	Electric Prunes	4	9
5/27/71	7/8/71	I Hear Those Church Bells Ringing	Dusk	9	10
4/14/66	4/14/66	I Hear Trumpets Blow	Tokens	xx	4
12/14/70	1/18/71	I Hear You Knocking	Dave Edmunds	1	11
11/14/68	12/12/68	I Heard It Through The Grapevine	Marvin Gaye	1	12

Debut	Peak	Title	Artist	Pos	Wks
11/9/67	1/4/68	I Heard It Through The Grapevine	Gladys Knight & the Pips	8	9
8/24/74	9/28/74	I Honestly Love You	Olivia Newton-John	1	18
7/13/70	8/17/70	I Just Can't Help Believing	B.J. Thomas	6	11
8/5/71	9/23/71	I Just Want To Celebrate	Rare Earth	4	10
4/7/66	4/21/66	I Lie Awake	New Colony Six	19	3
6/15/67	7/27/67	I Like The Way	Tommy James & the Shondells	14	7
2/16/74	3/23/74	I Like To Live The Love	B.B. King	20	8
12/29/73	2/9/74	I Love	Tom T. Hall	26	10
11/14/68	12/26/68	I Love How You Love Me	Bobby Vinton	3	10
12/20/75	2/7/76	I Love Music (Part 1)	O'Jays	7	10
7/28/66	7/28/66	I Love Onions	Susan Christie	xx	1
6/6/68	6/27/68	I Love You	People	3	7
4/8/71	5/20/71	I Love You For All Seasons	Fuzz	20	8
6/17/71	7/15/71	I Love You Lady Dawn	Bells	27	6
8/24/67	9/28/67	I Make A Fool Of Myself	Frankie Valli	12	8
9/19/68	9/26/68	I Met Her In Church	Box Tops	26	3
1/19/74	2/23/74	I Miss You	Dells	20	8
6/13/68	6/27/68	I Need Love	Third Booth	9	7
12/22/66	12/22/66	I Need Somebody	? & the Mysterians	xx	3
5/25/72	7/15/72	I Need You	America	5	11
3/30/67	3/30/67	I Never Loved A Man (The Way I Love You)	Aretha Franklin	30	1
3/11/71	4/8/71	I Play And Sing	Dawn	14	9
10/6/66	10/6/66	I Really Don't Want To Know	Ronnie Dove	xx	1
1/18/71	1/25/71	I Really Don't Want To Know	Elvis Presley	36	3
6/23/66	7/28/66	I Saw Her Again	Mamas & the Papas	4	10
4/13/72	6/1/72	I Saw The Light	Todd Rundgren	25	9
8/15/68	9/12/68	I Say A Little Prayer	Aretha Franklin	6	7
11/16/67	12/7/67	I Say A Little Prayer	Dionne Warwick	7	5
11/23/67	12/28/67	I Second That Emotion	Smokey Robinson & the Miracles	10	8
12/23/65	2/24/66	I See The Light	Five Americans	14	5

Debut	Peak	Title	Artist	Pos	Wks
8/3/74	9/21/74	I Shot The Sheriff	Eric Clapton	1	15
1/8/69	2/5/69	I Started A Joke	Bee Gees	5	7
7/27/67	8/24/67	I Thank The Lord For The Night Time	Neil Diamond	9	9
2/8/68	2/29/68	I Thank You	Sam & Dave	16	7
10/12/70	11/2/70	I Think I Love You	Partridge Family	1	14
1/26/67	3/2/67	I Think We're Alone Now	Tommy James & the Shondells	1	12
6/1/72	7/22/72	I Wanna Be Where You Are	Michael Jackson	6	11
11/18/72	12/30/72	I Wanna Be With You	Raspberries	6	11
5/3/75	5/24/75	I Wanna Dance Wit' Choo (Doo Dat Dance), Part 1	Disco Tex & the Sex-O-Lettes	26	5
10/27/66	11/17/66	I Wanna Meet You	Cryan' Shames	9	9
10/19/67	10/19/67	I Want Action	Ruby Winters	pr	1
3/3/66	3/3/66	I Want To Go With You	Eddy Arnold	xx	1
7/27/70	8/24/70	I Want To Take You Higher	Ike & Tina Turner & the Ikettes	13	11
7/7/66	7/7/66	I Want You	Bob Dylan	xx	4
1/12/70	1/12/70	I Want You Back	Jackson 5	8	3
8/27/69	9/24/69	I Want You To Know	New Colony Six	14	6
10/18/75	11/22/75	I Want'a Do Something Freaky To You	Leon Haywood	15	10
5/4/67	5/11/67	I Was Kaiser Bill's Batman	Whistling Jack Smith	19	3
7/6/67	8/24/67	I Was Made To Love Her	Stevie Wonder	5	9
1/25/68	4/4/68	I Will Always Think About You	New Colony Six	1	11
1/11/68	2/29/68	I Wish It Would Rain	Temptations	9	8
8/5/71	9/23/71	I Woke Up In Love This Morning	Partridge Family	3	11
1/4/68	2/8/68	I Wonder What She's Doing Tonite	Tommy Boyce & Bobby Hart	2	10
4/20/74	6/1/74	I Won't Last A Day Without You	Carpenters	8	13
11/15/75	2/7/76	I Write The Songs	Barry Manilow	1	15
12/23/71	1/20/72	I'd Like To Teach The World To Sing (In Perfect Harmony)	Hillside Singers	18	7
9/23/72	11/25/72	I'd Love You To Want Me	Lobo	1	15
8/6/69	9/17/69	I'd Wait A Million Years	Grass Roots	3	10

Debut	Peak	Title	Artist	Pos	Wks
3/25/71	5/13/71	If	Bread	4	12
12/22/66	12/22/66	If Every Day Was Like Christmas	Elvis Presley	pr	1
12/19/68	1/29/69	If I Can Dream	Elvis Presley	10	9
12/14/67	1/4/68	If I Could Build My Whole World Around You	Marvin Gaye & Tammi Terrell	18	6
9/30/72	12/2/72	If I Could Reach You	5th Dimension	5	13
1/12/70	1/19/70	If I Never Knew Your Name	Vic Dana	18	5
10/27/66	11/17/66	If I Were A Carpenter	Bobby Darin	15	4
4/11/68	6/13/68	If I Were A Carpenter	Four Tops	11	8
12/14/70	1/4/71	If I Were Your Woman	Gladys Knight & the Pips	10	7
10/21/71	11/25/71	If It's Alright With You	Rose Colored Glass	16	8
5/13/71	6/24/71	If Not For You	Olivia Newton-John	3	10
3/14/68	4/4/68	If You Can Want	Smokey Robinson & the Miracles	19	5
1/4/71	2/15/71	If You Could Read My Mind	Gordon Lightfoot	1	11
11/25/72	1/13/73	If You Don't Know Me By Now	Harold Melvin & the Blue Notes	7	11
6/8/74	7/6/74	If You Love Me (Let Me Know)	Olivia Newton-John	1	12
8/26/71	10/14/71	If You Really Love Me	Stevie Wonder	6	11
11/17/73	1/12/74	If You're Ready (Come Go With Me)	Staple Singers	11	12
4/6/72	5/11/72	Iko Iko	Dr. John	25	7
12/16/65	12/23/65	Il Silenzio	Nini Rosso	10	3
9/16/72	11/11/72	I'll Be Around	Spinners	1	13
9/7/70	10/5/70	I'll Be There	Jackson 5	1	14
4/7/66	5/5/66	I'll Go Crazy	Buckinghams	19	6
3/9/74	4/27/74	I'll Have To Say I Love You In A Song	Jim Croce	4	14
4/22/71	6/17/71	I'll Meet You Halfway	Partridge Family	5	13
7/2/69	8/13/69	I'll Never Fall In Love Again	Tom Jones	11	11
1/12/70	1/26/70	I'll Never Fall In Love Again	Dionne Warwick	6	7
6/29/67	6/29/67	I'll Never Need More Than This	Ike & Tina Turner	pr	1
2/1/75	2/15/75	I'll Still Love You	Jim Weatherly	32	3
3/9/67	3/9/67	I'll Take Care Of Your Cares	Frankie Laine	26	3
5/4/72	6/8/72	I'll Take You There	Staple Singers	12	11

Debut	Peak	Title	Artist	Pos	Wks
3/9/67	4/6/67	I'll Try Anything	Dusty Springfield	29	2
3/26/69	4/2/69	I'll Try Something New	Diana Ross & the Supremes & the Temptations	26	2
12/1/66	1/19/67	I'm A Believer	Monkees	1	13
4/6/67	4/20/67	I'm A Man	Spencer Davis Group	22	5
12/16/65	12/16/65	I'm A Man	Yardbirds	10	5
7/4/68	7/25/68	I'm A Midnight Mover	Wilson Pickett	18	5
4/13/74	5/11/74	I'm A Train	Albert Hammond	24	8
9/16/71	11/4/71	I'm Comin' Home	Tommy James	4	11
4/28/66	4/28/66	I'm Comin' Home, Cindy	Trini Lopez	xx	1
12/21/67	12/21/67	I'm Coming Home	Tom Jones	pr	1
7/22/72	8/12/72	I'm Coming Home	Stories	22	5
5/26/73	7/7/73	I'm Doin' Fine Now	New York City	13	11
4/28/73	6/30/73	I'm Gonna Love You Just A Little More Baby	Barry White	4	13
3/7/68	3/7/68	I'm Gonna Make You Love Me	Madeline Bell	24	2
12/5/68	1/15/69	I'm Gonna Make You Love Me	Diana Ross & the Supremes & the Temptations	1	11
9/3/69	9/24/69	I'm Gonna Make You Mine	Lou Christie	2	6
11/3/66	12/1/66	I'm Gonna Make You Mine	Shadows Of Knight	xx	3
10/24/68	10/31/68	I'm In A Different World	Four Tops	24	3
12/14/67	1/18/68	I'm In Love	Wilson Pickett	14	5
2/3/73	3/17/73	I'm Just A Singer (In A Rock And Roll Band)	Moody Blues	3	12
6/8/67	7/13/67	I'm Just Waiting Anticipating For Her To Show Up	New Colony Six	16	6
7/20/74	9/7/74	I'm Leaving It (All) Up To You	Donny & Marie Osmond	9	14
1/22/69	2/12/69	I'm Livin' In Shame	Diana Ross & the Supremes	13	7
8/24/70	9/28/70	(I Know) I'm Losing You	Rare Earth	5	13
12/1/66	12/1/66	(I Know) I'm Losing You	Temptations	xx	4
6/14/75	8/2/75	I'm Not In Love	10cc	4	16
5/31/75	7/12/75	I'm Not Lisa	Jessi Colter	6	13
11/30/70	12/14/70	I'm Not My Brothers Keeper	Flaming Ember	30	4
10/18/75	11/29/75	I'm On Fire	5000 Volts	12	11
6/7/75	6/28/75	I'm On Fire	Dwight Twilley Band	23	9

Debut	Peak	Title	Artist	Pos	Wks
3/10/66	3/10/66	I'm Ready	Little Boy Blues	xx	1
11/10/66	12/8/66	I'm Ready For Love	Martha & the Vandellas	18	5
3/17/66	4/21/66	I'm So Lonesome I Could Cry	B.J. Thomas & the Triumphs	9	7
9/20/75	11/1/75	I'm Sorry	John Denver	1	14
7/29/72	9/9/72	I'm Still In Love With You	Al Green	9	9
11/18/72	1/20/73	I'm Stone In Love With You	Stylistics	9	13
5/18/74	6/29/74	I'm The Leader Of The Gang	Brownsville Station	10	13
11/10/66	11/10/66	(Come 'Round Here) I'm The One You Need	Miracles	pr	1
10/5/67	11/2/67	I'm Wondering	Stevie Wonder	23	4
10/13/66	10/20/66	I'm Your Puppet	James & Bobby Purify	20	5
10/7/71	11/18/71	Imagine	John Lennon Plastic Ono Band	2	11
11/30/70	1/11/71	Immigrant Song	Led Zeppelin	2	10
6/1/72	7/6/72	In A Broken Dream	Python Lee Jackson	26	7
10/3/68	10/17/68	In-A-Gadda-Da-Vida	Iron Butterfly	17	3
11/9/67	12/28/67	In And Out Of Love	Diana Ross & the Supremes	16	7
3/7/68	3/7/68	In Need Of A Friend	Cowsills	pr	1
5/14/69	6/4/69	In The Ghetto	Elvis Presley	6	7
9/1/73	10/13/73	In The Midnight Hour	Cross Country	20	9
2/9/67	2/9/67	In The Midnight Hour	Dick Whittington's Cats	pr	1
1/19/74	2/16/74	In The Mood	Bette Midler	24	7
4/6/72	5/25/72	In The Rain	Dramatics	5	11
6/29/70	8/17/70	In The Summertime	Mungo Jerry	4	14
6/25/69	7/16/69	In The Year 2525 (Exordium & Terminus)	Zager & Evans	1	8
10/19/67	11/9/67	Incense And Peppermints	Strawberry Alarm Clock	2	9
2/16/67	2/23/67	Indescribably Blue	Elvis Presley	28	2
2/5/69	3/26/69	Indian Giver	1910 Fruitgum Co.	2	9
5/23/68	7/25/68	Indian Lake	Cowsills	5	6
9/5/68	9/26/68	(The Lament Of The Cherokee) Indian Reservation	Don Fardon	5	5
7/8/71	8/5/71	Indian Reservation (The Lament of The Cherokee Reservation Indian)	Raiders	1	9

Debut	Peak	Title	Artist	Pos	Wks
8/24/70	10/19/70	Indiana Wants Me	R. Dean Taylor	1	15
8/18/66	8/18/66	Indication	Zombies	xx	3
9/30/71	11/11/71	Inner City Blues (Make Me Wanna Holler)	Marvin Gaye	8	11
3/14/68	4/11/68	Inner Light, The	Beatles	1	8
3/17/66	3/17/66	Inside-Looking Out	Animals	xx	2
2/23/70	3/23/70	Instant Karma (We All Shine On)	John Lennon	3	10
10/8/69	10/8/69	Is That All There Is	Peggy Lee	30	1
10/11/75	11/22/75	Island Girl	Elton John	1	15
11/23/70	11/30/70	Isn't It A Pity	George Harrison	16	2
4/27/72	6/1/72	Isn't Life Strange	Moody Blues	8	9
5/28/69	6/25/69	Israelites	Desmond Dekker & the Aces	5	8
6/29/67	8/17/67	It Could Be We're In Love	Cryan' Shames	1	13
8/31/74	9/21/74	It Could Have Been Me	Sami Jo	20	7
4/29/71	6/10/71	It Don't Come Easy	Ringo Starr	2	10
9/21/70	10/19/70	It Don't Matter To Me	Bread	7	10
9/21/67	11/9/67	It Must Be Him	Vikki Carr	8	9
11/18/72	12/30/72	It Never Rains In Southern California	Albert Hammond	3	13
9/13/75	10/25/75	It Only Takes A Minute	Tavares	7	14
4/14/73	5/19/73	It Sure Took A Long, Long Time	Lobo	14	9
2/17/66	2/17/66	It Was A Very Good Year	Frank Sinatra	18	1
2/24/66	2/24/66	It Won't Be Wrong	Byrds	xx	1
11/2/67	2/15/68	Itchycoo Park	Small Faces	4	6
5/26/66	5/26/66	It's A Man's Man's Man's World	James Brown	xx	2
4/12/75	5/31/75	It's A Miracle	Barry Manilow	1	14
10/5/70	10/19/70	It's A Shame	Spinners	30	5
5/25/70	6/15/70	It's All In The Game	Four Tops	23	7
1/11/75	2/15/75	It's All Right	Jim Capaldi	22	8
5/31/75	6/21/75	It's All Up To You	Jim Capaldi	31	5
5/4/72	6/8/72	It's Going To Take Some Time	Carpenters	7	10
12/23/65	12/30/65	It's Good News Week	Hedgehoppers Anonymous	5	6
12/14/70	1/4/71	It's Impossible	Perry Como	27	5

Debut	Peak	Title	Artist	Pos	Wks
12/16/65	1/20/66	It's My Life	Animals	8	8
6/27/68	6/27/68	It's Nice To Be With You	Monkees	21	2
1/5/67	2/9/67	It's Now Winters Day	Tommy Roe	11	7
12/9/71	1/20/72	It's One Of Those Nights (Yes Love)	Partridge Family	6	10
10/20/66	12/15/66	It's Only Love	Tommy James & the Shondells	10	8
4/16/69	4/30/69	It's Only Love	B.J. Thomas	23	4
8/10/74	9/14/74	It's Only Rock 'N Roll (But I Like It)	Rolling Stones	10	11
6/2/66	6/2/66	It's That Time Of The Year	Len Barry	pr	1
7/20/67	7/20/67	It's The Little Things	Sonny & Cher	pr	1
2/10/66	3/10/66	It's Too Late	Bobby Goldsboro	xx	4
5/20/71	6/24/71	It's Too Late	Carole King	1	14
12/21/70	1/18/71	It's Up To You Petula	Edison Lighthouse	15	6
11/30/67	1/18/68	It's Wonderful	Young Rascals	10	7
10/19/67	11/2/67	(Loneliness Made Me Realize) It's You That I Need	Temptations	21	4
7/6/70	8/3/70	It's Your Life	Andy Kim	25	6
3/12/69	4/2/69	It's Your Thing	Isley Brothers	3	10
4/16/69	5/21/69	I've Been Hurt	Bill Deal & the Rhondels	11	6
6/15/72	7/6/72	I've Been Lonely For So Long	Frederick Knight	25	5
2/23/67	3/9/67	I've Been Lonely Too Long	Young Rascals	23	5
9/1/66	9/22/66	I've Been Wrong	Buckinghams	15	4
8/19/71	10/21/71	I've Found Someone Of My Own	Free Movement	2	13
10/19/74	11/30/74	I've Got The Music In Me	Kiki Dee Band	13	10
10/6/66	10/6/66	I've Got To Do A Little Bit Better	Joe Tex	pr	1
12/29/66	1/19/67	I've Got To Have A Reason	Dave Clark Five	xx	4
12/29/73	2/16/74	I've Got To Use My Imagination	Gladys Knight & the Pips	6	12
8/25/66	10/27/66	I've Got You Under My Skin	Four Seasons	20	5
1/29/69	3/5/69	I've Gotta Be Me	Sammy Davis, Jr.	3	8
9/19/68	10/31/68	I've Gotta Get A Message To You	Bee Gees	2	9
12/8/66	2/9/67	I've Passed This Way Before	Jimmy Ruffin	23	4

Debut	Peak	Title	Artist	Pos	Wks
9/24/69	10/8/69	Jack And Jill	Tommy Roe	26	3
3/22/75	5/10/75	Jackie Blue	Ozark Mountain Daredevils	3	15
7/13/67	7/20/67	Jackson	Nancy Sinatra & Lee Hazlewood	27	4
1/12/70	1/12/70	Jam Up Jelly Tight	Tommy Roe	3	5
12/16/72	2/10/73	Jambalaya (On The Bayou)	Blue Ridge Rangers	5	13
8/30/75	9/27/75	("Jaws", Theme From), Main Title	John Williams	16	10
10/19/74	11/23/74	Jazzman	Carole King	3	13
9/17/69	9/24/69	Jealous Kind Of Fella	Garland Green	26	2
2/8/68	2/8/68	Jealous Love	Wilson Pickett	pr	1
9/3/69	10/1/69	Jean	Oliver	4	6
6/6/68	6/13/68	Jelly Jungle (Of Orange Marmalade)	Lemon Pipers	21	2
2/29/68	5/16/68	Jennifer Eccles	Hollies	14	6
3/28/68	5/2/68	Jennifer Juniper	Donovan	12	6
3/9/70	3/23/70	Jennifer Tomkins	Street People	15	6
2/3/66	2/10/66	Jenny Take A Ride	Mitch Ryder & the Detroit Wheels	12	2
6/29/72	8/5/72	Jesahel	English Congregation	17	9
9/29/73	10/27/73	Jesse	Roberta Flack	28	6
10/8/69	10/8/69	Jesus Is A Soul Man	Lawrence Reynolds	23	1
2/16/74	4/6/74	Jet	Paul McCartney & Wings	5	13
12/29/73	3/2/74	Jim Dandy	Black Oak Arkansas	5	14
9/1/73	10/13/73	Jimmy Loves Mary-Anne	Looking Glass	5	12
3/16/67	4/27/67	Jimmy Mack	Martha & the Vandellas	6	8
1/12/70	1/12/70	Jingle Jangle	Archies	4	4
6/14/75	8/23/75	Jive Talkin'	Bee Gees	1	20
9/14/70	10/12/70	Joanne	Michael Nesmith & the First National Band	13	9
2/15/71	3/11/71	Jody's Got Your Girl And Gone	Johnnie Taylor	25	4
8/5/72	9/16/72	Join Together	Who	18	9
11/17/73	1/12/74	Joker, The	Steve Miller Band	1	15
9/1/66	9/29/66	Joker Went Wild, The	Brian Hyland	6	7
7/25/68	8/22/68	Journey To The Center Of The Mind	Amboy Dukes	6	7
1/13/72	3/2/72	Joy	Apollo 100	1	12

Debut	Peak	Title	Artist	Pos	Wks
4/1/71	4/29/71	Joy To The World	Three Dog Night	1	12
12/7/67	1/4/68	Judy In Disguise (With Glasses)	John Fred & his Playboy Band	1	10
9/8/66	9/8/66	Jug Band Music	Mugwumps	xx	2
7/20/70	8/24/70	Julie, Do Ya Love Me	Bobby Sherman	7	13
6/13/68	7/11/68	Jumpin' Jack Flash	Rolling Stones	1	8
2/2/74	3/23/74	Jungle Boogie	Kool & the Gang	6	12
3/9/72	4/13/72	Jungle Fever	Chakachas	5	8
11/9/74	12/21/74	Junior's Farm	Paul McCartney & Wings	3	13
2/21/76	2/21/76	Junk Food Junkie	Larry Groce	32	1
12/14/67	1/18/68	Just As Much As Ever	Bobby Vinton	23	6
3/2/74	5/4/74	Just Don't Want To Be Lonely	Main Ingredient	3	15
2/22/68	3/14/68	Just Dropped In (To See What Condition My Condition Was In)	First Edition	4	6
9/29/66	9/29/66	Just Like A Woman	Bob Dylan	xx	1
12/16/65	1/6/66	Just Like Me	Paul Revere & the Raiders featuring Mark Lindsay	8	5
2/1/71	3/25/71	Just My Imagination (Running Away With Me)	Temptations	1	15
12/8/66	1/5/67	Just One Smile	Gene Pitney	8	7
9/29/73	11/24/73	Just You 'N' Me	Chicago	4	14
8/27/69	9/3/69	Keem-O-Sabe	Electric Indian	16	3
12/16/65	12/16/65	Keep On Dancing	Gentrys	5	2
11/14/68	11/14/68	Keep On Lovin' Me Honey	Marvin Gaye & Tammi Terrell	25	1
3/30/74	5/11/74	Keep On Singing	Helen Reddy	12	11
7/20/74	8/24/74	Keep On Smilin'	Wet Willie	14	11
9/15/73	11/10/73	Keep On Truckin' (Part 1)	Eddie Kendricks	3	14
12/14/67	12/21/67	Keep The Ball Rollin'	Jay & the Techniques	27	2
11/18/72	1/13/73	Keeper Of The Castle	Four Tops	2	14
2/2/70	3/2/70	Kentucky Rain	Elvis Presley	10	8
11/28/68	12/19/68	Kentucky Woman	Deep Purple	22	5
10/5/67	11/9/67	Kentucky Woman	Neil Diamond	15	6
3/10/66	4/21/66	Kicks	Paul Revere & the Raiders featuring Mark Lindsay	1	14
5/5/66	5/5/66	Killer Joe	Kingsmen	xx	2

Debut	Peak	Title	Artist	Pos	Wks
4/12/75	6/7/75	Killer Queen	Queen	1	18
2/3/73	3/3/73	Killing Me Softly With His Song	Roberta Flack	1	11
11/24/66	12/22/66	Kind Of A Drag	Buckinghams	2	11
9/28/67	9/28/67	King Midas In Reverse	Hollies	pr	1
9/7/74	10/5/74	Kings Of The Party	Brownsville Station	18	8
12/23/71	2/10/72	Kiss An Angel Good Mornin'	Charley Pride	9	12
2/8/68	3/14/68	Kiss Me Goodbye	Petula Clark	10	7
8/18/66	8/18/66	Kissin' My Life Away	Hondells	pr	1
2/17/73	4/7/73	Kissing My Love	Bill Withers	1	11
12/15/66	1/26/67	Knight In Rusty Armour	Peter & Gordon	16	6
11/9/70	1/4/71	Knock Three Times	Dawn	1	14
10/6/73	11/17/73	Knockin' On Heaven's Door	Bob Dylan	16	10
5/19/73	7/14/73	Kodachrome	Paul Simon	1	15
10/19/74	12/21/74	Kung Fu Fighting	Carl Douglas	1	17
2/22/71	4/15/71	L.A. Goodbye	Ides Of March	2	12
5/18/74	6/29/74	La Grange	ZZ Top	2	15
1/12/70	1/12/70	La La La (If I Had You)	Bobby Sherman	6	3
2/29/68	4/4/68	La-La-Means I Love You	Delfonics	7	7
1/11/75	2/15/75	Lady	Styx	3	11
9/13/75	11/8/75	Lady Blue	Leon Russell	5	14
8/3/67	8/3/67	Lady Friend	Byrds	pr	1
10/6/66	12/1/66	Lady Godiva	Peter & Gordon	5	9
7/28/66	8/4/66	Lady Jane	Rolling Stones	11	3
3/14/68	4/11/68	Lady Madonna	Beatles	1	8
3/8/75	4/19/75	Lady Marmalade	Labelle	1	14
6/20/68	7/18/68	Lady Willpower	Gary Puckett & the Union Gap	4	7
8/18/66	9/1/66	Land Of 1000 Dances	Wilson Pickett	19	4
6/9/66	7/7/66	Land Of Milk And Honey, The	Vogues	16	6
4/14/66	5/5/66	Lara's Theme From "Dr. Zhivago"	Roger Williams	17	4
5/31/75	6/28/75	Last Farewell, The	Roger Whittaker	15	10

Debut	Peak	Title	Artist	Pos	Wks
11/15/75	12/13/75	Last Game Of The Season (A Blind Man In The Bleachers), The	David Geddes	20	7
1/26/74	3/16/74	Last Kiss	Wednesday	5	13
1/13/73	2/24/73	Last Song	Edward Bear	2	14
7/14/66	7/14/66	Last Time Around	Del-Vetts	xx	1
2/9/74	3/23/74	Last Time I Saw Him	Diana Ross	13	10
9/8/66	10/20/66	Last Train To Clarksville	Monkees	3	11
10/19/67	11/9/67	Last Waltz, The	Engelbert Humperdinck	23	3
3/9/67	3/16/67	Laudy Miss Clawdy	Buckinghams	24	2
7/23/69	8/13/69	Laughing	Guess Who	10	7
12/7/74	1/25/75	Laughter In The Rain	Neil Sedaka	1	14
6/8/70	7/13/70	Lay A Little Lovin' On Me	Robin McNamara	9	13
5/4/70	6/15/70	Lay Down (Candles In The Rain)	Melanie with the Edwin Hawkins Singers	5	13
7/30/69	8/27/69	Lay Lady Lay	Bob Dylan	1	9
3/11/71	4/8/71	Layla	Derek & the Dominos	18	6
11/2/67	11/2/67	Lazy Day	Spanky & Our Gang	29	1
6/15/72	7/15/72	Lean On Me	Bill Withers	1	11
4/14/66	5/12/66	Leaning On The Lamp Post	Herman's Hermits	11	5
11/3/73	1/12/74	Leave Me Alone (Ruby Red Dress)	Helen Reddy	8	14
1/12/70	1/12/70	Leaving On A Jet Plane	Peter, Paul & Mary	40	1
3/2/70	3/23/70	Let It Be	Beatles	1	13
9/28/67	10/26/67	Let It Out (Let It All Hang Out)	Hombres	3	9
3/9/74	4/13/74	Let It Ride	Bachman-Turner Overdrive	21	8
5/14/69	6/11/69	Let Me	Paul Revere & the Raiders featuring Mark Lindsay	8	9
12/8/73	2/2/74	Let Me Be There	Olivia Newton-John	2	14
9/15/73	11/3/73	Let Me In	Osmonds	14	11
11/3/73	12/15/73	Let Me Serenade You	Three Dog Night	8	12
6/27/68	7/4/68	Let Yourself Go	Elvis Presley	25	2
9/15/66	9/15/66	Let's Call It A Day Girl	Razor's Edge	xx	2
11/15/75	12/20/75	Let's Do It Again	Staple Singers	6	12
7/21/73	9/29/73	Let's Get It On	Marvin Gaye	1	15
12/16/65	12/16/65	Let's Hang On	Four Seasons	1	6

Debut	Peak	Title	Artist	Pos	Wks
5/25/67	6/29/67	Let's Live For Today	Grass Roots	4	9
4/28/73	6/23/73	Let's Pretend	Raspberries	4	12
9/7/74	10/5/74	Let's Put It All Together	Stylistics	10	10
5/5/66	5/5/66	Let's Start All Over Again	Ronnie Dove	xx	3
12/16/71	2/3/72	Let's Stay Together	Al Green	7	11
10/19/70	11/23/70	Let's Work Together	Canned Heat	6	8
3/12/69	4/9/69	Letter, The	Arbors	20	6
8/31/67	9/21/67	Letter, The	Box Tops	1	12
4/13/70	6/1/70	Letter, The	Joe Cocker	7	11
7/22/71	8/26/71	Liar	Three Dog Night	11	11
6/6/68	6/13/68	Licking Stick—Licking Stick (Part 1)	James Brown & the Famous Flames	20	4
1/20/66	2/10/66	Lies	Knickerbockers	4	5
9/30/71	11/11/71	Life Is A Carnival	Band	17	8
10/12/74	11/23/74	Life Is A Rock (But The Radio Rolled Me)	Reunion	4	12
7/6/67	8/10/67	Light My Fire	Doors	2	12
8/1/68	8/22/68	Light My Fire	José Feliciano	1	7
1/20/66	2/10/66	Lightnin' Strikes	Lou Christie	1	8
9/14/67	11/2/67	Lightning's Girl	Nancy Sinatra	22	5
10/12/67	10/12/67	Like An Old Time Movie	Scott McKenzie	pr	1
5/9/68	6/13/68	Like To Get To Know You	Spanky & Our Gang	6	7
6/30/66	8/11/66	Lil' Red Riding Hood	Sam the Sham & the Pharaohs	3	11
1/13/72	3/9/72	Lion Sleeps Tonight, The	Robert John	2	12
2/10/66	2/24/66	Listen People	Herman's Hermits	4	6
9/16/72	11/4/72	Listen To The Music	Doobie Brothers	3	11
6/7/75	8/2/75	Listen To What The Man Said	Wings	1	16
3/23/67	4/27/67	Little Bit Me, A Little Bit You, A	Monkees	1	10
8/3/67	8/24/67	Little Bit Now, A	Dave Clark Five	28	2
6/8/72	6/29/72	Little Bit O' Soul	Bullet	27	5
5/18/67	6/8/67	Little Bit O' Soul	Music Explosion	2	11
10/26/67	10/26/67	Little Bitty Pretty One	Jewel Akens	pr	1
4/13/72	6/1/72	Little Bitty Pretty One	Jackson 5	10	12

Debut	Peak	Title	Artist	Pos	Wks
12/23/65	12/23/65	Little Boy (In Grown Up Clothes)	Four Seasons	pr	1
4/6/67	4/6/67	Little Games	Yardbirds	pr	1
6/23/66	7/21/66	Little Girl	Syndicate Of Sound	19	5
12/23/65	12/23/65	Little Girl I Once Knew, The	Beach Boys	18	2
9/5/68	10/24/68	Little Green Apples	O.C. Smith	1	10
3/23/70	4/27/70	Little Green Bag	George Baker Selection	3	13
2/24/66	3/17/66	Little Latin Lupe Lu	Mitch Ryder & the Detroit Wheels	xx	3
9/22/66	10/20/66	Little Man	Sonny & Cher	xx	4
9/7/67	10/12/67	Little Ole Man (Uptight-Everything's Alright)	Bill Cosby	2	8
8/10/67	8/10/67	Little Ole Wine Drinker, Me	Dean Martin	pr	1
2/10/73	4/14/73	Little Willy	Sweet	1	15
9/10/69	10/1/69	Little Woman	Bobby Sherman	1	5
7/21/73	8/25/73	Live And Let Die	Wings	4	11
11/24/73	1/19/74	Living For The City	Stevie Wonder	10	12
5/18/72	7/6/72	Living In A House Divided	Cher	4	11
12/9/72	1/27/73	Living In The Past	Jethro Tull	2	12
1/20/73	2/24/73	Living Together, Growing Together	5th Dimension	19	9
12/19/68	1/8/69	Lo Mucho Que Te Quiero (The More I Love You)	Rene & Rene	18	5
3/9/74	5/11/74	Loco-Motion, The	Grand Funk	2	16
5/21/69	6/11/69	Lodi	Creedence Clearwater Revival	2	5
9/7/70	10/26/70	Lola	Kinks	2	13
11/30/70	1/4/71	Lonely Days	Bee Gees	6	9
6/22/67	8/3/67	Lonely Drifter	Pieces Of Eight	24	4
2/7/76	2/21/76	Lonely Night (Angel Face)	Captain & Tennille	19	3
2/15/75	3/29/75	Lonely People	America	4	12
5/18/70	6/22/70	Long And Winding Road, The	Beatles	9	10
7/6/72	8/19/72	Long Cool Woman (In A Black Dress)	Hollies	2	11
2/19/69	3/19/69	Long Green	Fireballs	18	5
1/27/66	2/10/66	Long Live Our Love	Shangri-Las	xx	4
3/2/70	4/6/70	Long Lonesome Highway	Michael Parks	6	10

Debut	Peak	Title	Artist	Pos	Wks
4/26/75	6/7/75	Long Tall Glasses (I Can Dance)	Leo Sayer	2	13
11/18/71	1/13/72	Long Time To Be Alone	New Colony Six	13	11
5/19/73	7/14/73	Long Train Runnin'	Doobie Brothers	3	15
10/12/74	12/7/74	Longfellow Serenade	Neil Diamond	5	15
6/6/68	6/27/68	Look Of Love, The	Sergio Mendes & Brasil '66	8	5
10/19/67	11/16/67	Look Of Love, The	Dusty Springfield	7	7
10/13/66	11/10/66	Look Through My Window	Mamas & the Papas	18	4
4/25/68	5/9/68	Look To Your Soul	Johnny Rivers	21	3
9/7/70	10/19/70	Look What They've Done To My Song Ma	New Seekers	8	11
4/20/72	6/8/72	Look What You Done For Me	Al Green	9	10
3/30/74	5/4/74	Lookin' For A Love	Bobby Womack	22	9
8/3/70	9/21/70	Lookin' Out My Back Door	Creedence Clearwater Revival	2	14
3/7/68	3/7/68	Looking For A Fox	Clarence Carter	29	1
12/16/71	1/20/72	Looking For A Love	J. Geils Band	16	9
3/2/74	4/13/74	Lord's Prayer, The	Sister Janet Mead	3	11
2/23/67	4/6/67	Loser (With A Broken Heart), The	Gary Lewis & the Playboys	26	2
10/13/66	12/1/66	Louie, Louie	Sandpipers	20	5
9/30/71	11/4/71	Love	Lettermen	12	10
4/16/69	5/14/69	Love (Can Make You Happy)	Mercy	1	10
4/12/75	5/3/75	L-O-V-E (Love)	Al Green	27	6
10/24/68	11/21/68	Love Child	Diana Ross & the Supremes	1	10
3/9/67	4/20/67	Love Eyes	Nancy Sinatra	25	5
2/9/70	3/9/70	Love Grows (Where My Rosemary Goes)	Edison Lighthouse	3	11
4/1/71	5/27/71	Love Her Madly	Doors	3	13
2/21/76	2/21/76	Love Hurts	Nazareth	30	1
3/23/67	3/23/67	Love I Saw In You Was Just A Mirage, The	Smokey Robinson & the Miracles	28	1
10/13/66	10/27/66	Love Is A Hurtin' Thing	Lou Rawls	17	3
2/29/68	4/4/68	Love Is All Around	Troggs	17	6
1/18/68	2/8/68	Love Is Blue	Paul Mauriat	1	11
1/19/67	2/23/67	Love Is Here And Now You're Gone	Supremes	7	9

Debut	Peak	Title	Artist	Pos	Wks
5/12/66	5/12/66	Love Is Like An Itching In My Heart	Supremes	xx	2
10/26/67	11/9/67	Love Is Strange	Peaches & Herb	17	3
2/7/76	2/21/76	Love Is The Drug	Roxy Music	25	3
1/20/73	3/17/73	Love Jones	Brighter Side Of Darkness	8	12
5/18/70	6/15/70	Love Land	Charles Wright & the Watts 103rd Street Rhythm Band	2	11
7/21/66	8/4/66	Love Letters	Elvis Presley	19	4
1/24/76	2/21/76	Love Machine (Part 1)	Miracles	13	5
8/15/68	9/5/68	Love Makes A Woman	Barbara Acklin	17	5
2/24/66	3/10/66	Love Makes The World Go Round	Deon Jackson	19	3
2/8/71	2/22/71	Love Makes The World Go Round	Odds & Ends	25	5
9/14/74	10/26/74	Love Me For A Reason	Osmonds	9	13
5/28/69	7/2/69	Love Me Tonight	Tom Jones	11	8
4/20/70	6/1/70	Love On A Two-Way Street	Moments	1	12
3/2/70	4/27/70	Love Or Let Me Be Lonely	Friends Of Distinction	8	16
11/29/75	1/31/76	Love Rollercoaster	Ohio Players	1	13
2/2/74	3/9/74	Love Song	Anne Murray	6	14
1/25/71	1/25/71	Love Story, Theme From	Francis Lai	19	2
1/4/71	1/18/71	Love Story, Theme From	Henry Mancini	19	5
1/20/72	2/24/72	(Love Me) Love The Life I Lead	Fantastics	23	7
12/7/70	1/18/71	Love The One You're With	Stephen Stills	3	9
12/27/75	2/7/76	Love To Love You Baby	Donna Summer	2	9
2/10/73	3/31/73	Love Train	O'Jays	2	11
6/14/75	7/12/75	Love Will Keep Us Together	Captain & Tennille	1	15
5/24/75	6/28/75	Love Won't Let Me Wait	Major Harris	13	12
5/25/70	6/29/70	Love You Save, The	Jackson 5	1	14
12/29/66	1/26/67	Love You So Much	New Colony Six	4	9
7/11/68	7/25/68	Lover's Holiday	Peggy Scott & Jo Jo Benson	25	4
2/15/71	4/1/71	Love's Lines, Angles And Rhymes	5th Dimension	9	10
3/24/66	4/21/66	Love's Made A Fool Of You	Bobby Fuller Four	xx	3
8/11/73	9/22/73	Loves Me Like A Rock	Paul Simon with the Dixie Hummingbirds	1	13

Debut	Peak	Title	Artist	Pos	Wks
12/15/73	2/9/74	Love's Theme	Love Unlimited Orchestra	2	15
2/19/69	3/5/69	Lovin' Things	Grass Roots	22	3
1/12/67	2/9/67	Lovin' You	Bobby Darin	24	4
2/22/75	4/5/75	Lovin' You	Minnie Riperton	1	13
8/26/72	10/14/72	Loving You Just Crossed My Mind	Sam Neely	14	11
10/12/70	11/2/70	Lucretia Mac Evil	Blood, Sweat & Tears	25	5
11/30/74	1/11/75	Lucy In The Sky With Diamonds	Elton John	1	14
3/3/66	3/3/66	Lullaby Of Love	Poppies	pr	1
3/5/69	4/2/69	L.U.V. (Let Us Vote)	Tommy Boyce & Bobby Hart	23	5
9/27/75	11/8/75	Lyin' Eyes	Eagles	4	14
1/12/70	2/9/70	Ma Belle Amie	Tee Set	7	9
9/2/71	10/7/71	MacArthur Park	Four Tops	24	7
4/18/68	6/20/68	MacArthur Park	Richard Harris	7	8
7/20/74	8/10/74	Machine Gun	Commodores	12	8
9/9/71	9/30/71	Maggie May	Rod Stewart	1	10
5/17/75	7/19/75	Magic	Pilot	2	17
8/29/68	9/19/68	Magic Bus	Who	9	4
10/10/68	11/7/68	Magic Carpet Ride	Steppenwolf	2	9
2/24/66	3/17/66	Magic Town	Vogues	9	6
11/29/75	1/31/76	Mahogany, Theme From (Do You Know Where You're Going To)	Diana Ross	3	13
3/9/67	3/9/67	Mairzy Doats	Innocence	30	2
9/17/69	10/8/69	Make Believe	Wind	13	4
6/29/70	7/27/70	Make It With You	Bread	1	12
4/20/70	6/1/70	Make Me Smile	Chicago	5	13
3/30/72	4/27/72	Make You, Break You	Gerry Rafferty	25	7
8/17/67	8/17/67	Making Every Minute Count	Spanky & Our Gang	pr	1
5/18/67	5/18/67	Making Memories	Frankie Laine	30	2
5/5/66	6/2/66	Mama	B.J. Thomas	xx	4
5/18/70	6/22/70	Mama Told Me (Not To Come)	Three Dog Night	1	14
1/11/71	2/22/71	Mama's Pearl	Jackson 5	1	11
11/10/66	12/8/66	Mame	Herb Alpert & the Tijuana Brass	19	4

Debut	Peak	Title	Artist	Pos	Wks
10/27/73	12/15/73	Mammy Blue	Stories	7	12
5/2/68	6/13/68	Man Without Love (Quando M'innamoro), A	Engelbert Humperdinck	19	5
12/28/74	2/8/75	Mandy	Barry Manilow	1	13
4/21/66	4/21/66	Marble Breaks And Iron Bends	Drafi	pr	1
8/19/71	9/30/71	Marianne	Stephen Stills	4	11
7/9/69	8/13/69	Marrakesh Express	Crosby, Stills & Nash	17	6
12/14/70	12/14/70	Marvelous Toy, The	Irish Rovers	xx	2
6/29/67	6/29/67	Mary In The Morning	Al Martino	28	1
12/7/67	12/14/67	(The Lights Went Out In) Massachusetts	Bee Gees	26	2
5/9/68	6/6/68	Master Jack	Four Jacks & A Jill	6	7
3/17/73	4/28/73	Masterpiece	Temptations	20	9
2/19/69	3/26/69	May I	Bill Deal & the Rhondels	11	6
3/28/68	3/28/68	May I Take A Giant Step (Into Your Heart)	1910 Fruitgum Co.	pr	1
7/22/71	8/26/71	Maybe Tomorrow	Jackson 5	2	10
2/1/71	4/1/71	Me And Bobby McGee	Janis Joplin	5	11
12/9/71	1/13/72	Me And Bobby McGee	Jerry Lee Lewis	25	7
12/2/72	1/13/73	Me And Mrs. Jones	Billy Paul	1	12
3/18/71	4/29/71	Me And You And A Dog Named Boo	Lobo	6	10
4/11/68	4/18/68	Me, The Peaceful Heart	Lulu	23	2
2/9/67	2/23/67	Mechanical Man, The	Bent Bolt & the Nuts	24	3
4/30/69	5/28/69	Medicine Man (Part I)	Buchanan Brothers	5	10
11/3/66	12/8/66	Mellow Yellow	Donovan	3	10
4/2/69	4/23/69	Memories	Elvis Presley	22	4
2/1/68	2/22/68	Men Are Gettin' Scarce	Joe Tex	30	3
1/6/66	1/20/66	Men In My Little Girl's Life, The	Mike Douglas	13	5
3/5/69	3/19/69	Mendocino	Sir Douglas Quintet	16	4
2/10/72	3/9/72	(Oh Lord Won't You Buy Me A) Mercedes Benz	Goose Creek Symphony	28	6
4/2/69	4/30/69	Mercy	Ohio Express	5	8
7/1/71	8/12/71	Mercy Mercy Me (The Ecology)	Marvin Gaye	6	12

Debut	Peak	Title	Artist	Pos	Wks
2/9/67	3/2/67	Mercy, Mercy, Mercy	"Cannonball" Adderley	20	4
6/15/67	7/27/67	Mercy, Mercy, Mercy	Buckinghams	7	9
12/14/70	12/14/70	Merry Christmas Darling	Carpenters	xx	2
5/5/66	5/26/66	Message To Michael	Dionne Warwick	17	5
4/13/74	6/8/74	Midnight At The Oasis	Maria Muldaur	1	15
6/28/75	8/9/75	Midnight Blue	Melissa Manchester	6	13
9/12/68	10/17/68	Midnight Confessions	Grass Roots	2	9
1/12/70	1/12/70	Midnight Cowboy	Ferrante & Teicher	12	3
4/27/67	6/1/67	Midnight Hour	Michael & the Messengers	5	8
12/15/73	1/26/74	Midnight Rider	Gregg Allman	15	10
9/22/73	11/17/73	Midnight Train To Georgia	Gladys Knight & the Pips	1	14
6/24/71	7/29/71	Mighty Clouds Of Joy	B.J. Thomas	16	9
3/16/70	4/6/70	Mighty Joe	Shocking Blue	28	4
3/7/68	4/11/68	Mighty Quinn (Quinn The Eskimo)	Manfred Mann	12	8
8/25/73	9/22/73	Million To One, A	Donny Osmond	16	8
11/10/73	12/29/73	Mind Games	John Lennon	1	14
10/11/75	11/22/75	Miracles	Jefferson Starship	2	15
4/13/67	5/18/67	Mirage	Tommy James & the Shondells	1	7
2/22/68	2/29/68	Mission-Impossible	Lalo Schifrin	22	2
6/1/70	7/6/70	Mississippi	John Phillips	7	10
6/29/70	8/3/70	Mississippi Queen	Mountain	7	10
3/23/72	5/11/72	Mister Can't You See	Buffy Sainte-Marie	9	10
8/4/66	8/4/66	Misty	Richard "Groove" Holmes	xx	2
7/12/75	8/2/75	Misty	Ray Stevens	19	8
2/9/74	3/23/74	Mockingbird	Carly Simon & James Taylor	1	13
3/31/66	5/5/66	Monday, Monday	Mamas & the Papas	1	10
5/26/73	7/21/73	Money	Pink Floyd	8	14
2/14/76	2/21/76	Money Honey	Bay City Rollers	28	2
10/12/70	11/23/70	Mongoose	Elephant's Memory	5	11
6/2/73	7/14/73	Monster Mash	Bobby "Boris" Pickett & the Crypt-Kickers	2	14
10/19/70	11/30/70	Montego Bay	Bobby Bloom	2	14
3/21/68	5/9/68	Mony Mony	Tommy James & the Shondells	1	11
6/4/69	6/18/69	Moody Woman	Jerry Butler	18	3

Debut	Peak	Title	Artist	Pos	Wks
6/17/71	8/12/71	Moon Shadow	Cat Stevens	7	12
6/25/69	7/16/69	More And More	Blood, Sweat & Tears	13	4
6/2/66	6/30/66	More I See You, The	Chris Montez	13	7
5/21/69	5/21/69	More Today Than Yesterday	Spiral Starecase	30	1
7/5/75	8/2/75	Mornin' Beautiful	Tony Orlando & Dawn	15	9
6/30/73	8/25/73	Morning After, The	Maureen McGovern	1	15
4/30/69	5/28/69	Morning Girl	Neon Philharmonic	4	8
4/13/72	6/1/72	Morning Has Broken	Cat Stevens	1	11
7/13/70	8/17/70	Morning Much Better	Ten Wheel Drive with Genya Ravan	16	8
12/28/74	2/1/75	Morning Side Of The Mountain	Donny & Marie Osmond	7	10
3/30/67	3/30/67	Morningtown Ride	Seekers	25	1
11/24/73	1/26/74	Most Beautiful Girl, The	Charlie Rich	5	15
1/11/71	1/25/71	Most Of All	B.J. Thomas	30	3
1/25/71	2/1/71	Mother	John Lennon	22	3
2/10/72	3/30/72	Mother And Child Reunion	Paul Simon	2	12
7/15/71	8/26/71	Mother Freedom	Bread	12	10
6/25/69	7/16/69	Mother Popcorn (You Got To Have A Mother For Me) Part I	James Brown	9	7
7/14/66	8/4/66	Mothers Little Helper	Rolling Stones	11	5
7/22/72	9/16/72	Motorcycle Mama	Sailcat	8	12
2/8/75	3/15/75	Movin' On	Bad Company	13	9
6/24/71	8/5/71	Mr. Big Stuff	Jean Knight	3	11
2/22/71	3/11/71	Mr. Bojangles	Nitty Gritty Dirt Band	28	4
9/15/66	9/29/66	Mr. Dieingly Sad	Critters	12	6
2/2/67	2/2/67	Mr. Farmer	Seeds	pr	1
9/6/75	10/4/75	Mr. Jaws	Dickie Goodman	5	10
3/5/69	4/23/69	Mr. Sun, Mr. Moon	Paul Revere & the Raiders featuring Mark Lindsay	3	10
3/16/67	4/6/67	Mr. Unreliable	Cryan' Shames	12	8
6/18/69	7/2/69	Mrs. Robinson	Booker T. & the MG's	22	4
4/18/68	6/6/68	Mrs. Robinson	Simon & Garfunkel	2	11
7/14/66	7/14/66	(I Washed My Hands In) Muddy Water	Johnny Rivers	xx	1
9/7/67	9/7/67	Museum	Herman's Hermits	28	2

Debut	Peak	Title	Artist	Pos	Wks
1/19/67	2/16/67	Music To Watch Girls By	Bob Crewe Generation	13	5
4/20/67	5/11/67	Music To Watch Girls By	Andy Williams	17	4
11/2/74	12/21/74	Must Of Got Lost	J. Geils Band	16	12
12/30/65	1/13/66	Must To Avoid, A	Herman's Hermits	5	6
5/11/67	5/11/67	My Babe	Ronnie Dove	27	1
4/20/70	6/8/70	My Baby Loves Lovin'	White Plains	1	15
3/23/67	3/23/67	My Back Pages	Byrds	pr	1
6/11/69	8/6/69	My Cherie Amour	Stevie Wonder	5	10
2/23/67	3/23/67	My Cup Runneth Over	Ed Ames	14	5
9/16/72	10/7/72	My Ding-A-Ling	Chuck Berry	1	8
1/18/75	3/22/75	My Eyes Adored You	Frankie Valli	1	17
1/20/66	1/20/66	My Generation	Who	pr	1
7/13/67	7/13/67	My Girl	Rolling Stones	pr	1
5/4/74	6/22/74	My Girl Bill	Jim Stafford	8	13
4/11/68	5/23/68	My Girl/Hey Girl	Bobby Vee	6	7
5/18/67	6/1/67	My Girl Josephine	Jerry Jaye	22	3
7/28/66	8/18/66	My Heart's Symphony	Gary Lewis & the Playboys	xx	3
5/5/66	6/2/66	My Little Red Book	Love	xx	3
11/29/75	1/24/76	My Little Town	Simon & Garfunkel	6	13
1/20/66	2/10/66	My Love	Petula Clark	11	7
5/5/73	6/23/73	My Love	Paul McCartney	1	14
7/6/67	7/27/67	My Mammy	Happenings	17	6
8/11/73	10/6/73	My Maria	B.W. Stevenson	3	13
6/22/70	7/6/70	My Marie	Engelbert Humperdinck	31	4
10/19/74	11/30/74	My Melody Of Love	Bobby Vinton	1	15
6/25/69	7/16/69	My Pledge Of Love	Joe Jeffrey Group	15	5
9/5/68	10/3/68	My Special Angel	Vogues	8	7
11/23/70	12/7/70	My Sweet Lord	George Harrison	1	10
2/26/69	3/19/69	My Whole World Ended (The Moment You Left Me)	David Ruffin	9	5
1/20/72	3/9/72	My World	Bee Gees	7	11
7/13/67	7/27/67	My World Fell Down	Sagittarius	19	4
1/13/66	2/17/66	My World Is Empty Without You	Supremes	17	5
1/12/70	1/12/70	Na Na Hey Hey Kiss Him Goodbye	Steam	19	2

Debut	Peak	Title	Artist	Pos	Wks
3/3/73	4/7/73	Names, Tags, Numbers & Labels	Association	12	8
12/22/66	1/5/67	Nashville Cats	Lovin' Spoonful	16	5
5/20/71	7/1/71	Nathan Jones	Supremes	5	11
6/9/73	7/14/73	Natural High	Bloodstone	18	10
9/28/67	11/2/67	Natural Woman (You Make Me Feel Like), A	Aretha Franklin	18	5
8/17/70	8/31/70	Neanderthal Man	Hotlegs	5	8
8/24/74	10/5/74	Need To Be, The	Jim Weatherly	12	11
3/10/73	4/14/73	Neither One Of Us (Wants To Be The First To Say Goodbye)	Gladys Knight & the Pips	13	9
11/23/67	12/28/67	Neon Rainbow	Box Tops	8	7
1/11/75	2/22/75	Never Can Say Goodbye	Gloria Gaynor	2	12
3/25/71	5/13/71	Never Can Say Goodbye	Jackson 5	2	12
6/3/71	8/12/71	Never Ending Song Of Love	Delaney & Bonnie & Friends	1	15
6/20/68	7/11/68	Never Give You Up	Jerry Butler	17	5
8/31/67	10/5/67	Never My Love	Association	2	10
9/7/74	10/12/74	Never My Love	Blue Swede	11	10
10/14/71	11/11/71	Never My Love	5th Dimension	23	5
12/15/73	2/9/74	Never, Never Gonna Give Ya Up	Barry White	5	13
12/28/67	12/28/67	New Orleans	Neil Diamond	pr	1
6/1/67	6/29/67	New York Mining Disaster 1941	Bee Gees	21	5
9/15/66	9/15/66	Next Time You See Me	Robbs	pr	1
4/20/72	6/15/72	Nice To Be With You	Gallery	1	15
7/6/74	8/24/74	Night Chicago Died, The	Paper Lace	1	15
3/24/73	4/21/73	Night The Lights Went Out In Georgia, The	Vicki Lawrence	1	11
8/12/71	9/23/71	Night They Drove Old Dixie Down, The	Joan Baez	2	11
1/20/66	1/20/66	Night Time	Strangeloves	pr	1
9/9/72	11/4/72	Nights In White Satin	Moody Blues	1	13
10/4/75	11/29/75	Nights On Broadway	Bee Gees	4	17
11/17/66	11/17/66	Nineteen Days	Dave Clark Five	xx	3
12/14/70	1/18/71	1900 Yesterday	Liz Damon's Orient Express	9	8
2/24/66	3/10/66	19th Nervous Breakdown	Rolling Stones	6	7

Debut	Peak	Title	Artist	Pos	Wks
12/22/66	1/19/67	98.6	Keith	14	7
9/15/66	10/20/66	96 Tears	? & the Mysterians	1	10
8/6/69	8/27/69	Nitty Gritty, The	Gladys Knight & the Pips	21	4
12/2/72	1/13/73	No	Bulldog	17	9
2/9/67	3/2/67	No Fair At All	Association	18	6
2/15/71	4/22/71	No Love At All	B.J. Thomas	15	11
11/9/70	12/14/70	No Matter What	Badfinger	10	10
1/13/66	1/27/66	No Matter What Shape (Your Stomach's In)	T-Bones	5	5
6/4/69	6/11/69	No Matter What Sign You Are	Diana Ross & the Supremes	21	4
4/28/73	6/30/73	No More Mr. Nice Guy	Alice Cooper	6	12
2/22/75	4/26/75	No No Song	Ringo Starr	3	15
3/5/69	3/12/69	No, Not Much	Vogues	11	3
9/15/66	9/15/66	No Salt On Her Tail	Mamas & the Papas	pr	1
3/23/70	4/20/70	No Sugar Tonight	Guess Who	1	12
1/12/70	2/2/70	No Time	Guess Who	1	9
12/5/68	12/5/68	Nobody	Three Dog Night	28	1
1/18/68	2/15/68	Nobody But Me	Human Beinz	3	8
12/29/66	1/26/67	(We Ain't Got) Nothin' Yet	Blues Magoos	5	9
1/29/69	6/4/69	Nothing But A Heartache	Flirtations	21	9
8/17/74	10/5/74	Nothing From Nothing	Billy Preston	2	16
4/6/70	4/27/70	Nothing Succeeds Like Success	Bill Deal & the Rhondels	16	5
11/18/71	1/13/72	Nothing To Hide	Tommy James	2	11
3/3/66	3/31/66	Nowhere Man	Beatles	4	7
1/11/75	3/1/75	#9 Dream	John Lennon	13	10
1/22/69	1/29/69	Ob-La-Di, Ob-La-Da	Arthur Conley	25	2
8/17/67	9/7/67	Ode To Billie Joe	Bobbie Gentry	1	9
12/16/72	2/10/73	Oh, Babe, What Would You Say	Hurricane Smith	17	11
4/27/72	6/8/72	Oh Girl	Chi-Lites	5	12
4/23/69	5/21/69	Oh Happy Day	Edwin Hawkins' Singers featuring Dorothy Combs Morrison	4	7
6/9/66	6/30/66	Oh How Happy	Shades Of Blue	18	5
2/9/70	3/2/70	Oh Me Oh My I'm A Fool For You Baby	Lulu	15	8

Debut	Peak	Title	Artist	Pos	Wks
3/9/74	4/13/74	Oh My My	Ringo Starr	13	12
3/16/67	3/16/67	Oh That's Good, No That's Bad	Sam the Sham & the Pharaohs	pr	1
5/4/74	6/1/74	Oh Very Young	Cat Stevens	17	11
9/3/69	9/3/69	Oh, What A Night	Dells	28	3
3/1/71	3/11/71	Oh Woman Oh Why	Paul McCartney	22	2
5/26/66	6/16/66	Oh Yeah	Shadows Of Knight	15	6
11/23/67	11/23/67	Okolona River Bottom Band	Bobbie Gentry	pr	1
6/4/69	7/16/69	Old Brown Shoe	Beatles	8	7
5/17/75	6/14/75	Old Days	Chicago	9	12
10/14/71	12/9/71	Old Fashioned Love Song, An	Three Dog Night	3	12
3/16/67	4/20/67	On A Carousel	Hollies	4	9
7/13/74	8/24/74	On And On	Gladys Knight & the Pips	7	12
9/5/68	10/3/68	On The Road Again	Canned Heat	6	6
3/1/75	4/12/75	Once You Get Started	Rufus featuring Chaka Khan	17	9
5/28/69	7/2/69	One	Three Dog Night	1	10
1/4/71	2/1/71	One Bad Apple	Osmonds	1	9
10/14/71	10/28/71	One Fine Morning	Lighthouse	23	5
11/23/70	12/14/70	One Less Bell To Answer	5th Dimension	2	10
11/9/70	12/7/70	One Man Band	Three Dog Night	19	7
2/17/73	4/7/73	One Man Band (Plays All Alone)	Ronnie Dyson	11	10
11/9/74	1/18/75	One Man Woman/One Woman Man	Paul Anka with Odia Coates	5	16
2/17/66	2/17/66	One More Heartache	Marvin Gaye	pr	1
5/5/73	7/7/73	One Of A Kind (Love Affair)	Spinners	9	12
5/24/75	7/26/75	One Of These Nights	Eagles	3	17
12/15/73	1/26/74	One Tin Soldier, The Legend Of Billy Jack	Coven	1	12
3/11/71	3/11/71	One Toke Over The Line	Brewer & Shipley	36	1
3/10/66	4/7/66	One Track Mind	Knickerbockers	xx	2
12/16/65	12/16/65	1-2-3	Len Barry	6	3
7/25/68	9/5/68	1, 2, 3, Red Light	1910 Fruitgum Co.	1	10
6/15/67	6/15/67	Only All The Time	Barbara Lewis	pr	1
1/31/76	2/21/76	Only Sixteen	Dr. Hook	21	4

Debut	Peak	Title	Artist	Pos	Wks
3/12/69	4/16/69	Only The Strong Survive	Jerry Butler	8	7
4/26/75	6/14/75	Only Women	Alice Cooper	6	14
5/3/75	6/14/75	Only Yesterday	Carpenters	2	16
12/14/74	1/25/75	Only You	Ringo Starr	6	10
9/16/71	11/11/71	Only You Know And I Know	Delaney & Bonnie	6	11
5/18/67	6/1/67	Oogum Boogum Song, The	Brenton Wood	19	4
2/2/67	2/2/67	Ooh Baby	Bo Diddley	xx	1
10/6/73	12/1/73	Ooh Baby	Gilbert O'Sullivan	6	13
6/8/70	7/13/70	O-o-h Child	Five Stairsteps	2	14
11/9/67	11/30/67	Open Letter To My Teenage Son, An	Victor Lundberg	9	4
7/28/66	7/28/66	Open The Door To Your Heart	Darrell Banks	xx	1
11/1/75	11/22/75	Operator	Manhattan Transfer	16	9
11/4/72	12/16/72	Operator (That's Not The Way It Feels)	Jim Croce	7	11
6/2/66	6/2/66	Opus 17 (Don't You Worry 'Bout Me)	Four Seasons	xx	1
12/28/67	1/4/68	Other Man's Grass Is Always Greener, The	Petula Clark	25	2
8/31/70	9/28/70	Our World	Blue Mink	19	7
8/10/67	8/17/67	Out & About	Tommy Boyce & Bobby Hart	29	3
8/24/70	9/28/70	Out In The Country	Three Dog Night	10	11
11/9/67	11/30/67	Out Of The Blue	Tommy James & the Shondells	19	4
5/25/72	6/29/72	Outa-Space	Billy Preston	1	11
7/14/66	7/14/66	Outside Chance	Turtles	pr	1
3/17/66	3/17/66	Outside The Gates Of Heaven	Lou Christie	xx	3
12/16/65	12/16/65	Over And Over	Dave Clark Five	4	5
7/15/71	7/29/71	Over And Over	Delfonics	30	4
1/17/76	2/21/76	Over My Head	Fleetwood Mac	8	6
6/9/73	7/14/73	Over The Hills And Far Away	Led Zeppelin	17	7
7/14/66	8/4/66	Over Under Sideways Down	Yardbirds	15	7
9/19/68	10/24/68	Over You	Gary Puckett & the Union Gap	2	8

Debut	Peak	Title	Artist	Pos	Wks
3/1/71	4/8/71	Oye Como Va	Santana	10	8
5/19/66	6/2/66	Paint It, Black	Rolling Stones	1	8
9/29/66	11/17/66	(You Don't Have To) Paint Me A Picture	Gary Lewis & the Playboys	18	6
11/3/73	12/29/73	Painted Ladies	Ian Thomas	4	13
1/17/76	2/7/76	Paloma Blanca	George Baker Selection	29	5
11/17/66	11/17/66	Pandora's Golden Heebie Jeebies	Association	pr	1
10/28/72	12/9/72	Papa Was A Rollin' Stone	Temptations	1	14
1/8/69	1/8/69	Papa's Got A Brand New Bag	Otis Redding	27	2
11/16/67	11/30/67	Paper Cup	5th Dimension	27	4
9/29/73	11/10/73	Paper Roses	Marie Osmond	8	13
6/2/66	6/30/66	Paperback Writer	Beatles	2	8
1/25/75	3/15/75	Part Of The Plan	Dan Fogelberg	10	11
7/27/70	9/7/70	Patches	Clarence Carter	4	14
5/18/67	6/22/67	Pay You Back With Interest	Hollies	13	6
11/9/67	12/14/67	Peace Of Mind	Paul Revere & the Raiders featuring Mark Lindsay	23	4
9/23/71	11/18/71	Peace Train	Cat Stevens	1	13
3/3/73	4/14/73	Peaceful	Helen Reddy	2	12
1/20/73	2/17/73	Peaceful Easy Feeling	Eagles	22	7
6/8/70	7/13/70	Pearl	Tommy Roe	17	10
2/16/67	3/23/67	Penny Lane	Beatles	4	9
9/21/67	10/26/67	People Are Strange	Doors	20	5
7/18/68	8/29/68	People Got To Be Free	Rascals	1	10
7/11/68	7/11/68	People Sure Act Funny	Arthur Conley	28	1
3/15/75	4/26/75	Philadelphia Freedom	Elton John Band	1	17
3/3/66	3/17/66	Phoenix Love Theme (Senza Fine), The	Brass Ring	19	3
10/13/73	12/1/73	Photograph	Ringo Starr	1	12
1/11/75	3/8/75	Pick Up The Pieces	AWB	3	13
1/11/68	1/11/68	Pick Up The Pieces	Carla Thomas	pr	1
6/13/68	7/4/68	Pictures Of Matchstick Men	Status Quo	2	8
10/17/68	10/31/68	Piece Of My Heart	Big Brother & the Holding Company	23	3
9/2/72	10/14/72	Piece Of Paper, A	Gladstone	22	8

Debut	Peak	Title	Artist	Pos	Wks
12/9/72	2/3/73	Pieces Of April	Three Dog Night	2	12
6/16/66	7/14/66	Pied Piper, The	Crispian St. Peters	3	10
4/14/73	6/2/73	Pillow Talk	Sylvia	1	12
4/14/66	4/14/66	Pin The Tail On The Donkey	Paul Peek	pr	1
4/2/69	5/14/69	Pinball Wizard	Who	5	9
11/3/66	11/17/66	Pipeline	Chantay's	19	3
11/17/66	11/17/66	Place In The Sun, A	Stevie Wonder	pr	1
5/25/67	5/25/67	Plastic Man	Sonny & Cher	pr	1
8/26/72	10/7/72	Play Me	Neil Diamond	4	11
11/23/74	12/21/74	Play Something Sweet (Brickyard Blues)	Three Dog Night	20	8
7/7/73	7/28/73	Playground In My Mind	Clint Holmes	2	10
7/13/67	8/17/67	Pleasant Valley Sunday	Monkees	2	9
12/1/66	12/1/66	Please Don't Ever Leave Me	Cyrkle	xx	4
10/26/67	11/23/67	Please Love Me Forever	Bobby Vinton	6	7
6/21/75	8/2/75	Please Mr. Please	Olivia Newton-John	2	13
12/21/74	2/1/75	Please Mr. Postman	Carpenters	1	13
8/15/68	9/5/68	Please Return Your Love To Me	Temptations	19	5
6/16/66	6/16/66	Please Tell Me Why	Dave Clark Five	xx	4
2/22/75	3/29/75	Poetry Man	Phoebe Snow	16	10
7/2/69	7/30/69	Polk Salad Annie	Tony Joe White	4	7
9/19/68	10/3/68	Poor Baby	Cowsills	20	4
9/8/66	11/17/66	Poor Side Of Town	Johnny Rivers	4	12
8/26/72	9/23/72	Pop That Thang	Isley Brothers	15	8
9/2/72	10/14/72	Popcorn	Hot Butter	8	11
5/26/66	7/21/66	Popsicle	Jan & Dean	20	5
8/5/72	9/16/72	Power Of Love	Joe Simon	15	8
5/6/71	6/3/71	Power To The People	John Lennon & the Plastic Ono Band	8	8
12/30/71	2/3/72	Precious And Few	Climax	4	9
1/25/71	2/1/71	Precious, Precious	Jackie Moore	35	2
2/9/67	3/2/67	Pretty Ballerina	Left Banke	14	5
7/7/66	7/14/66	Pretty Flamingo	Manfred Mann	15	4
12/28/74	1/25/75	Promised Land	Elvis Presley	16	7
11/21/68	12/5/68	Promises, Promises	Dionne Warwick	20	5

Debut	Peak	Title	Artist	Pos	Wks
2/5/69	3/19/69	Proud Mary	Creedence Clearwater Revival	4	9
1/25/71	3/11/71	Proud Mary	Ike & Tina Turner	2	10
1/12/70	2/9/70	Psychedelic Shack	Temptations	3	11
9/29/66	10/27/66	Psychotic Reaction	Count Five	9	7
4/13/70	5/11/70	Puppet Man	5th Dimension	15	7
5/20/71	6/17/71	Puppet Man	Tom Jones	8	8
2/17/72	3/30/72	Puppy Love	Donny Osmond	1	12
10/5/67	11/16/67	Purple Haze	Jimi Hendrix Experience	5	8
1/12/67	2/9/67	Pushin' Too Hard	Seeds	2	9
7/2/69	8/13/69	Put A Little Love In Your Heart	Jackie DeShannon	7	9
8/12/72	9/9/72	Put It Where You Want It	Crusaders	21	6
3/25/71	5/13/71	Put Your Hand In The Hand	Ocean	3	11
7/2/69	7/23/69	Quentin's Theme	Charles Randolph Grean Sounde	8	7
5/11/70	6/15/70	Question	Moody Blues	8	12
2/15/68	3/21/68	Question Of Temperature, A	Balloon Farm	11	6
11/7/68	12/5/68	Quick Joey Small (Run Joey Run)	Kasenetz-Katz Singing Orchestral Circus	10	6
5/19/66	6/9/66	Race With The Wind	Robbs	xx	5
6/29/74	8/10/74	Radar Love	Golden Earring	4	12
6/2/66	6/30/66	Rain	Beatles	2	8
10/27/66	11/3/66	Rain On The Roof	Lovin' Spoonful	13	6
10/12/67	11/16/67	Rain, The Park & Other Things, The	Cowsills	1	10
1/12/70	1/12/70	Raindrops Keep Fallin' On My Head	B.J. Thomas	2	9
8/25/66	8/25/66	Raining In My Heart	Legend	pr	1
4/14/66	5/12/66	Rainy Day Women #12 & 35	Bob Dylan	3	8
5/13/71	6/17/71	Rainy Days And Mondays	Carpenters	2	13
6/10/71	7/22/71	Rainy Jane	Davy Jones	7	11
1/19/70	2/23/70	Rainy Night In Georgia	Brook Benton	5	10
1/8/69	2/19/69	Ramblin' Gamblin' Man	Bob Seger System	1	11
8/18/73	10/20/73	Ramblin Man	Allman Brothers Band	3	14
1/19/70	2/23/70	Rapper, The	Jaggerz	2	12

Debut	Peak	Title	Artist	Pos	Wks
12/12/68	12/19/68	Ray Of Hope, A	Rascals	25	3
4/27/70	5/11/70	Reach Out And Touch (Somebody's Hand)	Diana Ross	29	8
9/15/66	11/10/66	Reach Out I'll Be There	Four Tops	1	12
4/22/71	6/10/71	Reach Out I'll Be There	Diana Ross	8	10
5/2/68	6/6/68	Reach Out Of The Darkness	Friend & Lover	4	8
4/25/68	5/16/68	Ready, Willing And Able	American Breed	27	4
7/2/69	7/30/69	Reconsider Me	Johnny Adams	23	5
12/23/65	12/23/65	Recovery	Fontella Bass	pr	1
1/4/68	1/4/68	Red, Green, Yellow And Blue	Dickey Lee	pr	1
6/9/66	7/21/66	Red Rubber Ball	Cyrkle	6	8
4/7/73	5/26/73	Reeling In The Years	Steely Dan	3	12
8/3/67	9/7/67	Reflections	Diana Ross & the Supremes	5	11
3/16/70	4/20/70	Reflections Of My Life	Marmalade	7	13
5/11/67	5/25/67	Release Me (And Let Me Love Again)	Engelbert Humperdinck	13	6
12/21/70	2/8/71	Remember Me	Diana Ross	4	10
4/7/66	4/7/66	Remember The Rain	Bob Lind	pr	1
4/19/75	5/31/75	Remember What I Told You To Forget	Tavares	19	9
8/2/75	9/6/75	Rendezvous	Hudson Brothers	14	9
1/31/76	2/21/76	Renegade	Michael Murphey	27	4
5/4/67	6/15/67	Respect	Aretha Franklin	7	9
11/18/71	1/13/72	Respect Yourself	Staple Singers	5	12
7/21/66	8/25/66	Respectable	Outsiders	11	7
7/22/71	9/2/71	Resurrection Shuffle	Ashton, Gardner & Dyke	8	10
3/2/67	3/23/67	Return Of The Red Baron, The	Royal Guardsmen	21	4
9/5/68	9/26/68	Revolution	Beatles	2	11
3/17/66	5/12/66	Rhapsody In The Rain	Lou Christie	14	10
7/5/75	9/6/75	Rhinestone Cowboy	Glen Campbell	1	21
5/4/70	6/15/70	Ride Captain Ride	Blues Image	3	14
1/12/67	1/12/67	Ride, Ride, Ride	Brenda Lee	pr	1
7/1/71	8/12/71	Riders On The Storm	Doors	2	11
2/21/76	2/21/76	Right Back Where We Started From	Maxine Nightingale	37	1

Debut	Peak	Title	Artist	Pos	Wks
4/29/71	6/10/71	Right On The Tip Of My Tongue	Brenda & the Tabulations	12	9
5/12/73	7/7/73	Right Place Wrong Time	Dr. John	3	14
4/21/73	6/16/73	Right Thing To Do, The	Carly Simon	1	13
6/8/74	7/27/74	Rikki Don't Lose That Number	Steely Dan	4	14
2/10/72	3/30/72	Ring The Living Bell	Melanie	3	11
7/22/71	8/26/71	Rings	Cymarron	3	10
12/7/70	1/11/71	River Deep—Mountain High	Supremes & the Four Tops	11	8
2/24/73	3/24/73	River Road	Uncle Dog	29	6
10/21/72	11/25/72	Roberta	Bones	19	7
7/6/72	9/2/72	Rock And Roll Part 2	Gary Glitter	1	13
11/29/75	2/14/76	Rock And Roll All Nite	Kiss	2	13
6/1/74	7/13/74	Rock And Roll Heaven	Righteous Brothers	12	12
2/23/74	3/16/74	Rock And Roll, Hoochie Koo	Rick Derringer	24	5
2/3/72	4/6/72	Rock And Roll Lullaby	B.J. Thomas	6	12
3/12/69	4/9/69	Rock Me	Steppenwolf	6	6
8/10/74	9/14/74	Rock Me Gently	Andy Kim	2	12
8/19/72	9/2/72	Rock Me On The Water	Jackson Browne	26	4
2/24/72	3/30/72	Rock Me On The Water	Linda Ronstadt	21	7
1/13/72	2/3/72	Rock 'N Roll	Detroit featuring Mitch Ryder	29	4
10/20/73	11/17/73	Rock 'N Roll (I Gave You The Best Years Of My Life)	Kevin Johnson	24	7
11/11/72	12/16/72	Rock 'N Roll Soul	Grand Funk Railroad	18	8
1/26/70	2/23/70	Rock Of All Ages	Badfinger	32	5
1/19/74	3/9/74	Rock On	David Essex	3	14
10/21/71	12/9/71	Rock Steady	Aretha Franklin	13	11
6/1/74	7/20/74	Rock The Boat	Hues Corporation	1	15
6/22/74	7/27/74	Rock Your Baby	George McCrae	1	13
7/19/75	8/23/75	Rockford Files, The	Mike Post	10	13
6/21/75	8/16/75	Rockin' Chair	Gwen McCrae	3	16
10/21/72	12/23/72	Rockin' Pneumonia— Boogie Woogie Flu	Johnny Rivers	2	15
3/2/72	4/13/72	Rockin' Robin	Michael Jackson	2	12

Debut	Peak	Title	Artist	Pos	Wks
12/1/73	1/26/74	Rockin' Roll Baby	Stylistics	12	13
1/20/73	3/10/73	Rocky Mountain High	John Denver	4	13
9/22/73	10/27/73	Rocky Mountain Way	Joe Walsh	22	8
7/29/71	9/16/71	Roll On	New Colony Six	10	12
2/1/75	3/22/75	Roll On Down The Highway	Bachman-Turner Overdrive	4	12
7/7/73	9/1/73	Roll Over Beethoven	Electric Light Orchestra	6	13
8/18/66	9/15/66	Roller Coaster	Ides Of March	xx	3
7/6/67	8/3/67	Romeo And Juliet	Michael & the Messengers	14	6
5/21/69	6/11/69	Romeo & Juliet, Love Theme From	Henry Mancini	1	10
12/14/70	1/25/71	Rose Garden	Lynn Anderson	21	7
5/4/67	5/4/67	Round Round	Jonathan King	pr	1
2/3/72	3/23/72	Roundabout	Yes	4	11
9/15/73	11/3/73	Rubber Bullets	10cc	7	13
8/24/70	9/14/70	Rubber Duckie	Ernie (Jim Henson)	7	7
10/1/69	10/8/69	Ruben James	Kenny Rogers & the First Edition	19	2
6/18/69	7/23/69	Ruby, Don't Take Your Love To Town	Kenny Rogers & the First Edition	2	7
1/19/67	2/16/67	Ruby Tuesday	Rolling Stones	1	10
3/12/69	3/26/69	Run Away Child, Running Wild	Temptations	10	4
8/2/75	9/13/75	Run Joey Run	David Geddes	7	12
3/9/72	5/11/72	Run Run Run	Jo Jo Gunne	2	14
8/17/67	8/31/67	Run, Run, Run	Third Rail	23	3
8/5/72	9/16/72	Run To Me	Bee Gees	16	8
10/17/68	11/21/68	Run To Me	Montanas	9	6
3/1/75	4/26/75	Runaway	Charlie Kulis	8	13
4/14/66	4/14/66	Running Round In Circles	Ivy League	pr	1
7/15/72	8/19/72	Runway, The	Grass Roots	10	8
8/29/68	9/5/68	Sally Had A Party	Flavor	27	2
6/15/67	7/13/67	San Francisco (Be Sure To Wear Flowers In Your Hair)	Scott McKenzie	4	9
9/19/68	10/10/68	San Francisco Girls (Return Of The Native)	Fever Tree	26	4

Debut	Peak	Title	Artist	Pos	Wks
1/13/66	2/3/66	Sandy	Ronny & the Daytonas	8	5
12/14/70	12/14/70	Santa Claus Is Comin' To Town	Jackson 5	xx	2
8/4/66	8/25/66	Satisfied With You	Dave Clark Five	xx	3
8/5/72	9/23/72	Saturday In The Park	Chicago	3	12
11/22/75	1/17/76	Saturday Night	Bay City Rollers	2	14
7/28/73	9/22/73	Saturday Night's Alright For Fighting	Elton John	4	13
2/9/67	2/9/67	Save Me	Dave Dee, Dozy, Beaky, Mick & Tich	pr	1
6/8/70	6/29/70	Save The Country	5th Dimension	19	6
1/26/70	2/9/70	Save The Country	Thelma Houston	23	4
4/27/74	5/25/74	Save The Last Dance For Me	DeFranco Family featuring Tony DeFranco	19	9
7/14/73	9/22/73	Say, Has Anybody Seen My Sweet Gypsy Rose	Dawn featuring Tony Orlando	8	13
7/14/66	8/18/66	Say I Am (What I Am)	Tommy James & the Shondells	3	9
10/10/68	10/24/68	Say It Loud—I'm Black And I'm Proud (Part 1)	James Brown	21	3
11/28/68	12/12/68	Scarborough Fair	Sergio Mendes & Brasil '66	21	5
2/15/68	4/11/68	Scarborough Fair (/Canticle)	Simon & Garfunkel	20	4
6/15/72	8/5/72	School's Out	Alice Cooper	2	11
12/2/71	1/13/72	Scorpio	Dennis Coffey & the Detroit Guitar Band	4	11
7/11/68	8/8/68	Sealed With A Kiss	Gary Lewis & the Playboys	7	8
3/23/74	5/18/74	(I've Been) Searchin' So Long	Chicago	7	15
8/18/66	8/18/66	Searching For My Love	Bobby Moore & the Rhythm Aces	xx	2
1/12/74	3/2/74	Seasons In The Sun	Terry Jacks	1	16
4/30/69	5/21/69	Seattle	Perry Como	21	5
2/10/66	2/10/66	Second Hand Rose	Barbra Streisand	20	1
3/31/66	4/21/66	Secret Agent Man	Johnny Rivers	2	8
11/22/75	12/6/75	Secret Love	Freddy Fender	26	6
9/29/66	11/17/66	Secret Love	Billy Stewart	20	3
5/28/69	6/4/69	See	Rascals	19	4
11/2/70	11/30/70	See Me, Feel Me	Who	3	10

Debut	Peak	Title	Artist	Pos	Wks
11/28/68	12/12/68	See Saw	Aretha Franklin	24	4
10/20/66	11/3/66	See See Rider	Eric Burdon & the Animals	16	6
8/4/66	9/8/66	See You In September	Happenings	4	9
4/13/70	5/11/70	Seeker, The	Who	16	7
1/13/66	1/13/66	Set You Free This Time	Byrds	pr	1
5/18/67	6/8/67	7 Rooms Of Gloom	Four Tops	24	4
2/9/74	3/16/74	Sexy Mama	Moments	11	10
11/16/74	12/21/74	Sha-La-La (Make Me Happy)	Al Green	12	10
8/25/73	10/6/73	Shady Lady	Shepstone & Dibbens	19	8
10/21/71	11/25/71	Shaft, Theme From	Isaac Hayes	1	11
10/31/68	12/19/68	Shake	Shadows Of Knight	10	9
4/13/67	4/13/67	Shake A Tail Feather	James & Bobby Purify	pr	1
4/27/67	5/11/67	Shake Hands And Walk Away Cryin'	Lou Christie	22	4
2/17/66	2/17/66	Shake Me, Wake Me (When It's Over)	Four Tops	pr	1
5/26/73	7/21/73	Shambala	Three Dog Night	7	15
10/31/68	11/28/68	Shame, Shame	Magic Lanterns	4	6
3/29/75	5/3/75	Shame, Shame, Shame	Shirley (And Company)	4	11
8/29/68	10/3/68	Shape Of Things To Come	Max Frost & the Troopers	3	9
3/10/66	3/31/66	Shapes Of Things	Yardbirds	3	9
11/23/70	12/14/70	Share The Land	Guess Who	12	8
1/12/70	1/12/70	She	Tommy James & the Shondells	30	2
1/12/70	1/26/70	She Came In Through The Bathroom Window	Joe Cocker	32	4
12/1/66	12/1/66	(When She Needs Good Lovin') She Comes To Me	Chicago Loop	xx	1
11/16/67	11/23/67	She Is Still A Mystery	Lovin' Spoonful	22	2
1/26/70	2/23/70	She Let Her Hair Down (Early In The Morning)	Don Young	17	7
5/11/67	6/22/67	She'd Rather Be With Me	Turtles	4	7
3/7/68	5/9/68	Sherry Don't Go	Lettermen	27	3
6/6/68	6/27/68	She's A Heartbreaker	Gene Pitney	7	8
2/8/71	4/1/71	She's A Lady	Tom Jones	1	14
12/30/65	1/20/66	She's Just My Style	Gary Lewis & the Playboys	9	5
3/28/68	5/23/68	She's Lookin' Good	Wilson Pickett	16	8

Debut	Peak	Title	Artist	Pos	Wks
10/26/67	12/21/67	She's My Girl	Turtles	11	9
1/29/69	2/5/69	She's Not There	Road	22	2
1/26/70	4/6/70	Shilo	Neil Diamond	12	8
5/10/75	6/21/75	Shining Star	Earth, Wind & Fire	6	14
5/10/75	5/24/75	Shoeshine Boy	Eddie Kendricks	29	5
4/18/68	6/6/68	Shoo-Be-Doo-Be-Doo-Da-Day	Stevie Wonder	8	8
11/10/73	1/12/74	Show And Tell	Al Wilson	5	14
3/16/74	5/18/74	Show Must Go On, The	Three Dog Night	3	15
7/6/74	8/3/74	Sideshow	Blue Magic	15	9
3/17/66	3/31/66	Sign Of The Times, A	Petula Clark	xx	6
7/6/70	8/10/70	Signed, Sealed, Delivered I'm Yours	Stevie Wonder	4	12
7/20/67	8/24/67	Silence Is Golden	Tremeloes	11	7
7/13/70	8/10/70	Silver Bird	Mark Lindsay	19	9
1/4/71	1/11/71	Silver Moon	Michael Nesmith & the First National Band	31	3
2/15/68	3/14/68	Simon Says	1910 Fruitgum Co.	2	7
3/16/74	4/13/74	Simone	Henry Gross	25	7
3/23/72	4/27/72	Simple Song Of Freedom	Buckwheat	11	9
2/15/68	3/28/68	(Sweet Sweet Baby) Since You've Been Gone	Aretha Franklin	8	8
3/17/73	5/12/73	Sing	Carpenters	1	13
12/27/75	1/31/76	Sing A Song	Earth, Wind & Fire	14	9
12/8/66	12/8/66	Single Girl	Sandy Posey	xx	4
5/10/75	6/21/75	Sister Golden Hair	America	1	17
12/15/73	1/19/74	Sister Mary Elephant (Shudd-Up!)	Cheech & Chong	2	11
3/7/68	3/7/68	Sit With The Guru	Strawberry Alarm Clock	pr	1
11/25/72	1/27/73	Sitting	Cat Stevens	6	14
8/29/68	9/5/68	Six Man Band	Association	25	2
4/20/67	6/1/67	Six O'Clock	Lovin' Spoonful	17	5
3/10/66	3/10/66	634-5789 (Soulsville, U.S.A.)	Wilson Pickett	xx	3
9/21/74	10/26/74	Skin Tight	Ohio Players	15	10
11/9/67	12/7/67	Skinny Legs And All	Joe Tex	10	7
12/28/67	1/25/68	Skip A Rope	Henson Cargill	14	6
10/25/75	12/20/75	Sky High	Jigsaw	2	16

Debut	Peak	Title	Artist	Pos	Wks
7/18/68	8/8/68	Sky Pilot (Part One)	Eric Burdon & the Animals	11	5
12/22/66	12/22/66	Sleep In Heavenly Peace (Silent Night)	Barbra Streisand	pr	1
4/18/68	4/18/68	Sleepy Joe	Herman's Hermits	pr	1
8/1/68	8/29/68	Slip Away	Clarence Carter	12	5
3/24/66	5/12/66	Sloop John B	Beach Boys	10	8
2/21/76	2/21/76	Slow Ride	Foghat	35	1
6/22/70	7/20/70	Sly, Slick, And The Wicked, The	Lost Generation	19	8
7/6/72	8/12/72	Small Beginnings	Flash	23	7
7/8/71	8/19/71	Smiling Faces Sometimes	Undisputed Truth	1	11
1/13/73	2/24/73	Smoke Gets In Your Eyes	Blue Haze	11	10
6/2/73	8/4/73	Smoke On The Water	Deep Purple	3	15
11/10/73	1/12/74	Smokin' In The Boy's Room	Brownsville Station	2	14
10/3/68	10/3/68	Snake, The	Al Wilson	24	1
12/15/66	12/29/66	Snoopy vs. The Red Baron	Royal Guardsmen	1	9
12/7/67	12/21/67	Snoopy's Christmas	Royal Guardsmen	6	5
9/21/70	10/5/70	Snowbird	Anne Murray	17	6
7/14/66	8/4/66	(You Make Me Feel) So Good	McCoys	xx	2
5/21/69	5/21/69	So I Can Love You	Emotions	27	1
5/4/70	5/18/70	So Much Love	Faith Hope & Charity	32	3
6/2/73	7/14/73	So Very Hard To Go	Tower Of Power	24	9
11/9/74	12/7/74	So You Are A Star	Hudson Brothers	16	8
1/19/67	2/23/67	So You Want To Be A Rock 'N' Roll Star	Byrds	22	3
7/20/67	8/17/67	Society's Child (Baby I've Been Thinking)	Janis Ian	12	7
2/2/67	3/9/67	Sock It To Me-Baby	Mitch Ryder & the Detroit Wheels	9	8
12/30/71	2/24/72	Softly Whispering I Love You	English Congregation	3	12
4/21/66	4/21/66	Solitary Man	Neil Diamond	pr	1
8/3/70	9/7/70	Solitary Man	Neil Diamond	2	12
12/21/74	2/22/75	Some Kind Of Wonderful	Grand Funk	5	14
7/4/68	7/4/68	Some Things You Never Get Used To	Diana Ross & the Supremes	26	1
7/11/68	8/8/68	Somebody Cares	Tommy James & the Shondells	20	4

Debut	Peak	Title	Artist	Pos	Wks
7/20/67	8/10/67	Somebody Help Me	Spencer Davis Group	20	4
4/27/67	5/25/67	Somebody To Love	Jefferson Airplane	1	9
9/21/70	10/26/70	Somebody's Been Sleeping	100 Proof Aged In Soul	10	10
1/12/70	1/12/70	Someday We'll Be Together	Diana Ross & the Supremes	10	5
7/5/75	8/30/75	Someone Saved My Life Tonight	Elton John	1	16
3/9/72	4/20/72	Someone, Sometime	New Colony Six	19	9
3/23/67	5/11/67	Somethin' Stupid	Nancy Sinatra & Frank Sinatra	1	10
3/23/70	4/20/70	Something's Burning	Kenny Rogers & the First Edition	2	11
10/28/72	12/16/72	Something's Wrong With Me	Austin Roberts	12	12
7/28/66	7/28/66	Somewhere, My Love	Ray Conniff	xx	1
12/12/68	1/22/69	Son-Of-A Preacher Man	Dusty Springfield	9	8
2/24/72	4/20/72	Son Of My Father	Chicory	9	11
5/11/74	6/15/74	Son Of Sagittarius	Eddie Kendricks	21	9
5/25/70	6/29/70	Song Of Joy (Himno A La Alegria), A	Miguel Rios	12	11
4/27/72	6/22/72	Song Sung Blue	Neil Diamond	2	14
4/20/70	5/11/70	Soolaimón (African Trilogy II)	Neil Diamond	11	8
2/5/69	2/19/69	Sophisticated Cissy	Meters	27	3
4/23/69	4/30/69	Sorry Suzanne	Hollies	28	4
9/27/75	11/22/75	SOS	ABBA	4	17
3/10/66	5/5/66	(You're My) Soul And Inspiration	Righteous Brothers	8	12
7/16/69	9/3/69	Soul Deep	Box Tops	4	10
8/22/68	10/10/68	Soul Drippin'	Mauds	16	8
8/1/68	8/29/68	Soul-Limbo	Booker T. & the MG's	17	5
9/28/67	11/2/67	Soul Man	Sam & Dave	12	8
4/4/68	4/11/68	Soul Serenade	Willie Mitchell	25	2
8/10/70	8/24/70	Soul Shake	Delaney & Bonnie & Friends	27	4
1/22/69	1/22/69	Soul Sister, Brown Sugar	Sam & Dave	27	1
12/12/68	1/22/69	Soulful Strut	Young-Holt Unlimited	3	9
2/12/69	2/19/69	Soulshake	Peggy Scott & Jo Jo Benson	25	2
2/29/68	4/4/68	Sound Asleep	Turtles	20	3
5/4/67	6/15/67	Sound Of Love	Five Americans	17	7

Debut	Peak	Title	Artist	Pos	Wks
12/16/65	1/6/66	Sounds Of Silence, The	Simon & Garfunkel	1	10
2/8/75	3/15/75	South's Gonna Do It, The	Charlie Daniels Band	18	9
10/27/73	12/22/73	Space Race	Billy Preston	3	14
1/27/66	1/27/66	Spanish Eyes	Al Martino	20	1
7/29/71	9/9/71	Spanish Harlem	Aretha Franklin	3	10
8/5/72	8/26/72	Speak To The Sky	Rick Springfield	30	5
5/14/69	6/4/69	Special Delivery	1910 Fruitgum Co.	11	7
8/29/68	9/26/68	Special Occasion	Smokey Robinson & the Miracles	21	4
3/2/74	4/20/74	Spiders & Snakes	Jim Stafford	3	11
6/29/70	8/10/70	Spill The Wine	Eric Burdon & War	2	15
6/25/69	7/16/69	Spinning Wheel	Blood, Sweat & Tears	13	6
10/27/66	10/27/66	Spinout	Elvis Presley	xx	2
2/16/70	3/16/70	Spirit In The Sky	Norman Greenbaum	1	12
1/11/68	2/22/68	Spooky	Classics IV	2	9
1/17/76	2/21/76	Squeeze Box	Who	9	6
10/26/67	11/23/67	Stag-O-Lee	Wilson Pickett	23	6
8/12/71	9/30/71	Stagger Lee	Tommy Roe	9	11
4/5/75	5/3/75	Stand By Me	John Lennon	24	6
1/26/67	1/26/67	Stand By Me	Spyder Turner	xx	1
10/19/70	11/16/70	Stand By Your Man	Candi Staton	20	7
3/30/74	5/25/74	Standing At The End Of The Line	Lobo	12	13
12/8/66	1/26/67	Standing In The Shadows Of Love	Four Tops	10	10
4/6/74	6/1/74	Star Baby	Guess Who	3	16
9/23/72	10/21/72	Starting All Over Again	Mel & Tim	19	8
3/11/71	4/15/71	Stay Awhile	Bells	1	11
7/11/68	8/22/68	Stay In My Corner	Dells	15	7
12/23/71	2/3/72	Stay With Me	Faces	1	12
6/8/67	7/13/67	Step Out Of Your Mind	American Breed	10	7
10/5/74	11/2/74	Steppin' Out (Gonna Boogie Tonight)	Tony Orlando & Dawn	14	8
12/15/66	1/19/67	(I'm Not Your) Steppin' Stone	Monkees	1	6
9/9/71	10/14/71	Stick-Up	Honey Cone	9	8
10/19/70	11/23/70	Still Water (Love)	Four Tops	13	8

Debut	Peak	Title	Artist	Pos	Wks
3/10/73	4/21/73	Stir It Up	Johnny Nash	5	11
2/23/70	3/16/70	Stir It Up And Serve It	Tommy Roe	22	6
11/23/70	1/4/71	Stoned Love	Supremes	2	10
5/16/68	7/18/68	Stoned Soul Picnic	5th Dimension	2	10
11/4/71	12/9/71	Stones	Neil Diamond	7	9
1/4/71	1/25/71	Stoney End	Barbra Streisand	2	6
9/7/74	10/26/74	Stop And Smell The Roses	Mac Davis	3	14
9/15/66	9/15/66	Stop, Look And Listen	Chiffons	pr	1
11/3/66	11/24/66	Stop Stop Stop	Hollies	9	7
12/7/70	1/4/71	Stop The War Now	Edwin Starr	19	6
11/14/68	1/8/69	Stormy	Classics IV featuring Dennis Yost	4	10
8/26/71	10/7/71	Story In Your Eyes, The	Moody Blues	3	10
7/4/68	7/4/68	Story Of Rock And Roll, The	Turtles	29	1
11/28/68	12/12/68	Straight Life, The	Bobby Goldsboro	23	3
10/5/74	11/2/74	Straight Shootin' Woman	Steppenwolf	20	7
5/26/66	6/16/66	Strangers In The Night	Frank Sinatra	3	8
2/16/67	3/23/67	Strawberry Fields Forever	Beatles	4	9
4/20/74	5/18/74	Streak, The	Ray Stevens	1	12
3/10/73	4/28/73	Stuck In The Middle With You	Stealers Wheel	2	12
4/6/72	5/18/72	Suavecito	Malo	1	11
7/7/66	7/28/66	Sugar And Spice	Cryan' Shames	7	8
12/9/71	1/20/72	Sugar Daddy	Jackson 5	2	10
2/1/71	2/8/71	Sugar Mountain	Neil Young	34	3
9/17/69	10/8/69	Sugar On Sunday	Clique	21	4
8/6/69	9/3/69	Sugar, Sugar	Archies	1	10
11/24/66	12/15/66	Sugar Town	Nancy Sinatra	8	9
10/8/69	10/8/69	Suite: Judy Blue Eyes	Crosby, Stills & Nash	25	1
11/4/72	12/16/72	Summer Breeze	Seals & Crofts	2	12
7/7/66	8/4/66	Summer In The City	Lovin' Spoonful	1	11
12/21/67	1/18/68	Summer Rain	Johnny Rivers	9	7
9/22/66	9/29/66	Summer Samba (So Nice)	Walter Wanderley	20	3
6/10/71	7/22/71	Summer Sand	Dawn	13	11
7/22/72	8/26/72	Summer Sun	Jamestown Massacre	20	7

Debut	Peak	Title	Artist	Pos	Wks
9/29/66	9/29/66	Summer Wind	Frank Sinatra	xx	2
8/4/66	8/25/66	Summertime	Billy Stewart	15	5
3/14/68	4/25/68	Summertime Blues	Blue Cheer	5	9
5/5/66	5/26/66	Sun Ain't Gonna Shine (Anymore), The	Walker Brothers	14	4
12/16/65	12/16/65	Sunday And Me	Jay & the Americans	15	2
3/9/67	4/20/67	Sunday For Tea	Peter & Gordon	27	3
6/8/67	7/6/67	Sunday Will Never Be The Same	Spanky & Our Gang	16	7
5/4/74	6/29/74	Sundown	Gordon Lightfoot	1	17
7/28/66	8/18/66	Sunny	Bobby Hebb	4	9
6/16/66	9/15/66	Sunny Afternoon	Kinks	16	7
6/22/67	6/22/67	Sunrise Highway	Peter Anders	pr	1
11/18/71	12/30/71	Sunshine	Jonathan Edwards	1	12
6/1/67	6/8/67	Sunshine Girl	Parade	27	2
1/11/68	2/15/68	Sunshine Of Your Love	Cream	10	6
8/8/68	8/22/68	Sunshine Of Your Love	Cream	11	3
1/26/74	3/9/74	Sunshine On My Shoulders	John Denver	2	15
8/11/66	9/8/66	Sunshine Superman	Donovan	1	10
12/30/72	2/3/73	Superfly	Curtis Mayfield	11	10
3/22/75	4/12/75	Supernatural Thing—Part I	Ben E. King	29	5
9/9/71	10/21/71	Superstar	Carpenters	1	10
4/8/71	5/20/71	Superstar	Murray Head with the Trinidad Singers	5	10
11/25/71	12/23/71	Superstar (Remember How You Got Where You Are)	Temptations	14	8
12/16/72	2/3/73	Superstition	Stevie Wonder	3	12
7/27/74	8/31/74	Sure As I'm Sittin' Here	Three Dog Night	11	11
3/3/66	3/31/66	Sure Gonna Miss Her	Gary Lewis & the Playboys	13	5
4/25/68	4/25/68	Surprise, Surprise (I Need You)	Troggs	pr	1
11/23/67	1/18/68	Susan	Buckinghams	6	9
10/1/69	10/8/69	Suspicious Minds	Elvis Presley	12	2
11/2/67	11/2/67	Suzanne	Noel Harrison	30	1
9/19/68	10/17/68	Suzie Q. (Part One)	Creedence Clearwater Revival	10	6
1/24/76	2/21/76	S.W.A.T., Theme From	Rhythm Heritage	10	5

Debut	Peak	Title	Artist	Pos	Wks
6/28/75	8/2/75	Swearin' To God	Frankie Valli	11	11
4/8/71	5/27/71	Sweet And Innocent	Donny Osmond	1	13
10/31/68	11/14/68	Sweet Blindness	5th Dimension	18	4
7/9/69	8/13/69	Sweet Caroline (Good Times Never Seemed So Good)	Neil Diamond	2	9
7/28/73	9/29/73	Sweet Charlie Babe	Jackie Moore	13	13
4/9/69	5/14/69	Sweet Cherry Wine	Tommy James & the Shondells	21	5
8/26/71	10/7/71	Sweet City Woman	Stampeders	2	11
7/21/66	8/4/66	Sweet Dreams	Tommy McLain	16	4
7/8/71	8/12/71	Sweet Hitch-Hiker	Creedence Clearwater Revival	9	10
8/31/74	10/19/74	Sweet Home Alabama	Lynyrd Skynyrd	1	15
3/21/68	4/18/68	Sweet Inspiration	Sweet Inspirations	11	6
1/18/71	3/1/71	Sweet Mary	Wadsworth Mansion	2	11
6/30/66	8/4/66	Sweet Pea	Tommy Roe	10	8
4/13/67	5/11/67	Sweet Soul Music	Arthur Conley	4	9
11/25/72	1/20/73	Sweet Surrender	Bread	10	12
1/18/75	2/15/75	Sweet Surrender	John Denver	20	8
5/26/66	6/16/66	Sweet Talkin' Guy	Chiffons	18	5
2/21/76	2/21/76	Sweet Thing	Rufus featuring Chaka Khan	36	1
3/16/67	4/6/67	Sweets For My Sweet	Riddles	22	6
4/13/72	6/8/72	Sylvia's Mother	Dr. Hook & the Medicine Show	1	12
5/26/66	5/26/66	S.Y.S.L.J.F.M. (The Letter Song)	Joe Tex	xx	1
2/23/70	3/9/70	Take A Look Around	Smith	24	4
4/18/68	5/9/68	Take Good Care Of My Baby	Bobby Vinton	17	5
5/18/72	7/22/72	Take It Easy	Eagles	2	13
1/17/76	2/21/76	Take It To The Limit	Eagles	17	6
8/3/67	8/24/67	Take Me Back	Flock	17	3
11/7/68	11/14/68	Take Me For A Little While	Vanilla Fudge	26	2
1/6/66	1/6/66	Take Me For What I'm Worth	Searchers	pr	1
8/19/71	9/23/71	Take Me Girl, I'm Ready	Jr. Walker & the All Stars	15	8
7/1/71	8/19/71	Take Me Home, Country Roads	John Denver	2	12

Debut	Peak	Title	Artist	Pos	Wks
5/17/75	7/5/75	Take Me In Your Arms (Rock Me)	Doobie Brothers	4	15
4/11/68	4/18/68	Take Time To Know Her	Percy Sledge	24	4
6/15/74	8/10/74	Takin' Care Of Business	Bachman-Turner Overdrive	5	14
9/2/71	10/7/71	Talk It Over In The Morning	Anne Murray	25	6
11/24/66	12/8/66	Talk Talk	Music Machine	9	6
3/7/68	3/21/68	Tapioca Tundra	Monkees	1	7
12/16/65	12/16/65	Taste Of Honey	Herb Alpert & the Tijuana Brass	3	4
4/6/72	5/18/72	Taurus	Dennis Coffey & the Detroit Guitar Band	12	8
6/15/70	6/22/70	Teach Your Children	Crosby, Stills, Nash & Young	34	2
10/5/70	11/23/70	Tears Of A Clown, The	Smokey Robinson & the Miracles	1	15
4/28/73	5/19/73	Teddy Bear Song	Barbara Fairchild	28	5
12/22/73	2/9/74	Teenage Lament '74	Alice Cooper	9	12
10/12/67	10/12/67	Teenage Opera, Excerpt From A (Grocer Jack)	Keith West	pr	1
2/10/72	3/9/72	Tell 'Em Willie Boy's A'Comin'	Tommy James	25	7
11/17/73	12/29/73	Tell Her She's Lovely	El Chicano	20	9
12/22/66	1/19/67	Tell It Like It Is	Aaron Neville	9	8
12/8/66	2/2/67	Tell It To The Rain	Four Seasons	20	5
12/21/67	1/11/68	Tell Mama	Etta James	18	4
7/20/74	9/7/74	Tell Me Something Good	Rufus	3	13
3/23/70	3/30/70	Temma Harbour	Mary Hopkin	30	3
3/11/71	3/25/71	Temptation Eyes	Grass Roots	31	3
3/23/70	4/13/70	Tennessee Bird Walk	Jack Blanchard & Misty Morgan	20	6
5/3/75	6/14/75	Thank God I'm A Country Boy	John Denver	4	13
1/12/70	1/26/70	Thank You Falettinme Be Mice Elf Agin	Sly & the Family Stone	1	10
9/8/73	10/20/73	That Lady (Part 1)	Isley Brothers	10	10
12/1/66	1/5/67	That's Life	Frank Sinatra	15	6
11/8/75	12/13/75	That's The Way (I Like It)	KC & the Sunshine Band	1	15
5/6/71	6/10/71	That's The Way I've Always Heard It Should Be	Carly Simon	3	10
9/10/69	10/8/69	That's The Way Love Is	Marvin Gaye	9	5

Debut	Peak	Title	Artist	Pos	Wks
9/6/75	9/20/75	That's The Way Of The World	Earth, Wind & Fire	18	9
9/21/70	10/12/70	That's Where I Went Wrong	Poppy Family featuring Susan Jacks	9	9
8/17/74	10/12/74	Then Came You	Dionne Warwick & Spinners	3	14
2/2/67	2/23/67	Then You Can Tell Me Goodbye	Casinos	13	8
7/27/67	8/3/67	There Goes My Everything	Engelbert Humperdinck	26	2
1/18/68	2/1/68	There Is	Dells	16	5
9/7/67	9/21/67	There Is A Mountain	Donovan	22	3
1/18/68	2/1/68	There Was A Time	James Brown	14	5
4/6/67	4/6/67	There Was A Time	Trolls	pr	1
8/25/66	8/25/66	There Will Never Be Another You	Chris Montez	xx	4
2/16/67	3/9/67	There's A Kind Of Hush	Herman's Hermits	3	8
9/7/67	9/7/67	There's Always Me	Elvis Presley	pr	1
1/22/69	2/12/69	There's Gonna Be A Showdown	Archie Bell & the Drells	12	5
1/5/67	1/5/67	There's Got To Be A Word	Innocence	xx	2
6/9/73	7/14/73	There's No Me Without You	Manhattans	26	7
8/9/75	8/30/75	(I Believe) There's Nothing Stronger Than Our Love	Paul Anka with Odia Coates	22	9
2/10/66	3/10/66	These Boots Are Made For Walkin'	Nancy Sinatra	2	9
4/9/69	5/14/69	These Eyes	Guess Who	2	10
8/30/75	11/1/75	They Just Can't Stop It The (Games People Play)	Spinners	3	18
7/21/66	7/28/66	They're Coming To Take Me Away, Ha-Haaa!	Napoleon XIV	2	3
8/24/67	8/24/67	Things I Should Have Said	Grass Roots	30	1
11/21/68	12/19/68	Things I'd Like To Say	New Colony Six	3	9
5/16/68	6/13/68	Think	Aretha Franklin	12	7
5/12/73	6/23/73	Thinking Of You	Loggins & Messina	10	9
8/9/75	9/20/75	Third Rate Romance	Amazing Rhythm Aces	10	14
3/25/71	5/13/71	13 Questions	Seatrain	14	9
6/30/66	7/28/66	This Door Swings Both Ways	Herman's Hermits	12	7
8/27/69	9/10/69	This Girl Is A Woman Now	Gary Puckett & the Union Gap	2	7

Debut	Peak	Title	Artist	Pos	Wks
2/19/69	3/19/69	This Girl's In Love With You	Dionne Warwick	7	6
5/9/68	6/13/68	This Guy's In Love With You	Herb Alpert	1	10
6/15/74	7/20/74	This Heart	Gene Redding	17	10
3/16/67	3/30/67	This Is My Song	Petula Clark	9	7
2/15/68	2/29/68	This Is The Thanks I Get	Barbara Lynn	27	2
1/22/69	2/26/69	This Magic Moment	Jay & the Americans	3	7
9/27/75	11/8/75	This Will Be	Natalie Cole	8	12
10/3/68	10/31/68	Those Were The Days	Mary Hopkin	1	10
1/12/70	2/2/70	Thrill Is Gone, The	B.B. King	14	6
9/30/72	11/18/72	Thunder And Lightning	Chi Coltrane	4	12
1/12/70	2/9/70	Ticket To Ride	Carpenters	14	8
3/10/73	5/5/73	Tie A Yellow Ribbon Round The Ole Oak Tree	Dawn featuring Tony Orlando	3	13
9/9/72	10/14/72	Tight Rope	Leon Russell	11	10
4/4/68	5/16/68	Tighten Up	Archie Bell & the Drells	3	10
6/15/70	7/13/70	Tighter, Tighter	Alive And Kicking	4	14
7/12/75	8/16/75	Til The World Ends	Three Dog Night	14	10
11/21/68	12/12/68	Till	Vogues	18	6
3/31/66	5/5/66	Till The End Of The Day	Kinks	16	4
11/17/66	12/8/66	Time After Time	Chris Montez	17	5
5/9/68	6/13/68	Time For Livin'	Association	14	5
9/26/68	10/17/68	Time Has Come Today	Chambers Brothers	9	5
12/1/73	1/12/74	Time In A Bottle	Jim Croce	6	13
3/26/69	4/16/69	Time Is Tight	Booker T. & the MG's	13	5
2/5/69	3/19/69	Time Of The Season	Zombies	1	10
2/16/70	3/9/70	Time To Get It Together	Country Coalition	31	5
3/31/66	4/21/66	Time Won't Let Me	Outsiders	6	8
1/24/76	2/7/76	Times Of Your Life	Paul Anka	19	5
1/11/71	5/20/71	Timothy	Buoys	8	16
11/2/74	11/30/74	Tin Man	America	2	12
2/22/68	2/22/68	Tin Soldier	Small Faces	pr	1
6/6/68	6/20/68	Tip-Toe Thru' The Tulips With Me	Tiny Tim	20	3
9/23/71	11/4/71	Tired Of Being Alone	Al Green	5	10
12/21/67	1/25/68	To Give (The Reason I Live)	Frankie Valli	11	7
4/9/69	5/7/69	To Know You Is To Love You	Bobby Vinton	21	5

Debut	Peak	Title	Artist	Pos	Wks
9/28/67	11/2/67	To Sir With Love	Lulu	1	11
2/8/75	3/8/75	To The Door Of The Sun (Alle Porte Del Sole)	Al Martino	25	8
9/19/68	9/19/68	To Wait For Love	Herb Alpert	28	1
3/25/71	4/29/71	Toast And Marmalade For Tea	Tin Tin	23	8
7/20/70	8/24/70	Tommy, Overture From (A Rock Opera)	Assembled Multitude	8	10
1/18/68	2/15/68	Tomorrow	Strawberry Alarm Clock	14	6
5/7/69	6/4/69	Too Busy Thinking About My Baby	Marvin Gaye	2	10
6/8/72	7/29/72	Too Late To Turn Back Now	Cornelius Brothers & Sister Rose	2	11
5/18/67	5/25/67	Too Many Fish In The Sea & Three Little Fishes	Mitch Ryder & the Detroit Wheels	26	2
2/1/68	3/14/68	Too Much Talk	Paul Revere & the Raiders featuring Mark Lindsay	11	7
12/19/68	1/8/69	Too Weak To Fight	Clarence Carter	19	6
6/8/72	7/15/72	Too Young	Donny Osmond	3	10
10/13/73	12/15/73	Top Of The World	Carpenters	1	18
4/13/74	5/4/74	Touch A Hand, Make A Friend	Staple Singers	25	6
1/8/69	2/12/69	Touch Me	Doors	1	9
7/7/73	8/18/73	Touch Me In The Morning	Diana Ross	5	11
2/26/69	3/26/69	Traces	Classics IV featuring Dennis Yost	3	7
5/25/67	7/6/67	Tracks Of My Tears, The	Johnny Rivers	13	6
9/17/69	10/8/69	Tracy	Cuff Links	5	4
8/27/69	9/10/69	Train, The	1910 Fruitgum Co.	3	7
6/16/66	6/16/66	Train Of Life	Roger Miller	pr	1
6/1/74	6/29/74	Train Of Thought	Cher	13	9
7/21/66	7/21/66	Trains And Boats And Planes	Dionne Warwick	xx	3
1/19/67	1/19/67	Tramp	Lowell Fulsom	xx	3
1/19/70	2/23/70	Travelin' Band	Creedence Clearwater Revival	7	8
9/21/67	11/23/67	Treat Her Groovy	New Colony Six	12	8
5/27/71	7/1/71	Treat Her Like A Lady	Cornelius Brothers & Sister Rose	10	9
6/1/72	7/6/72	Troglodyte (Cave Man)	Jimmy Castor Bunch	1	10

Debut	Peak	Title	Artist	Pos	Wks
1/13/73	2/10/73	Trouble Man	Marvin Gaye	18	8
8/13/69	8/13/69	True Grit	Glen Campbell	30	1
5/27/71	6/10/71	Try Some, Buy Some	Ronnie Spector	31	3
3/24/66	4/14/66	Try Too Hard	Dave Clark Five	14	7
2/23/74	3/23/74	Trying To Hold On To My Woman	Lamont Dozier	24	7
3/23/74	5/11/74	TSOP (The Sound Of Philadelphia)	MFSB featuring the Three Degrees	5	13
3/16/74	5/4/74	Tubular Bells	Mike Oldfield	2	14
8/15/68	9/19/68	Tuesday Afternoon (Forever Afternoon)	Moody Blues	7	7
4/20/72	6/22/72	Tumbling Dice	Rolling Stones	1	14
6/27/68	8/15/68	Turn Around, Look At Me	Vogues	2	9
3/16/70	4/20/70	Turn Back The Hands Of Time	Tyrone Davis	8	10
9/8/66	9/22/66	Turn-Down Day	Cyrkle	13	4
12/16/65	12/16/65	Turn! Turn! Turn! (To Everything There Is A Season)	Byrds	8	3
7/26/75	9/13/75	Tush	ZZ Top	2	14
3/31/73	5/19/73	Twelfth Of Never, The	Donny Osmond	3	11
8/17/67	9/28/67	Twelve Thirty (Young Girls Are Coming To The Canyon)	Mamas & the Papas	20	5
3/19/69	4/9/69	Twenty-Five Miles	Edwin Starr	12	5
7/20/70	8/24/70	25 Or 6 To 4	Chicago	3	12
5/5/66	5/5/66	Twinkle Toes	Roy Orbison	xx	3
7/18/68	7/25/68	Two-Bit Manchild	Neil Diamond	22	3
11/18/71	12/23/71	Two Divided By Love	Grass Roots	5	10
5/11/67	6/29/67	Two In The Afternoon	Dino, Desi & Billy	26	3
8/3/70	8/31/70	Two Little Rooms	Trella Hart	34	7
7/29/71	8/26/71	Uncle Albert/Admiral Halsey	Paul & Linda McCartney	1	11
6/16/73	8/11/73	Uneasy Rider	Charlie Daniels	10	13
4/4/68	5/16/68	Unicorn, The	Irish Rovers	7	8
5/11/70	6/8/70	United We Stand	Brotherhood Of Man	9	9
4/11/68	4/11/68	Unknown Soldier, The	Doors	pr	1
2/2/70	3/2/70	Until It's Time For You To Go	Neil Diamond	30	5

Debut	Peak	Title	Artist	Pos	Wks
1/12/74	2/23/74	Until You Come Back To Me (That's What I'm Gonna Do)	Aretha Franklin	14	10
2/3/66	2/3/66	Up And Down	McCoys	pr	1
4/13/70	5/11/70	Up Around The Bend	Creedence Clearwater Revival	3	10
1/25/75	3/8/75	Up In A Puff Of Smoke	Polly Brown	12	10
1/12/70	1/12/70	Up On Cripple Creek	Band	24	2
2/22/68	3/14/68	Up On The Roof	Cryan' Shames	7	8
3/2/70	4/6/70	Up The Ladder To The Roof	Supremes	3	11
6/1/67	6/22/67	Up-Up And Away	5th Dimension	5	7
2/23/67	3/23/67	Ups And Downs	Paul Revere & the Raiders	7	6
2/17/66	2/17/66	Uptight (Everything's Alright)	Stevie Wonder	xx	2
4/11/68	5/9/68	U.S. Male	Elvis Presley	15	6
9/23/72	10/28/72	Use Me	Bill Withers	6	9
3/23/72	5/18/72	Vahevala	Kenny Loggins & Jim Messina	3	11
3/7/68	3/21/68	Valleri	Monkees	1	7
2/8/68	2/22/68	(Theme From) Valley Of The Dolls	Dionne Warwick	7	6
3/9/70	4/20/70	Vehicle	Ides Of March	3	13
10/21/72	12/16/72	Ventura Highway	America	5	13
1/12/70	1/12/70	Venus	Shocking Blue	1	7
11/8/75	12/6/75	Venus And Mars Rock Show	Wings	13	11
3/2/74	4/20/74	Virginia (Touch Me Like You Do)	Bill Amesbury	11	12
10/12/67	10/12/67	Visit To A Sad Planet, A	Leonard Nimoy	27	1
8/4/66	8/4/66	Wade In The Water	Ramsey Lewis	xx	5
3/24/66	3/24/66	Wait A Minute	Tim Tam & the Turn-Ons	xx	1
10/12/67	10/12/67	Wake Up, Wake Up	Grass Roots	pr	1
1/12/70	2/2/70	Walk A Mile In My Shoes	Joe South & the Believers	8	6
7/1/71	7/29/71	Walk Away	James Gang	17	7
12/6/75	1/24/76	Walk Away From Love	David Ruffin	13	12
1/18/68	2/22/68	Walk Away Renee	Four Tops	11	6
4/6/72	5/18/72	Walk In The Night	Jr. Walker & the All Stars	15	9
12/15/73	2/2/74	Walk Like A Man	Grand Funk	16	10
4/21/73	6/9/73	Walk On The Wild Side	Lou Reed	3	11

Debut	Peak	Title	Artist	Pos	Wks
3/2/67	4/13/67	Walk Tall	2 Of Clubs	10	7
1/12/70	2/9/70	Walkin' In The Rain	Jay & the Americans	11	7
5/11/72	6/15/72	Walkin' In The Rain With The One I Love	Love Unlimited	16	8
3/3/66	3/31/66	Walkin' My Cat Named Dog	Norma Tanega	xx	3
4/29/71	6/10/71	Want Ads	Honey Cone	1	11
7/20/70	8/10/70	War	Edwin Starr	1	16
8/30/75	9/13/75	Wasted Days And Wasted Nights	Freddy Fender	20	9
11/2/67	11/30/67	Watch The Flowers Grow	Four Seasons	12	5
1/11/71	2/22/71	Watching Scotty Grow	Bobby Goldsboro	11	8
5/25/74	7/20/74	Waterloo	ABBA	2	15
10/25/75	11/29/75	Way I Want To Touch You, The	Captain & Tennille	2	15
2/3/72	3/9/72	Way Of Love, The	Cher	5	10
12/22/73	2/9/74	Way We Were, The	Barbra Streisand	1	16
5/24/75	7/12/75	Way We Were, The/Try To Remember	Gladys Knight & the Pips	8	14
1/4/68	2/8/68	We Can Fly	Cowsills	21	5
8/31/70	9/21/70	We Can Make Music	Tommy Roe	18	8
12/16/65	1/13/66	We Can Work It Out	Beatles	1	11
3/1/71	4/29/71	We Can Work It Out	Stevie Wonder	8	12
1/11/71	1/25/71	We Gotta Get You A Woman	Runt	32	3
9/29/73	11/17/73	We May Never Pass This Way (Again)	Seals & Crofts	9	12
4/4/68	4/4/68	Wear It On Our Face	Dells	pr	1
12/21/67	1/18/68	Wear Your Love Like Heaven	Donovan	22	3
10/1/69	10/8/69	Wedding Bell Blues	5th Dimension	15	2
7/15/71	9/9/71	Wedding Song (There Is Love)	Paul Stookey	2	13
10/25/75	11/29/75	Welcome To My Nightmare	Alice Cooper	16	9
1/6/66	1/20/66	Well Respected Man, A	Kinks	15	4
1/18/68	2/22/68	We're A Winner	Impressions	21	6
7/28/73	9/15/73	We're An American Band	Grand Funk	3	13
5/25/72	7/6/72	We're On Our Way	Chris Hodge	21	10
3/2/67	3/30/67	Western Union	Five Americans	7	8

Debut	Peak	Title	Artist	Pos	Wks
9/7/70	10/26/70	We've Only Just Begun	Carpenters	1	16
9/27/75	10/25/75	What A Diff'rence A Day Makes	Esther Phillips	17	8
3/29/75	5/3/75	What Am I Gonna Do With You	Barry White	14	9
9/23/71	11/25/71	What Are You Doing Sunday	Dawn featuring Tony Orlando	3	14
9/1/66	11/24/66	What Becomes Of The Brokenhearted	Jimmy Ruffin	10	13
6/11/69	7/23/69	What Does It Take (To Win Your Love)	Jr. Walker & the All Stars	5	9
3/10/66	3/17/66	What Goes On	Beatles	5	2
2/22/71	3/25/71	What Is Life	George Harrison	9	9
3/30/70	4/20/70	What Is Truth	Johnny Cash	21	8
8/27/69	9/10/69	What Kind Of Fool Do You Think I Am	Bill Deal & the Rhondels	16	3
3/24/66	3/24/66	What Now My Love	Herb Alpert & the Tijuana Brass	xx	2
9/14/67	9/14/67	What Now My Love	Mitch Ryder	pr	1
2/10/66	3/3/66	What Now My Love	Sonny & Cher	20	5
7/29/71	9/16/71	Whatcha See Is Whatcha Get	Dramatics	8	10
10/26/74	12/7/74	Whatever Gets You Thru The Night	John Lennon with the Plastic Ono Nuclear Band	6	10
2/8/71	3/25/71	What's Going On	Marvin Gaye	3	12
9/17/69	9/17/69	What's The Use Of Breaking Up	Jerry Butler	21	4
12/14/74	1/18/75	When A Child Is Born	Michael Holm	19	8
5/12/66	6/23/66	When A Man Loves A Woman	Percy Sledge	8	7
8/27/69	10/1/69	When I Die	Motherlode	16	7
3/30/67	5/11/67	When I Was Young	Eric Burdon & the Animals	21	5
1/11/71	2/8/71	When I'm Dead And Gone	Bob Summers	15	5
1/13/66	2/17/66	When Liking Turns To Loving	Ronnie Dove	xx	2
11/9/70	11/30/70	When The Party Is Over	Robert John	19	6
4/8/71	4/29/71	When There's No You	Engelbert Humperdinck	28	4
5/10/75	6/21/75	When Will I Be Loved	Linda Ronstadt	2	15
11/30/74	1/11/75	When Will I See You Again	Three Degrees	4	13

Debut	Peak	Title	Artist	Pos	Wks
12/2/71	1/27/72	Where Did Our Love Go	Donnie Elbert	3	12
6/22/72	8/12/72	Where Is The Love	Roberta Flack & Donny Hathaway	2	11
8/11/66	8/11/66	Where Were You When I Needed You	Grass Roots	xx	2
1/5/67	2/9/67	Where Will The Words Come From	Gary Lewis & the Playboys	17	7
3/23/70	4/20/70	Which Way You Goin' Billy	Poppy Family featuring Susan Jacks	9	12
11/25/71	1/27/72	White Lies, Blue Eyes	Bullet	4	13
6/8/67	7/27/67	White Rabbit	Jefferson Airplane	4	9
10/3/68	11/14/68	White Room	Cream	5	8
7/6/67	8/10/67	Whiter Shade Of Pale, A	Procol Harum	15	7
10/13/66	11/24/66	Who Am I	Petula Clark	20	4
8/17/74	9/28/74	Who Do You Think You Are	Bo Donaldson & the Heywoods	10	12
10/18/75	11/29/75	Who Loves You	Four Seasons	1	15
12/7/67	1/18/68	Who Will Answer	Ed Ames	15	5
1/12/70	1/12/70	Whole Lotta Love	Led Zeppelin	5	5
1/19/70	2/23/70	Who'll Stop The Rain	Creedence Clearwater Revival	7	8
11/17/73	12/22/73	Who's In The Strawberry Patch With Sally	Tony Orlando & Dawn	20	9
10/31/68	11/28/68	Who's Making Love	Johnnie Taylor	10	9
3/15/75	4/12/75	Who's Sorry Now	Marie Osmond	26	7
2/23/70	3/30/70	Who's Your Baby	Archies	13	8
9/30/72	11/18/72	Why	Donny Osmond	7	11
6/22/70	8/3/70	(If You Let Me Make Love To You Then) Why Can't I Touch You	Ronnie Dyson	4	13
6/21/75	8/16/75	Why Can't We Be Friends	War	1	17
12/9/72	1/20/73	Why Can't We Live Together	Timmy Thomas	2	12
2/10/66	2/10/66	Why Can't You Bring Me Home	Jay & the Americans	pr	1
7/16/69	7/16/69	Why I Sing The Blues	B.B. King	27	2
2/16/70	2/23/70	Why Should I Cry	Gentrys	30	3
11/21/68	12/12/68	Wichita Lineman	Glen Campbell	10	6
4/28/73	6/23/73	Wild About My Lovin'	Adrian Smith	13	12

Debut	Peak	Title	Artist	Pos	Wks
7/1/71	7/29/71	Wild Horses	Rolling Stones	22	6
10/7/71	12/2/71	Wild Night	Van Morrison	7	12
6/29/74	8/17/74	Wild Thing	Fancy	5	14
1/12/67	1/19/67	Wild Thing	Senator Bobby	20	2
6/23/66	7/14/66	Wild Thing	Troggs	1	9
3/25/71	5/13/71	Wild World	Cat Stevens	8	10
5/24/75	7/5/75	Wildfire	Michael Murphey	1	16
3/10/73	5/19/73	Wildflower	Skylark	4	15
7/6/74	8/24/74	Wildwood Weed	Jim Stafford	5	11
5/26/73	7/14/73	Will It Go Round In Circles	Billy Preston	4	13
4/2/69	4/16/69	Will You Be Staying After Sunday	Peppermint Rainbow	15	5
2/15/68	3/14/68	Will You Love Me Tomorrow	Four Seasons	22	6
3/30/67	3/30/67	Willie Jean	Shadows Of Knight	26	2
10/27/66	12/1/66	Winchester Cathedral	New Vaudeville Band	1	12
9/28/67	9/28/67	Windows Of The World, The	Dionne Warwick	30	2
5/18/67	6/8/67	Windy	Association	1	12
11/1/75	12/27/75	Winners And Losers	Hamilton, Joe Frank & Reynolds	2	16
1/12/70	1/19/70	Winter World Of Love	Engelbert Humperdinck	15	6
12/22/66	12/22/66	Winters Children	Capes Of Good Hope	pr	1
8/25/66	9/29/66	Wipe Out	Surfaris	3	9
1/26/67	1/26/67	Wish Me A Rainbow	Gunter Kallmann Chorus	xx	1
11/3/66	11/3/66	Wish You Were Here, Buddy	Pat Boone	xx	1
10/26/74	12/7/74	Wishing You Were Here	Chicago	15	10
6/1/70	7/6/70	Witch, The	Rattles	20	9
12/30/71	2/17/72	Witch Queen Of New Orleans, The	Redbone	3	12
2/12/69	2/12/69	Witchi-Tai-To	Jim Pepper	30	1
10/7/72	12/2/72	Witchy Woman	Eagles	6	11
7/21/66	9/1/66	With A Girl Like You	Troggs	15	7
6/11/69	6/25/69	With Pen In Hand	Vikki Carr	26	3
7/18/68	7/18/68	With Pen In Hand	Billy Vera	30	1
1/12/70	1/26/70	Without Love (There Is Nothing)	Tom Jones	5	7

Debut	Peak	Title	Artist	Pos	Wks
1/13/72	2/24/72	Without You	Nilsson	1	11
2/24/66	3/24/66	Woman	Peter & Gordon	13	5
12/7/67	12/28/67	Woman, Woman	Union Gap featuring Gary Puckett	4	10
5/4/70	6/15/70	Wonder Of You, The	Elvis Presley	14	12
1/12/70	1/12/70	Wonderful World, Beautiful People	Jimmy Cliff	16	3
7/8/71	9/9/71	Won't Get Fooled Again	Who	4	12
2/22/71	4/8/71	Woodstock	Matthews' Southern Comfort	12	11
1/18/68	1/18/68	Words	Bee Gees	pr	1
7/20/67	8/17/67	Words	Monkees	2	8
12/8/66	1/19/67	Words Of Love	Mamas & the Papas	5	8
6/23/66	7/7/66	Work Song, The	Herb Alpert & the Tijuana Brass	xx	5
6/29/74	8/3/74	Workin' At The Car Wash Blues	Jim Croce	11	10
8/1/68	8/22/68	Workin' On A Groovy Thing	Patti Drew	25	4
7/30/69	8/13/69	Workin' On A Groovy Thing	5th Dimension	14	6
9/1/66	9/1/66	Working In The Coal Mine	Lee Dorsey	xx	3
1/13/66	3/17/66	Working My Way Back To You	Four Seasons	12	7
2/3/73	3/10/73	World Is A Ghetto, The	War	5	9
7/27/67	8/24/67	World We Knew (Over And Over), The	Frank Sinatra	27	2
12/19/68	2/12/69	Worst That Could Happen	Brooklyn Bridge	2	9
8/11/66	8/25/66	Wouldn't It Be Nice	Beach Boys	4	7
3/23/67	6/8/67	Yellow Balloon	Yellow Balloon	12	7
10/19/70	11/9/70	Yellow River	Christie	4	9
8/11/66	9/8/66	Yellow Submarine	Beatles	3	10
9/22/73	11/10/73	Yes We Can Can	Pointer Sisters	9	12
1/12/70	1/12/70	Yester-Me, Yester-You, Yesterday	Stevie Wonder	23	2
12/7/67	12/7/67	Yesterday	Ray Charles	30	2
6/23/73	7/28/73	Yesterday Once More	Carpenters	1	13
7/16/69	7/16/69	Yesterday, When I Was Young	Roy Clark	30	1

Debut	Peak	Title	Artist	Pos	Wks
8/8/68	8/8/68	Yesterday's Dreams	Four Tops	30	1
1/17/76	1/17/76	Yesterday's Hero	John Paul Young	32	3
9/9/71	11/11/71	Yo-Yo	Osmonds	1	14
2/1/68	2/15/68	You	Marvin Gaye	28	3
10/12/74	11/16/74	You Ain't Seen Nothing Yet	Bachman-Turner Overdrive	1	12
7/13/74	8/24/74	You And Me Against The World	Helen Reddy	8	13
2/15/75	4/19/75	You Are So Beautiful	Joe Cocker	2	15
2/17/72	4/13/72	You Are The One	Sugar Bears	6	12
4/7/73	5/12/73	You Are The Sunshine Of My Life	Stevie Wonder	10	10
3/3/66	4/7/66	You Baby	Turtles	4	8
6/9/66	6/23/66	You Better Run	Young Rascals	xx	6
11/2/67	12/14/67	You Better Sit Down Kids	Cher	3	7
9/21/70	10/26/70	You Better Think Twice	Poco	26	8
7/16/69	7/30/69	You Can't Always Get What You Want	Rolling Stones	1	7
4/21/73	5/19/73	You Can't Always Get What You Want	Rolling Stones	19	7
8/4/66	9/22/66	You Can't Hurry Love	Supremes	2	11
3/30/72	5/18/72	You Could Have Been A Lady	April Wine	7	11
12/30/65	1/27/66	You Didn't Have To Be So Nice	Lovin' Spoonful	9	7
11/23/70	12/14/70	You Don't Have To Say You Love Me	Elvis Presley	15	7
6/9/66	7/7/66	You Don't Have To Say You Love Me	Dusty Springfield	8	8
7/2/69	7/2/69	You Don't Have To Walk In The Rain	Turtles	29	1
5/19/66	5/19/66	You Don't Love Me	Gary Walker	xx	1
7/29/72	9/9/72	You Don't Mess Around With Jim	Jim Croce	1	13
3/12/69	3/26/69	You Gave Me A Mountain	Frankie Laine	26	3
9/15/73	10/20/73	(I Don't Want To Love You But) You Got Me Anyway	Sutherland Brothers & Quiver	14	9
1/12/70	2/16/70	You Got Me Hummin	Cold Blood	29	7
12/14/74	1/18/75	You Got The Love	Rufus featuring Chaka Khan	10	10
2/9/67	3/9/67	You Got To Me	Neil Diamond	16	5

Debut	Peak	Title	Artist	Pos	Wks
3/23/67	5/4/67	You Got What It Takes	Dave Clark Five	6	8
8/24/74	9/28/74	You Haven't Done Nothin'	Stevie Wonder	12	10
12/21/67	12/21/67	You Haven't Seen My Love	Ones	pr	1
8/27/69	10/1/69	You, I	Rugbys	7	7
10/20/66	11/24/66	You Keep Me Hangin' On	Supremes	3	10
8/8/68	9/5/68	You Keep Me Hangin' On	Vanilla Fudge	6	6
9/7/67	10/12/67	You Keep Running Away	Four Tops	24	3
8/17/67	9/14/67	You Know What I Mean	Turtles	15	9
9/14/74	11/2/74	You Little Trustmaker	Tymes	4	14
4/20/74	5/25/74	You Make Me Feel Brand New	Stylistics	16	11
8/1/68	8/1/68	You Met Your Match	Stevie Wonder	28	2
6/1/67	6/29/67	You Must Have Been A Beautiful Baby	Dave Clark Five	23	5
4/6/70	4/20/70	You Need Love Like I Do (Don't You)	Gladys Knight & the Pips	19	5
11/11/72	12/16/72	You Ought To Be With Me	Al Green	14	10
11/1/75	1/17/76	You Sexy Thing	Hot Chocolate	9	15
1/15/69	2/12/69	You Showed Me	Turtles	3	9
12/23/72	2/10/73	You Turn Me On, I'm A Radio	Joni Mitchell	13	11
9/30/72	11/4/72	You Wear It Well	Rod Stewart	16	9
5/25/74	7/13/74	You Won't See Me	Anne Murray	2	15
5/12/66	6/23/66	You Wouldn't Listen	Ides Of March	10	8
5/23/68	6/27/68	Young Birds Fly	Cryan' Shames	12	6
2/22/68	4/18/68	Young Girl	Union Gap featuring Gary Puckett	2	10
9/14/67	9/14/67	Younger Generation Blues	Janis Ian	pr	1
4/28/66	4/28/66	Younger Girl	Hondells	pr	1
1/11/75	2/1/75	Your Bulldog Drinks Champagne	Jim Stafford	29	5
7/30/69	9/10/69	Your Good Thing (Is About To End)	Lou Rawls	22	10
12/16/72	2/10/73	Your Mama Don't Dance	Kenny Loggins & Jim Messina	8	14
9/30/71	11/25/71	Your Move	Yes	4	12
9/28/67	11/2/67	Your Precious Love	Marvin Gaye & Tammi Terrell	14	6
12/7/70	2/1/71	Your Song	Elton John	7	11

Debut	Peak	Title	Artist	Pos	Wks
10/6/73	11/3/73	You're A Special Part Of Me	Diana Ross & Marvin Gaye	28	6
2/22/71	3/25/71	You're All I Need To Get By	Aretha Franklin	27	5
8/8/68	9/12/68	You're All I Need To Get By	Marvin Gaye & Tammi Terrell	8	6
3/16/67	4/27/67	You're Gonna Be Mine	New Colony Six	12	7
8/17/67	9/14/67	You're My Everything	Temptations	17	5
1/11/75	3/1/75	You're No Good	Linda Ronstadt	4	14
4/21/66	4/21/66	You're Ready Now	Frankie Valli	pr	1
12/15/73	2/2/74	You're Sixteen	Ringo Starr	1	14
12/16/72	1/20/73	You're So Vain	Carly Simon	1	17
8/19/72	10/7/72	You're Still A Young Man	Tower Of Power	11	11
11/30/74	1/11/75	You're The First, The Last, My Everything	Barry White	3	12
4/6/70	4/13/70	You're The One-Part I	Little Sister	28	3
5/27/71	7/15/71	You've Got A Friend	James Taylor	1	12
2/22/68	3/7/68	You've Got To Be Loved	Montanas	19	5
9/28/67	9/28/67	You've Got To Pay The Price	Al Kent	26	2
3/19/69	4/16/69	You've Made Me So Very Happy	Blood, Sweat & Tears	1	8
5/2/68	6/6/68	Yummy Yummy Yummy	Ohio Express	1	9
8/17/67	8/31/67	Zip Code	Five Americans	17	4
1/20/66	2/3/66	Zorba The Greek	Herb Alpert & the Tijuana Brass	13	5

WCFL Number One Hits

Date	Wks	Title	Artist
(* denotes non-consecutive weeks at #1)			
12/16/65	2	Let's Hang On	Four Seasons
12/30/65	1	Five O'Clock World	Vogues
1/6/66	1	The Sounds Of Silence	Simon & Garfunkel
1/13/66	4	We Can Work It Out/Day Tripper	Beatles
2/10/66	3	Lightnin' Strikes	Lou Christie
3/3/66	4	California Dreamin'	Mamas & the Papas
3/31/66	3	Gloria	Shadows Of Knight
4/21/66	2	Kicks	Paul Revere & the Raiders featuring Mark Lindsay
5/5/66	4	Monday, Monday	Mamas & the Papas
6/2/66	3	Paint It, Black	Rolling Stones
6/23/66	3	Hanky Panky	Tommy James & the Shondells
7/14/66	3	Wild Thing	Troggs
8/4/66	4	Summer In The City	Lovin' Spoonful
9/1/66	1	Bus Stop	Hollies
9/8/66	1	Sunshine Superman	Donovan
9/15/66	5	Cherish	Association
10/20/66	3	96 Tears	? & the Mysterians
11/10/66	1	Reach Out I'll Be There	Four Tops
11/17/66	2	Good Vibrations	Beach Boys
12/1/66	4	Winchester Cathedral	New Vaudeville Band
12/29/66	3	Snoopy vs. The Red Baron	Royal Guardsmen
1/19/67	2	I'm A Believer	Monkees
1/19/67	1	/(I'm Not Your) Steppin' Stone	Monkees
2/2/67	2	Georgy Girl	Seekers
2/16/67	2	Ruby Tuesday	Rolling Stones
3/2/67	*3	I Think We're Alone Now	Tommy James & the Shondells
3/16/67	*5	Happy Together	Turtles

Date	Wks	Title	Artist
4/27/67	2	A Little Bit Me, A Little Bit You	Monkees
5/11/67	1	Somethin' Stupid	Nancy Sinatra & Frank Sinatra
5/18/67	1	Mirage	Tommy James & the Shondells
5/25/67	2	Somebody To Love	Jefferson Airplane
6/8/67	6	Windy	Association
7/20/67	1	Come On Down To My Boat	Every Mothers' Son
7/27/67	3	Can't Take My Eyes Off You	Frankie Valli
8/17/67	3	It Could Be We're In Love	Cryan' Shames
9/7/67	2	Ode To Billie Joe	Bobbie Gentry
9/21/67	6	The Letter	Box Tops
11/2/67	2	To Sir With Love	Lulu
11/16/67	3	The Rain, The Park & Other Things	Cowsills
12/7/67	2	Daydream Believer	Monkees
12/21/67	2	Hello Goodbye/I Am The Walrus	Beatles
1/4/68	2	Judy In Disguise (With Glasses)	John Fred & his Playboy Band
1/18/68	3	Bend Me, Shape Me	American Breed
2/8/68	6	Love Is Blue	Paul Mauriat
3/21/68	2	Valleri/Tapioca Tundra	Monkees
4/4/68	1	I Will Always Think About You	New Colony Six
4/11/68	1	Lady Madonna/The Inner Light	Beatles
4/18/68	3	Honey	Bobby Goldsboro
5/9/68	4	Mony Mony	Tommy James & the Shondells
6/6/68	1	Yummy Yummy Yummy	Ohio Express
6/13/68	4	This Guy's In Love With You	Herb Alpert
7/11/68	4	Jumpin' Jack Flash	Rolling Stones
8/8/68	1	Hello, I Love You	Doors
8/15/68	1	Born To Be Wild	Steppenwolf
8/22/68	1	Light My Fire	José Feliciano
8/29/68	1	People Got To Be Free	Rascals
9/5/68	1	1, 2, 3, Red Light	1910 Fruitgum Co.
9/12/68	1	Do It Again	Beach Boys
9/19/68	1	Harper Valley P.T.A.	Jeannie C. Riley
9/26/68	4	Fire	Crazy World Of Arthur Brown
10/24/68	1	Little Green Apples	O.C. Smith
10/31/68	3	Those Were The Days	Mary Hopkin

Date	Wks	Title	Artist
11/21/68	1	Love Child	Diana Ross & the Supremes
11/28/68	2	Abraham, Martin And John	Dion
12/12/68	5	I Heard It Through The Grapevine	Marvin Gaye
1/15/69	2	I'm Gonna Make You Love Me	Diana Ross & the Supremes & the Temptations
1/29/69	2	Everyday People	Sly & the Family Stone
2/12/69	1	Touch Me	Doors
2/19/69	3	Ramblin' Gamblin' Man	Bob Seger System
3/12/69	1	Dizzy	Tommy Roe
3/19/69	2	Time Of The Season	Zombies
4/2/69	2	Hair	Cowsills
4/16/69	1	You've Made Me So Very Happy	Blood, Sweat & Tears
4/23/69	1	Aquarius/Let The Sunshine In (The Flesh Failures)	Fifth Dimension
4/30/69	2	Gitarzan	Ray Stevens
5/14/69	1	Love (Can Make You Happy)	Mercy
5/21/69	2	Get Back/Don't Let Me Down	Beatles with Billy Preston
6/4/69	1	Grazing In The Grass	Friends Of Distinction
6/11/69	3	Love Theme From Romeo & Juliet	Henry Mancini
7/2/69	2	One	Three Dog Night
7/16/69	2	In The Year 2525 (Exordium & Terminus)	Zager & Evans
7/30/69	4	Honky Tonk Women/You Can't Always Get What You Want	Rolling Stones
8/27/69	1	Lay Lady Lay	Bob Dylan
9/3/69	4	Sugar, Sugar	Archies
10/1/69	2	Little Woman	Bobby Sherman
		(No surveys from 10/8/69 through 1/11/70)	
1/12/70	2	Venus	Shocking Blue
1/26/70	1	Thank You Falettinme Be Mice Elf Agin	Sly & the Family Stone
2/2/70	2	No Time	Guess Who
2/16/70	4	Bridge Over Troubled Water	Simon & Garfunkel
3/16/70	1	Spirit In The Sky	Norman Greenbaum
3/23/70	2	Let It Be	Beatles
4/6/70	2	ABC	Jackson 5
4/20/70	2	American Woman/No Sugar Tonight	Guess Who

Date	Wks	Title	Artist
5/4/70	2	Cecilia	Simon & Garfunkel
5/18/70	2	Hitchin' A Ride	Vanity Fare
6/1/70	1	Love On A Two-Way Street	Moments
6/8/70	2	My Baby Loves Lovin'	White Plains
6/22/70	1	Mama Told Me (Not To Come)	Three Dog Night
6/29/70	2	The Love You Save	Jackson 5
7/13/70	2	(They Long To Be) Close To You	Carpenters
7/27/70	2	Make It With You	Bread
8/10/70	6	War	Edwin Starr
9/21/70	2	Candida	Dawn
10/5/70	2	I'll Be There	Jackson 5
10/19/70	1	Indiana Wants Me	R. Dean Taylor
10/26/70	1	We've Only Just Begun	Carpenters
11/2/70	3	I Think I Love You	Partridge Family
11/23/70	2	The Tears Of A Clown	Smokey Robinson & the Miracles
12/7/70	4	My Sweet Lord	George Harrison
1/4/71	2	Knock Three Times	Dawn
1/18/71	2	I Hear You Knocking	Dave Edmunds
2/1/71	2	One Bad Apple	Osmonds
2/15/71	1	If You Could Read My Mind	Gordon Lightfoot
2/22/71	2	Mama's Pearl	Jackson 5
3/11/71	2	Doesn't Somebody Want To Be Wanted	Partridge Family
3/25/71	1	Just My Imagination (Running Away With Me)	Temptations
4/1/71	2	She's A Lady	Tom Jones
4/15/71	2	Stay Awhile	Bells
4/29/71	4	Joy To The World	Three Dog Night
5/27/71	2	Sweet And Innocent	Donny Osmond
6/10/71	2	Want Ads	Honey Cone
6/24/71	3	It's Too Late	Carole King
7/15/71	1	You've Got A Friend	James Taylor
7/22/71	1	Don't Pull Your Love	Hamilton, Joe Frank & Reynolds
7/29/71	1	How Can You Mend A Broken Heart	Bee Gees
8/5/71	1	Indian Reservation (The Lament Of The Cherokee Reservation Indian)	Raiders

Date	Wks	Title	Artist
8/12/71	1	Never Ending Song Of Love	Delaney & Bonnie & Friends
8/19/71	1	Smiling Faces Sometimes	Undisputed Truth
8/26/71	4	Uncle Albert/Admiral Halsey	Paul & Linda McCartney
9/23/71	1	Go Away Little Girl	Donny Osmond
9/30/71	3	Maggie May	Rod Stewart
10/21/71	1	Superstar	Carpenters
10/28/71	2	Gypsys, Tramps & Thieves	Cher
11/11/71	1	Yo-Yo	Osmonds
11/18/71	1	Peace Train	Cat Stevens
11/25/71	2	Theme From Shaft	Isaac Hayes
12/9/71	3	Brand New Key	Melanie
12/30/71	2	Sunshine	Jonathan Edwards
1/13/72	3	American Pie—Parts I & II	Don McLean
2/3/72	2	Stay With Me	Faces
2/17/72	1	Hurting Each Other	Carpenters
2/24/72	1	Without You	Nilsson
3/2/72	1	Joy	Apollo 100
3/9/72	2	Down By The Lazy River	Osmonds
3/23/72	1	Heart Of Gold	Neil Young
3/30/72	1	Puppy Love	Donny Osmond
4/6/72	1	A Horse With No Name	America
4/13/72	2	The First Time Ever I Saw Your Face	Roberta Flack
4/27/72	2	A Cowboy's Work Is Never Done	Sonny & Cher
5/11/72	1	Doctor My Eyes	Jackson Browne
5/18/72	1	Suavecito	Malo
5/25/72	1	Back Off Boogaloo	Ringo Starr
6/1/72	1	Morning Has Broken	Cat Stevens
6/8/72	1	Sylvia's Mother	Dr. Hook & the Medicine Show
6/15/72	1	Nice To Be With You	Gallery
6/22/72	1	Tumbling Dice	Rolling Stones
6/29/72	1	Outa-Space	Billy Preston
7/6/72	1	Troglodyte (Cave Man)	Jimmy Castor Bunch
7/15/72	3	Lean On Me	Bill Withers
8/5/72	2	Alone Again (Naturally)	Gilbert O'Sullivan
8/19/72	2	Brandy (You're A Fine Girl)	Looking Glass

Date	Wks	Title	Artist
9/2/72	1	Rock And Roll Part 2	Gary Glitter
9/9/72	2	You Don't Mess Around With Jim	Jim Croce
9/23/72	1	Back Stabbers	O'Jays
9/30/72	1	Black & White	Three Dog Night
10/7/72	2	My Ding-A-Ling	Chuck Berry
10/21/72	1	Beautiful Sunday	Daniel Boone
10/28/72	1	Everybody Plays The Fool	Main Ingredient
11/4/72	1	Nights In White Satin	Moody Blues
11/11/72	2	I'll Be Around	Spinners
11/25/72	1	I'd Love You To Want Me	Lobo
12/2/72	1	I Am Woman	Helen Reddy
12/9/72	2	Papa Was A Rollin' Stone	Temptations
12/23/72	3	Clair	Gilbert O'Sullivan
1/13/73	1	Me And Mrs. Jones	Billy Paul
1/20/73	3	You're So Vain	Carly Simon
2/10/73	2	Crocodile Rock	Elton John
2/24/73	1	Dancing In The Moonlight	King Harvest
3/3/73	3	Killing Me Softly With His Song	Roberta Flack
3/24/73	2	Also Sprach Zarathustra (2001)	Deodato
4/7/73	1	Kissing My Love	Bill Withers
4/14/73	1	Little Willy	Sweet
4/21/73	3	The Night The Lights Went Out In Georgia	Vicki Lawrence
5/12/73	1	Sing	Carpenters
5/19/73	1	Frankenstein	Edgar Winter Group
5/26/73	1	Hocus Pocus	Focus
6/2/73	2	Pillow Talk	Sylvia
6/16/73	1	The Right Thing To Do	Carly Simon
6/23/73	1	My Love	Paul McCartney
6/30/73	2	Give Me Love—(Give Me Peace On Earth)	George Harrison
7/14/73	1	Kodachrome	Paul Simon
7/21/73	1	Boogie Woogie Bugle Boy	Bette Midler
7/28/73	2	Yesterday Once More	Carpenters
8/11/73	1	Get Down	Gilbert O'Sullivan
8/18/73	1	Brother Louie	Stories

Date	Wks	Title	Artist
8/25/73	2	The Morning After	Maureen McGovern
9/8/73	2	Delta Dawn	Helen Reddy
9/22/73	1	Loves Me Like A Rock	Paul Simon
9/29/73	1	Let's Get It On	Marvin Gaye
10/6/73	1	The Hurt	Cat Stevens
10/13/73	2	Half-Breed	Cher
10/27/73	2	Angie	Rolling Stones
11/10/73	1	Heartbeat—It's A Lovebeat	DeFranco Family featuring Tony DeFranco
11/17/73	2	Midnight Train To Georgia	Gladys Knight & the Pips
12/1/73	1	Photograph	Ringo Starr
12/8/73	1	Hello It's Me	Todd Rundgren
12/15/73	2	Top Of The World	Carpenters
12/29/73	2	Mind Games	John Lennon
1/12/74	2	The Joker	Steve Miller Band
1/26/74	1	One Tin Soldier, The Legend Of Billy Jack	Coven
2/2/74	1	You're Sixteen	Ringo Starr
2/9/74	3	The Way We Were	Barbra Streisand
3/2/74	3	Seasons In The Sun	Terry Jacks
3/23/74	3	Mockingbird	Carly Simon & James Taylor
4/13/74	2	Hooked On A Feeling	Blue Swede
4/27/74	3	Come And Get Your Love	Redbone
5/18/74	3	The Streak	Ray Stevens
6/8/74	1	Midnight At The Oasis	Maria Muldaur
6/15/74	2	Band On The Run	Paul McCartney & Wings
6/29/74	1	Sundown	Gordon Lightfoot
7/6/74	2	If You Love Me (Let Me Know)	Olivia Newton-John
7/20/74	1	Rock The Boat	Hues Corporation
7/27/74	1	Rock Your Baby	George McCrae
8/3/74	2	Annie's Song	John Denver
8/17/74	1	Don't Let The Sun Go Down On Me	Elton John
8/24/74	1	The Night Chicago Died	Paper Lace
8/31/74	1	Feel Like Makin' Love	Roberta Flack
9/7/74	2	(You're) Having My Baby	Paul Anka with Odia Coates
9/21/74	1	I Shot The Sheriff	Eric Clapton

Date	Wks	Title	Artist
9/28/74	3	I Honestly Love You	Olivia Newton-John
10/19/74	2	Sweet Home Alabama	Lynyrd Skynyrd
11/2/74	1	Can't Get Enough	Bad Company
11/9/74	1	The Bitch Is Back	Elton John
11/16/74	2	You Ain't Seen Nothing Yet	Bachman-Turner Overdrive
11/30/74	2	My Melody Of Love	Bobby Vinton
12/14/74	1	Cat's In The Cradle	Harry Chapin
12/21/74	1	Kung Fu Fighting	Carl Douglas
12/28/74	2	I Can Help	Billy Swan
1/11/75	2	Lucy In The Sky With Diamonds	Elton John
1/25/75	1	Laughter In The Rain	Neil Sedaka
2/1/75	1	Please Mr. Postman	Carpenters
2/8/75	1	Mandy	Barry Manilow
2/15/75	2	Best Of My Love	Eagles
3/1/75	2	Black Water	Doobie Brothers
3/15/75	1	Fire	Ohio Players
3/22/75	1	My Eyes Adored You	Frankie Valli
3/29/75	1	Have You Never Been Mellow	Olivia Newton-John
4/5/75	2	Lovin' You	Minnie Riperton
4/19/75	1	Lady Marmalade	Labelle
4/26/75	2	Philadelphia Freedom	Elton John Band
5/10/75	1	Chevy Van	Sammy Johns
5/17/75	2	(Hey Won't You Play) Another Somebody Done Somebody Wrong Song	B.J. Thomas
5/31/75	1	It's A Miracle	Barry Manilow
6/7/75	2	Killer Queen	Queen
6/21/75	2	Sister Golden Hair	America
7/5/75	1	Wildfire	Michael Murphey
7/12/75	3	Love Will Keep Us Together	Captain & Tennille
8/2/75	2	Listen To What The Man Said	Wings
8/16/75	1	Why Can't We Be Friends	War
8/23/75	1	Jive Talkin'	Bee Gees
8/30/75	1	Someone Saved My Life Tonight	Elton John
9/6/75	1	Rhinestone Cowboy	Glen Campbell
9/13/75	1	Fallin' In Love	Hamilton, Joe Frank & Reynolds

Date	Wks	Title	Artist
9/20/75	2	Get Down Tonight	KC & the Sunshine Band
10/4/75	2	Ballroom Blitz	Sweet
10/18/75	2	Fame	David Bowie
11/1/75	1	I'm Sorry	John Denver
11/8/75	2	Bad Blood	Neil Sedaka
11/22/75	1	Island Girl	Elton John
11/29/75	2	Who Loves You	Four Seasons
12/13/75	1	That's The Way (I Like It)	KC & the Sunshine Band
12/20/75	1	Feelings	Morris Albert
12/27/75	3	Fox On The Run	Sweet
1/17/76	2	Convoy	C.W. McCall
1/31/76	1	Love Rollercoaster	Ohio Players
2/7/76	1	I Write The Songs	Barry Manilow
2/14/76	2	50 Ways To Leave Your Lover	Paul Simon

YEARLY TOP 40 CHARTS

Top 40 Hits of 1966:

1.	Cherish	Association
2.	Winchester Cathedral	New Vaudeville Band
3.	California Dreamin'	Mamas & the Papas
4.	We Can Work It Out/DayTripper	Beatles
5.	Summer In The City	Lovin' Spoonful
6.	Monday, Monday	Mamas & the Papas
7.	Gloria	Shadows Of Knight
8.	96 Tears	? & the Mysterians
9.	Hanky Panky	Tommy James & the Shondells
10.	Snoopy vs. The Red Baron	Royal Guardsmen
11.	Wild Thing	Troggs
12.	Paint It, Black	Rolling Stones
13.	Lightnin' Strikes	Lou Christie
14.	Kicks	Paul Revere & the Raiders
15.	Good Vibrations	Beach Boys
16.	Reach Out I'll Be There	Four Tops
17.	The Sounds Of Silence	Simon & Garfunkel
18.	Sunshine Superman	Donovan
19.	Bus Stop	Hollies
20.	You Can't Hurry Love	Supremes
21.	Kind Of A Drag	Buckinghams
22.	These Boots Are Made For Walkin'	Nancy Sinatra
23.	Barbara Ann	Beach Boys
24.	I Am A Rock	Simon & Garfunkel
25.	Secret Agent Man	Johnny Rivers
26.	Paperback Writer/Rain	Beatles
27.	They're Coming To Take Me Away, Ha-Haaa!	Napoleon XIV
28.	A Groovy Kind Of Love	Mindbenders

29.	The Pied Piper	Crispian St. Peters
30.	Last Train To Clarksville	Monkees
31.	Shapes Of Things	Yardbirds
32.	Yellow Submarine/Eleanor Rigby	Beatles
33.	You Keep Me Hangin' On	Supremes
34.	Mellow Yellow	Donovan
35.	Say I Am (What I Am)	Tommy James & the Shondells
36.	Good Lovin'	Young Rascals
37.	Dirty Water	Standells
38.	Lil' Red Riding Hood	Sam the Sham & the Pharaohs
39.	Hooray For Hazel	Tommy Roe
40.	Wipe Out	Surfaris

Top 40 Hits of 1967:

1.	The Letter	Box Tops
2.	Windy	Association
3.	Happy Together	Turtles
4.	Can't Take My Eyes Off You	Frankie Valli
5.	It Could Be We're In Love	Cryan' Shames
6.	I Think We're Alone Now	Tommy James & the Shondells
7.	The Rain, The Park & Other Things	Cowsills
8.	I'm A Believer/(I'm Not Your) Steppin' Stone	Monkees
9.	Daydream Believer	Monkees
10.	To Sir With Love	Lulu
11.	Georgy Girl	Seekers
12.	A Little Bit Me, A Little Bit You	Monkees
13.	Ruby Tuesday	Rolling Stones
14.	Ode To Billie Joe	Bobbie Gentry
15.	Hello Goodbye/I Am The Walrus	Beatles
16.	Somebody To Love	Jefferson Airplane
17.	Come On Down To My Boat	Every Mothers' Son
18.	Somethin' Stupid	Nancy Sinatra & Frank Sinatra
19.	Mirage	Tommy James & the Shondells
20.	Little Bit O' Soul	Music Explosion
21.	Never My Love	Association
22.	Incense And Peppermints	Strawberry Alarm Clock
23.	Light My Fire	Doors
24.	I Got Rhythm	Happenings
25.	Don't You Care	Buckinghams
26.	Pushin' Too Hard	Seeds
27.	Come Back When You Grow Up	Bobby Vee
28.	Pleasant Valley Sunday/Words	Monkees
29.	Little Ole Man (Uptight-Everything's Alright)	Bill Cosby
30.	For What It's Worth	Buffalo Springfield
31.	Groovin'	Young Rascals
32.	Let It Out (Let It All Hang Out)	Hombres
33.	Good Thing	Paul Revere & the Raiders
34.	There's A Kind Of Hush	Herman's Hermits
35.	Blue's Theme	Davie Allan & the Arrows
36.	Brown Eyed Girl	Van Morrison
37.	You Better Sit Down Kids	Cher

38.	On A Carousel	Hollies
39.	Let's Live For Today	Grass Roots
40.	Penny Lane/Strawberry Fields Forever	Beatles

Top 40 Hits of 1968:

1.	Love Is Blue	Paul Mauriat
2.	I Heard It Through The Grapevine	Marvin Gaye
3.	Mony Mony	Tommy James & the Shondells
4.	This Guy's In Love With You	Herb Alpert
5.	Fire	Crazy World Of Arthur Brown
6.	Jumpin' Jack Flash	Rolling Stones
7.	Bend Me, Shape Me	American Breed
8.	Honey	Bobby Goldsboro
9.	Those Were The Days	Mary Hopkin
10.	Judy In Disguise (With Glasses)	John Fred & his Playboy Band
11.	Abraham, Martin And John	Dion
12.	Valleri/Tapioca Tundra	Monkees
13.	I Will Always Think About You	New Colony Six
14.	Love Child	Diana Ross & the Supremes
15.	Born To Be Wild	Steppenwolf
16.	People Got To Be Free	Rascals
17.	1, 2, 3, Red Light	1910 Fruitgum Co.
18.	Little Green Apples	O.C. Smith
19.	Yummy Yummy Yummy	Ohio Express
20.	Do It Again	Beach Boys
21.	Lady Madonna/The Inner Light	Beatles
22.	Hello, I Love You	Doors
23.	Light My Fire	José Feliciano
24.	Harper Valley P.T.A.	Jeannie C. Riley
25.	Hey Jude/Revolution	Beatles
26.	Stoned Soul Picnic	5th Dimension
27.	Spooky	Classics IV
28.	Mrs. Robinson	Simon & Garfunkel
29.	I Wonder What She's Doing Tonite	Tommy Boyce & Bobby Hart
30.	Pictures Of Matchstick Men	Status Quo
31.	For Once In My Life	Stevie Wonder
32.	Young Girl	Gary Puckett & the Union Gap
33.	Green Tambourine	Lemon Pipers
34.	Magic Carpet Ride	Steppenwolf
35.	Cry Like A Baby	Box Tops
36.	Turn Around, Look At Me	Vogues
37.	I've Gotta Get A Message To You	Bee Gees

Top 40 Hits of 1969:

(No surveys were published from 10/8/69 through 1/11/70)

1. Honky Tonk Women
   /You Can't Always Get What You Want — Rolling Stones
2. Sugar, Sugar — Archies
3. Ramblin' Gamblin' Man — Bob Seger System
4. Love Theme From Romeo & Juliet — Henry Mancini
5. I'm Gonna Make You Love Me
   — Diana Ross & the Supremes & the Temptations
6. Hair — Cowsills
7. Everyday People — Sly & the Family Stone
8. One — Three Dog Night
9. Time Of The Season — Zombies
10. Get Back/Don't Let Me Down — Beatles
11. In The Year 2525 — Zager & Evans
12. Gitarzan — Ray Stevens
13. Little Woman — Bobby Sherman
14. Aquarius/Let The Sunshine In — 5th Dimension
15. Dizzy — Tommy Roe
16. Love (Can Make You Happy) — Mercy
17. Touch Me — Doors
18. Lay Lady Lay — Bob Dylan
19. You've Made Me So Very Happy — Blood, Sweat & Tears
20. Grazing In The Grass — Friends of Distinction
21. I'm Gonna Make You Mine — Lou Christie
22. Sweet Caroline — Neil Diamond
23. The Boxer — Simon & Garfunkel
24. Bad Moon Rising/Lodi — Creedence Clearwater Revival
25. This Girl Is A Woman Now — Gary Puckett & the Union Gap
26. Hurt So Bad — Lettermen
27. Crystal Blue Persuasion — Tommy James & the Shondells
28. Too Busy Thinking About My Baby — Marvin Gaye
29. These Eyes — Guess Who
30. Worst That Could Happen — Brooklyn Bridge
31. Indian Giver — 1910 Fruitgum Co.
32. Build Me Up Buttercup — Foundations
33. Ruby, Don't Take Your Love To Town — Kenny Rogers & the First Edition

34.	Baby, I Love You	Andy Kim
35.	Crimson And Clover	Tommy James & the Shondells
36.	It's Your Thing	Isley Brothers
37.	Good Morning Starshine	Oliver
38.	Baby, Baby Don't Cry	Smokey Robinson & the Miracles
39.	I'd Wait A Million Years	Grass Roots
40.	Mr. Sun, Mr. Moon	Paul Revere & the Raiders

Top 40 Hits of 1970:

1.	War	Edwin Starr
2.	Bridge Over Troubled Water	Simon & Garfunkel
3.	My Sweet Lord	George Harrison
4.	I Think I Love You	Partridge Family
5.	Hitchin' A Ride	Vanity Fare
6.	The Tears Of A Clown	Smokey Robinson & the Miracles
7.	My Baby Loves Lovin'	White Plains
8.	(They Long To Be) Close To You	Carpenters
9.	Candida	Dawn
10.	The Love You Save	Jackson 5
11.	I'll Be There	Jackson 5
12.	Let It Be	Beatles
13.	American Woman/No Sugar Tonight	Guess Who
14.	Make It With You	Bread
15.	Cecilia	Simon & Garfunkel
16.	ABC	Jackson 5
17.	No Time	Guess Who
18.	Venus	Shocking Blue
19.	We've Only Just Begun	Carpenters
20.	Indiana Wants Me	R. Dean Taylor
21.	Mama Told Me (Not To Come)	Three Dog Night
22.	Love On A Two-Way Street	Moments
23.	Spirit In The Sky	Norman Greenbaum
24.	Thank You Falettinme Be Mice Elf Agin	Sly & the Family Stone
25.	Ain't No Mountain High Enough	Diana Ross
26.	Get Ready	Rare Earth
27.	Gypsy Woman	Brian Hyland
28.	O-o-h Child	Five Stairsteps
29.	The Rapper	Jaggerz
30.	Something's Burning	Kenny Rogers & the First Edition
31.	Love Land	
	Charles Wright & the Watts 103rd Street Rhythm Band	
32.	Hey There Lonely Girl	Eddie Holman
33.	House Of The Rising Sun	Frijid Pink
34.	Spill The Wine	Eric Burdon & War
35.	Cracklin' Rosie	Neil Diamond
36.	Montego Bay	Bobby Bloom

37. Lookin' Out My Back Door   Creedence Clearwater Revival
38. Lola   Kinks
39. Solitary Man   Neil Diamond
40. One Less Bell To Answer   5th Dimension

Top 40 Hits of 1971:

1.	Joy To The World	Three Dog Night
2.	Uncle Albert/Admiral Halsey	Paul & Linda McCartney
3.	Brand New Key	Melanie
4.	It's Too Late	Carole King
5.	Maggie May	Rod Stewart
6.	Knock Three Times	Dawn
7.	She's A Lady	Tom Jones
8.	Sweet And Innocent	Donny Osmond
9.	Doesn't Somebody Want To Be Wanted	Partridge Family
10.	Sunshine	Jonathan Edwards
11.	I Hear You Knocking	Dave Edmunds
12.	Mama's Pearl	Jackson 5
13.	Stay Awhile	Bells
14.	Gypsys, Tramps & Thieves	Cher
15.	Want Ads	Honey Cone
16.	Theme From Shaft	Isaac Hayes
17.	One Bad Apple	Osmonds
18.	Just My Imagination (Running Away With Me)	Temptations
19.	Never Ending Song Of Love	Delaney & Bonnie
20.	Yo-Yo	Osmonds
21.	Peace Train	Cat Stevens
22.	Don't Pull Your Love	Hamilton, Joe Frank & Reynolds
23.	You've Got A Friend	James Taylor
24.	Go Away Little Girl	Donny Osmond
25.	How Can You Mend A Broken Heart	Bee Gees
26.	If You Could Read My Mind	Gordon Lightfoot
27.	Smiling Faces Sometimes	Undisputed Truth
28.	Superstar	Carpenters
29.	Indian Reservation	Raiders
30.	Rainy Days And Mondays	Carpenters
31.	Wedding Song (There Is Love)	Paul Stookey
32.	Hey Girl	Donny Osmond
33.	The Night They Drove Old Dixie Down	Joan Baez
34.	Maybe Tomorrow	Jackson 5
35.	All I Ever Need Is You	Sonny & Cher
36.	I've Found Someone Of My Own	Free Movement
37.	Draggin' The Line	Tommy James

38.	Never Can Say Goodbye	Jackson 5
39.	L.A. Goodbye	Ides Of March
40.	Absolutely Right	Five Man Electrical Band

Top 40 Hits of 1972:

1.	American Pie	Don McLean
2.	Clair	Gilbert O'Sullivan
3.	Lean On Me	Bill Withers
4.	Down By The Lazy River	Osmonds
5.	Brandy (You're A Fine Girl)	Looking Glass
6.	A Cowboy's Work Is Never Done	Sonny & Cher
7.	Papa Was A Rollin' Stone	Temptations
8.	Alone Again (Naturally)	Gilbert O'Sullivan
9.	I'll Be Around	Spinners
10.	You Don't Mess Around With Jim	Jim Croce
11.	The First Time Ever I Saw Your Face	Roberta Flack
12.	Stay With Me	Faces
13.	My Ding-A-Ling	Chuck Berry
14.	Doctor My Eyes	Jackson Browne
15.	Nice To Be With You	Gallery
16.	I'd Love You To Want Me	Lobo
17.	Heart Of Gold	Neil Young
18.	Tumbling Dice	Rolling Stones
19.	I Am Woman	Helen Reddy
20.	A Horse With No Name	America
21.	Beautiful Sunday	Daniel Boone
22.	Back Stabbers	O'Jays
23.	Nights In White Satin	Moody Blues
24.	Rock And Roll Part 2	Gary Glitter
25.	Back Off Boogaloo	Ringo Starr
26.	Puppy Love	Donny Osmond
27.	Sylvia's Mother	Dr. Hook & the Medicine Show
28.	Joy	Apollo 100
29.	Everybody Plays The Fool	Main Ingredient
30.	Suavecito	Malo
31.	Black & White	Three Dog Night
32.	Hurting Each Other	Carpenters
33.	Outa-Space	Billy Preston
34.	Morning Has Broken	Cat Stevens
35.	Without You	Nilsson
36.	Troglodyte (Cave Man)	Jimmy Castor Bunch
37.	I Can See Clearly Now	Johnny Nash

38.	Black Dog	Led Zeppelin
39.	Rockin' Robin	Michael Jackson
40.	(Last Night) I Didn't Get To Sleep At All	5th Dimension

Top 40 Hits of 1973:

1.	You're So Vain	Carly Simon
2.	Killing Me Softly With His Song	Roberta Flack
3.	The Night The Lights Went Out In Georgia	Vicki Lawrence
4.	Top Of The World	Carpenters
5.	The Morning After	Maureen McGovern
6.	Half-Breed	Cher
7.	Angie	Rolling Stones
8.	Mind Games	John Lennon
9.	Crocodile Rock	Elton John
10.	Delta Dawn	Helen Reddy
11.	Midnight Train To Georgia	Gladys Knight & the Pips
12.	Yesterday Once More	Carpenters
13.	Give Me Love—(Give Me Peace On Earth)	George Harrison
14.	Pillow Talk	Sylvia
15.	Also Sprach Zarathustra (2001)	Deodato
16.	Heartbeat—It's A Lovebeat	DeFranco Family
17.	Let's Get It On	Marvin Gaye
18.	Kodachrome	Paul Simon
19.	Little Willy	Sweet
20.	My Love	Paul McCartney
21.	Hello It's Me	Todd Rundgren
22.	The Right Thing To Do	Carly Simon
23.	Hocus Pocus	Focus
24.	Frankenstein	Edgar Winter Group
25.	Loves Me Like A Rock	Paul Simon
26.	Brother Louie	Stories
27.	Sing	Carpenters
28.	Get Down	Gilbert O'Sullivan
29.	Me And Mrs. Jones	Billy Paul
30.	Photograph	Ringo Starr
31.	Dancing In The Moonlight	King Harvest
32.	Boogie Woogie Bugle Boy	Bette Midler
33.	Kissing My Love	Bill Withers
34.	The Hurt	Cat Stevens
35.	Monster Mash	Bobby "Boris" Pickett
36.	Last Song	Edward Bear
37.	Dueling Banjos	Eric Weissberg & Steve Mandell

38. Playground In My Mind — Clint Holmes
39. Keeper Of The Castle — Four Tops
40. I Got A Name — Jim Croce

Top 40 Hits of 1974:

1.	I Honestly Love You	Olivia Newton-John
2.	Seasons In The Sun	Terry Jacks
3.	The Way We Were	Barbra Streisand
4.	Mockingbird	Carly Simon & James Taylor
5.	The Streak	Ray Stevens
6.	Come And Get Your Love	Redbone
7.	Band On The Run	Paul McCartney & Wings
8.	Annie's Song	John Denver
9.	Hooked On A Feeling	Blue Swede
10.	The Joker	Steve Miller Band
11.	My Melody Of Love	Bobby Vinton
12.	Sweet Home Alabama	Lynyrd Skynyrd
13.	(You're) Having My Baby	Paul Anka
14.	I Can Help	Billy Swan
15.	If You Love Me (Let Me Know)	Olivia Newton-John
16.	You Ain't Seen Nothing Yet	Bachman-Turner Overdrive
17.	Sundown	Gordon Lightfoot
18.	Kung Fu Fighting	Carl Douglas
19.	Don't Let The Sun Go Down On Me	Elton John
20.	I Shot The Sheriff	Eric Clapton
21.	Rock The Boat	Hues Corporation
22.	Midnight At The Oasis	Maria Muldaur
23.	The Night Chicago Died	Paper Lace
24.	Can't Get Enough	Bad Company
25.	You're Sixteen	Ringo Starr
26.	Cat's In The Cradle	Harry Chapin
27.	The Bitch Is Back	Elton John
28.	Rock Your Baby	George McCrae
29.	One Tin Soldier, The Legend Of Billy Jack	Coven
30.	Feel Like Makin' Love	Roberta Flack
31.	The Loco-Motion	Grand Funk
32.	Sunshine On My Shoulders	John Denver
33.	Nothing From Nothing	Billy Preston
34.	Bennie And The Jets	Elton John
35.	Billy, Don't Be A Hero	Bo Donaldson & the Heywoods
36.	La Grange	ZZ Top
37.	Tin Man	America

38. Sister Mary Elephant (Shudd-Up!)　　　　Cheech & Chong
39. The Entertainer　　　　Marvin Hamlisch
40. You Won't See Me　　　　Anne Murray

Top 40 Hits of 1975:

1.	Love Will Keep Us Together	Captain & Tennille
2.	Fox On The Run	Sweet
3.	Bad Blood	Neil Sedaka
4.	Killer Queen	Queen
5.	Another Somebody Done Somebody Wrong Song	B.J. Thomas
6.	Sister Golden Hair	America
7.	Philadelphia Freedom	Elton John Band
8.	Ballroom Blitz	Sweet
9.	Listen To What The Man Said	Wings
10.	Get Down Tonight	KC & the Sunshine Band
11.	Best Of My Love	Eagles
12.	Who Loves You	Four Seasons
13.	Fame	David Bowie
14.	Lucy In The Sky With Diamonds	Elton John
15.	Lovin' You	Minnie Riperton
16.	Black Water	Doobie Brothers
17.	Rhinestone Cowboy	Glen Campbell
18.	Jive Talkin'	Bee Gees
19.	Fallin' In Love	Hamilton, Joe Frank & Reynolds
20.	Why Can't We Be Friends	War
21.	My Eyes Adored You	Frankie Valli
22.	Chevy Van	Sammy Johns
23.	Have You Never Been Mellow	Olivia Newton-John
24.	Someone Saved My Life Tonight	Elton John
25.	Wildfire	Michael Murphey
26.	That's The Way (I Like It)	KC & the Sunshine Band
27.	Island Girl	Elton John
28.	Lady Marmalade	Labelle
29.	I'm Sorry	John Denver
30.	Laughter In The Rain	Neil Sedaka
31.	It's A Miracle	Barry Manilow
32.	Feelings	Morris Albert
33.	Mandy	Barry Manilow
34.	Please Mr. Postman	Carpenters
35.	Fire	Ohio Players
36.	Winners And Losers	Hamilton, Joe Frank & Reynolds
37.	The Way I Want To Touch You	Captain & Tennille

38. Dance With Me   Orleans
39. He Don't Love You (Like I Love You)   Tony Orlando & Dawn
40. When Will I Be Loved   Linda Ronstadt

WCFL Top 40 Hits of All-Time

1.	War	Edwin Starr
2.	The Letter	Box Tops
3.	Windy	Association
4.	Love Is Blue	Paul Mauriat
5.	Happy Together	Turtles
6.	Cherish	Association
7.	I Heard It Through The Grapevine	Marvin Gaye
8.	Bridge Over Troubled Water	Simon & Garfunkel
9.	Winchester Cathedral	New Vaudeville Band
10.	Joy To The World	Three Dog Night
11.	California Dreamin'	Mamas & the Papas
12.	We Can Work It Out/DayTripper	Beatles
13.	Summer In The City	Lovin' Spoonful
14.	Mony Mony	Tommy James & the Shondells
15.	Uncle Albert/Admiral Halsey	Paul & Linda McCartney
16.	Monday, Monday	Mamas & the Papas
17.	This Guy's In Love With You	Herb Alpert
18.	My Sweet Lord	George Harrison
19.	Fire	Crazy World Of Arthur Brown
20.	Jumpin' Jack Flash	Rolling Stones
21.	I Honestly Love You	Olivia Newton-John
22.	You're So Vain	Carly Simon
23.	Seasons In The Sun	Terry Jacks
24.	Brand New Key	Melanie
25.	The Way We Were	Barbra Streisand
26.	Love Will Keep Us Together	Captain & Tennille
27.	I Think I Love You	Partridge Family
28.	It's Too Late	Carole King
29.	American Pie	Don McLean
30.	Can't Take My Eyes Off You	Frankie Valli
31.	It Could Be We're In Love	Cryan' Shames
32.	Clair	Gilbert O'Sullivan

33. Mockingbird — Carly Simon & James Taylor
34. Bend Me, Shape Me — American Breed
35. I Think We're Alone Now — Tommy James & the Shondells
36. The Streak — Ray Stevens
37. Come And Get Your Love — Redbone
38. Gloria — Shadows Of Knight
39. Killing Me Softly With His Song — Roberta Flack
40. Lean On Me — Bill Withers

WCFL Top 100 Artists

1. Beatles
2. Neil Diamond
3. Supremes
4. Tommy James & the Shondells
5. Rolling Stones
6. Three Dog Night
7. Stevie Wonder
8. Aretha Franklin
9. 5th Dimension
10. Marvin Gaye
11. Temptations
12. Paul Revere & the Raiders
13. Carpenters
14. Four Tops
15. Elvis Presley
16. New Colony Six
17. Creedence Clearwater Revival
18. Elton John
19. Jackson 5
20. Chicago
21. Simon & Garfunkel
22. Gladys Knight & the Pips
23. Rascals
24. Paul McCartney/Wings
25. Bee Gees
26. Monkees
27. Donny Osmond
28. Tony Orlando & Dawn
29. Hollies
30. Beach Boys
31. Four Seasons
32. B.J. Thomas

33. John Lennon
34. Grass Roots
35. Guess Who
36. Mamas & the Papas
37. Tom Jones
38. Tommy Roe
39. Turtles
40. Buckinghams
41. Herman's Hermits
42. Dionne Warwick
43. Smokey Robinson & the Miracles
44. Bread
45. John Denver
46. Glen Campbell
47. Who
48. Association
49. Lovin' Spoonful
50. Bobby Vinton
51. Al Green
52. Cher
53. Helen Reddy
54. Cat Stevens
55. Wilson Pickett
56. Osmonds
57. Eagles
58. Cryan' Shames
59. Diana Ross
60. Donovan
61. Petula Clark
62. Gary Lewis & the Playboys
63. Ringo Starr
64. Jim Croce
65. America
66. Johnny Rivers
67. Bobby Sherman
68. Grand Funk
69. Alice Cooper
70. Vogues
71. Lobo
72. Paul Anka

73. Engelbert Humperdinck
74. Herb Alpert/Tijuana Brass
75. Dave Clark Five
76. Olivia Newton-John
77. Gary Puckett & the Union Gap
78. Doobie Brothers
79. Doors
80. 1910 Fruitgum Co.
81. Moody Blues
82. Dells
83. Spinners
84. Andy Kim
85. George Harrison
86. Bachman-Turner Overdrive
87. Staple Singers
88. Box Tops
89. Nancy Sinatra
90. Frank Sinatra
91. Ray Stevens
92. James Brown
93. Jr. Walker & the All Stars
94. Carly Simon
95. Partridge Family
96. James Taylor
97. War
98. Led Zeppelin
99. Barry White
100. Roberta Flack

About the Author

Ron Smith has been involved in oldies radio for over 30 years as a disk jockey, program and music director, most recently as the Music Director and Evening DJ at Real Oldies 1690 in Chicago. He also served for more than eight years as Music Director of WJMK-FM, Oldies 104.3 in the Windy City. He was Senior Music Programmer of Internet Radio for RadioWave.com and created and hosted streaming channels for MusicNow.com, including the Net's only all-Elvis station. Since 1995, he has delighted fans of '50s, '60s and '70s music with the Internet's premiere oldies Web site—www.oldiesmusic.com.

Smith is the author of three reference books of the WLS and WYTZ Silver Dollar Surveys—*Chicago Top 40 Charts 1960-1969, 1970-1979* and *1980-1990*. He resides in suburban Chicago with his vast music and book libraries.

978-0-595-43180-9
0-595-43180-1

Printed in the United States
75618LV00005B/202-237

9 780595 431809